MORNING BY MORNING

MORNING BY MORNING

CHARLES H. SPURGEON

Bridge-Logos

Alachua, Florida 32615 USA

Bridge-Logos

Alachua, Florida 32615 USA

Copyright ©2000 by Bridge-Logos

Library of Congress Catalog Card Number: 00-105-360
International Standard Book Number 978-0-88270-821-8

G616.318.FBM.m802.35250

Acknowledgment

Our thanks to Beverlee J. Chadwick
for her help in preparing this book for publication.

Preface

I use far too often the expression, "This is a marvelous book!" But that's exactly what this book is—a marvelous book! So, with your indulgence, I'll use it one more time.

This is a marvelous book!

It's a marvelous book because it contains the writings of a marvelous preacher—perhaps the most marvelous since the Apostle Paul. Think of every good thing, every superlative thing that could be said about a preacher of the Gospel of Jesus Christ, and they've all been said about Charles Haddon Spurgeon.

"To me he is master and friend. I have neither known nor heard of any other, in my time, so many-sided, so commanding, so simple, so humble, so selfless, so entirely Christ's man. Proudly I stand at the salute!" (W. Y. Fullerton, close friend and biographer)

"Charles Haddon Spurgeon, whose name is a household word the world over, is the most remarkable minister of Christ now living!" (Thomas Armitage, 1887, Pastor of 5th Avenue Baptist Church in New York City)

"Charles Spurgeon is the world's greatest divine. His life contains so much that is strange, unusual, wonderful, and even truly miraculous, that it will require most careful statement and most conservative reasoning to convince the reader that the record is literally true." (Russell Conwell, author of *Acres of Diamonds*)

Charles Haddon Spurgeon was born June 19, 1834, born-again on January 6, 1850, and preached his first sermon that same year. It is estimated that by the time he died on January 31, 1892, he had preached over 6,000 sermons, and never preached the same sermon twice. Yet, every sermon had only one theme: Jesus Christ and Him crucified.

It was Spurgeon's fixed focus upon that one theme that gave his sermons and writings so much power, and encouraged and strengthened so many Christians. Over 4.000 of his sermons are in print, and nearly 110 years after his death, they are the most popular and widely read of any sermons outside of Paul's epistles. They are so full of spirit and life that it could nearly be said about them what Jesus said about His own words, "They are spirit, and they are life." Without question, they are full of the spirit and love of Christ.

Spurgeon was an absolute believer in the sovereign grace and goodness of God and the all-sufficiency of Jesus Christ. His writings are filled with the glory and joy of both. About himself he once wrote, "My life seems to me like a fairy dream. I am often both amazed and dazed with its mercies and its love. How good God has been to me! I used to think that I should sing among the saints above as loudly as any, for I owe so much to the grace of God; and I said so once in a sermon, long ago, quoting these lines, 'Then loudest of the crowd I'll sing, while Heaven's resounding mansions ring with shouts of sovereign grace.'"

In this Pure Gold Classics version of *Morning by Morning*, there are the sounds of trumpets and glory-bells and crowns being cast before the throne and multitudes of heavenly choirs singing praises to the Lamb of God. All those marvelous eternal joys and wonders spring out of the fountain of Jesus Christ on your behalf to your mind, heart, soul, and daily life.

Pick any day, it doesn't matter which, and you'll be enlightened, encouraged, strengthened, and blessed. I guarantee you'll learn things about your Lord and Savior that you never knew or dreamed before. It's a book by which saints on higher ground are made.

And if you're not yet a Christian, but God is drawing you to His beloved Son so that you might have eternal life, then this book will be a blessing to you beyond your wildest imagination. It will show you the true way to a true Christ and a true God. Before God, I wish I could walk the way with you just to see your joy when Christ first becomes your all-sufficient Savior.

Charles Spurgeon died in 1892, but yet he lives, and will continue to so long as there are seekers after God. A month before he died, he wrote this, not knowing that he was literally prophesying about himself:

Those preachers whose voices were clear and mighty for truth during life continue to preach in their graves. Being dead, they yet speak, and whether people put their ears to their tombs or not, they cannot help but hear them. Often the death of a man is a kind of new birth to him, when he himself is gone physically, he spiritually survives, and from his grave there shoots up a tree of life whose leaves heal nations. Oh, worker for God, death cannot touch your sacred mission! Be content to die if the truth will live the better because you die. Be content to die, because death may be the enlargement of your influence. Good men die as dies the seed, which thereby no longer abides alone. When saints are apparently laid in the earth, they quit the earth, and rise and mount to Heaven's gate and enter into immortality. No, when the sepulcher receives this mortal frame, we will not die, but live.

And live Charles Spurgeon does, especially in the writings in this book. I know you will agree.

Harold J. Chadwick

Charles Haddon Spurgeon

From Boy Preacher to Prince of Preachers, Charles Haddon Spurgeon moved tens of thousands to trust Christ for their eternal salvation and left a treasure trove of sermons and writings that continue to move and touch his readers. And Spurgeon did all through great infirmities and trials, living humbly even as he became a world-renowned celebrity.

The 15-year-old boy entered the Primitive Methodist Church amid a howling snowstorm that had kept him from reaching his intended church. The unusual English storm also kept the preacher from reaching the church. Only a handful of hearty believers made it, and the young lad, Charles, joined them in the service with singing.

Charles describes the events this way:

> "At last, a very thin looking man, a shoemaker, went up into the pulpit to preach … He was forced to stick to his Scripture text, for the simple reason that he had little else to say. The text was, 'Look unto me, and be ye saved, all the ends of the earth' (Isaiah 45:22).
>
> "When he had managed to spin out 10 minutes or so, he was at the end of his tether. Then he looked at me under the gallery, and I daresay, with so few present, he knew me to be a stranger. Just fixing his eyes on me, as if he knew all my heart, he said, 'Young man, you look very miserable.' Well, I did, but I had not been

1

accustomed to have remarks made from the pulpit on my personal appearance before. However, it was a good blow, struck right home. He continued, 'And you always will be miserable—miserable in life, and miserable in death—if you don't obey my text; but if you obey now, this moment, you will be saved.' Then, lifting up his hands, he shouted as only a Primitive Methodist could do, 'Young man, look to Jesus Christ. Look! Look! Look! You have nothing to do but to look and live.'

"I saw at once the way of salvation ... I had been waiting to do fifty things, but when I heard the word, 'Look!' what a charming word it seemed to me! Oh! I looked until I could almost have looked my eyes away. There and then the cloud was gone, the darkness had rolled away, and that moment I saw the sun; and I could have risen that instant, and sung with the most enthusiastic of them, of the precious blood of Christ, and the simple faith which looks alone to HIM ...

> E'er since by faith I saw the stream
> Thy flowing wounds supply
> Redeeming love has been my theme
> And shall be till I die."

God's hand was in a snowstorm, an absent preacher, a faithful little shoemaker, and an aptly spoken word. And He brought forth the salvation of a man who would see tens of thousands of souls converted under his ministry, and tens of millions influenced by his writings that are reprinted and absorbed by Christians to this day. Once in the Kingdom, God lit a fire in Charles that would light the way for millions of people.

The bedraggled 15-year-old boy who heard the word of the Lord that day and looked up to see Jesus was Charles Haddon Spurgeon, often called the Prince of Preachers, a teacher and man who lived the Word and was used by God.

Young Beginnings

Spurgeon's Christian roots can be traced back to persecuted Dutchmen who fled to England centuries earlier only to find different persecution. Job Spurgeon was imprisoned in 1677 for six years and had all of his belongings confiscated for attending a worship service not sanctioned by the Church of England. A few years after being released from prison, he was sent back for the same offense.

Spurgeon's father and grandfather were both Congregationalist ministers and strong Christians.

Into this godly heritage, Charles Haddon Spurgeon was born June 19, 1834 in Kelvedon, Essex, England—the first of 17 children. Interestingly, as an infant, he was sent to live with his grandparents and stayed with them until he was six years old. There, he was given a complete youngster's understanding of Scriptures, and by age six he had learned to love John Bunyan's classic *Pilgrim's Progress*.

Back with his parents, he grew up in a home with strong Puritan teachings and faithful, restrained lives to match. There was no known hypocrisy in his parents' lives. And the Spurgeons did not allow it in their offspring. By outward standards, he and his siblings were exemplary children.

Little Charles once lost his pencil and decided to buy one at the store on credit. When his father found out, he gave him a lecture on the sins of debt that he never forgot.

> "I was marched off to the shop like a deserter marched into barracks, crying bitterly all down the street and feeling dreadfully ashamed, because I thought everybody knew I was in debt. The farthing was paid amid solemn warnings, and the poor debtor was set free like a bird out of a cage."

Spurgeon spent some time at a boarding school, and here we see a flash of his occasional fieriness. When he first started there, he knelt to pray before going to bed and was pelted by other boys with slippers and other items. He arose and struck at the mocking boys to his right and then to his left. After several were knocked down, the others stopped and stayed still. Then he knelt back down and returned to his prayers. He reported not being interrupted again.

From his earliest days, Spurgeon struggled with the sin in his life. Although his sinfulness might appear small from the outside, it weighed heavily on the boy's heart. No doubt at least part of this reason was all the talk and teaching in the home of fallen nature. In addition to Scripture, Spurgeon was reared on the writings of John Bunyan and Richard Baxter, making him keenly aware of the soul's struggle with sin. He had a sharp sense of the justice of God.

> "Sin, whatever it might be to other people, became to me an intolerable burden. It was not so much that I feared hell as that I feared sin, and all the while I had upon my mind a deep concern for the honour of God's name. I felt that it would not satisfy my conscience if I could be forgiven unjustly, but then there came the question, how could God be just and yet justify me, who had been so guilty?"

During that cold Sunday morning in January 1850, Spurgeon was making his way toward his own church, but the fateful snowstorm forced him to the Primitive Methodist Church where the faithful cobbler showed him the way to salvation through the words of the prophet Isaiah.

Spurgeon, of course, knew the Gospel well from his upbringing, but God chose to use a vehicle outside his family to draw him to His Son. It was the longing of his heart, and Christ filled it.

> "I do from my soul confess that I was never satisfied till I came to Christ ... Since that dear hour when my soul cast itself on Jesus, I have found solid joy and peace, but before that all those supposed gaieties of early youth, all the imagined joy and ease of boyhood, were but vanity and vexation of spirit to me. That happy day when I found the Saviour and learnt to cling to His dear feet was a day never to be forgotten by me, an obscure child,

unknown, unheard of. I listened to the word of God, and that precious text led me to the Cross of Christ."

Spurgeon attended Oxford for a while. However, because he was not a member of the Church of England, he was not allowed to earn a degree. But he studied diligently, and his keen mind was obvious. And he was free to preach as he desired, taking part in street preaching.

Spurgeon was never able to keep his joy and the basic message of the Gospel to himself. It spilled out of him naturally. Almost immediately, he set out as a servant of God, putting his hand to the plow and not looking back. There was nothing too small or trivial; he only wanted to do God's will. The Lord began him small, found him faithful, and in a stunningly short time, brought him to great things.

"The very first service which my youthful heart rendered to Christ was the placing of tracts in envelopes, and then sealing them up, that I might send them. I might have done nothing for Christ if I had not been encouraged by finding myself able to do a little. Then I sought to do something more, and from that something more, and I do not doubt that many servants of God have been led on to higher and nobler labours for their Lord, because they began to serve Him in the right spirit and manner."

His spirit was to share Christ in any way he could—writing verses on a scrap of paper and leaving it for someone to find.

"I could scarcely content myself even for five minutes without trying to do something for Christ."

Nothing could stop him.

"It may be that in the young dawn of my Christian life, I did imprudent things in order to serve the cause of Christ, but I still say, give me back that time again, with all its imprudence and with all its hastiness, if I may but have the same love to my Master, the same overwhelming influence in my spirit, making me obey my Lord's commands because it was a pleasure to me to do anything to serve my God."

Deceived Onto the Path of Greatness

Spurgeon was actually tricked into his first sermon. James Vinter, who headed the Local Preachers' Association in Cambridge, heard of Spurgeon's success giving the closing address after Sunday school. Vinter invited Spurgeon to accompany a man to the village of Teversham where he was to preach. Enroute, Spurgeon said he would be praying for him, and the man stopped in surprise. He had never preached, he said, and never intended to. He assumed Spurgeon was preaching and suggested that if he were not, they should turn back.

Spurgeon realized he had been tricked, but he decided to give a message anyway, even though he was completely unprepared and had never preached. He chose the Scripture "Unto you therefore which believe He is precious" on which to preach, and God greatly blessed the 16-year-old. When he finished, a woman's voice piped up and asked, "Bless your dear heart. How old are you?" Spurgeon very solemnly replied, "You must wait till the service is over before making such inquiries. Let us now sing."

And so the boy preacher was launched at 16.

Within 18 months of his conversion, Spurgeon was made pastor of the small Waterbeach Baptist Chapel.

He said he became a Baptist because of studying the New Testament in Greek. "According to my reading of Holy Scripture, the believer in Christ should be buried with Him in baptism, and so enter upon his open Christian life."

Spurgeon's mother once proclaimed, "Ah, Charles! I often prayed the Lord to make you a Christian, but I never asked that you become a Baptist."

Spurgeon with a smile responded quickly, "Ah, mother! The Lord has answered your prayer with His usual bounty, and given you exceeding abundantly above what you asked or thought."

England was in a state of considerable spiritual darkness, with corruption and apathy in the Church of England. While there were firm remnants of Christianity, the overall picture was dismal. The Rev. Desmond Morse-Boycott of the Church of England wrote:

> "England was a land of closed churches and unstoled clergy ... The parson was often an absentee, not infrequently a drunkard ... The rich went to church to doze in upholstered curtained pews fitted with fireplaces, while the poor were herded together on uncomfortable benches."

The small town of Waterbeach was in a similarly, spiritually dilapidated state. But God was with the 17-year-old pastor, and the work of Charles Spurgeon began to bear fruit almost immediately. The thatched-roof church was soon crammed with people, and some men who were the lowest and most noxious in the village became great blessings in the church.

Many of the villagers helped out their young pastor with his needs, knowing that the tiny amount of income he was provided could not support even such a modest lifestyle. Spurgeon was determined to stick it out as long as God desired it. He seemed to want little for himself and truly delighted in the changed lives of those in the village.

> "I can testify that great numbers of humble country folk accepted the Saviour's invitation, and it was delightful to see what a firm grip they afterwards had on the verities of the faith. Many of them became perfect masters of divinity. I used to think sometimes that if they had degrees who deserved them, diplomas would often be transferred and given to those who hold the plough handle or work at the carpenter's bench."

This attitude toward the simple man remained with Spurgeon, a country boy himself, who remained comfortable and approachable by any class even when he became a worldwide name.

He spent three years in Waterbeach and although a mere teenager most of the time, the church and the village flourished under his care and ministering. He wrote:

> "It was a pleasant thing to walk through that place when drunkenness had almost ceased, when debauchery in the case of many was dead, when men and women went forth to labour with joyful hearts, singing the praises of the ever-living God."

New Park Street: Great Church, Little Preacher

In November 1853, the young man received an invitation to preach a Sunday service at New Park Street Chapel in London. New Park Street was famous among Baptists and Londoners and most Christians as a place of great godly influence and preaching in the 1700s. Spurgeon thought at first it was a mistake. Why would such a great church be interested in this little, country lay preacher?

But after he determined that the invitation was indeed not an error, he replied in sincere humility, informing them that he was only 19 and had never preached in a large church. He went on to say he had a prior commitment for the date they requested and offered December 11. The New Park Street deacons accepted.

New Park Street Chapel was symbolic of the decline in Baptist churches in England in the middle 1800s. The once vibrant church was a shell of its former glory. Few congregations in the whole of London topped 300 people, and all the talk was of the decline in church attendance. In fact, the Baptist denomination was divided on several issues.

Spurgeon arrived in London on a cold and dreary day, staying in a tiny little apartment where the other young men boarding there ridiculed him for claiming that he would be preaching at New Park Street. He felt completely alone, without a friend in the city. When he tried to sleep, it was torture in the cramped room with the cacophony of horses and cabs all night. He already hated London.

And yet he considered that perhaps God was in all of it.

When he arrived at New Park Street the next morning, he was in awe of the magnificent building, and wondered how such a sophisticated and perhaps critical congregation would receive him. But more surprises were in store. As the time of the service approached, the great chapel did not fill up. In fact, it was dotted with just a few souls. It felt practically empty.

Spurgeon rose and spoke on "Every good gift and every perfect gift is from above and cometh down from the Father of Lights, with Whom is no variableness neither shadow of turning." Every thread of Spurgeon's preaching led up to the Cross. He did not preach on moral issues or anything in modern debate. He simply preached Christ crucified and let everything else fall as it may.

The people seemed unsure of the young preacher who knew Scripture so well and seemed to already have a vast wealth of knowledge and experience. But when the evening service came about, everyone returned and brought a good number more with them. He preached from Revelation, "They are without fault before the throne of God."

In one day, his future and the church's future were cemented together. He was invited to pastor the church. And while he could not accept immediately, and did not treasure leaving his flock in Waterbeach, he received peace from God to take the position.

Spurgeon Breaks the Mold

Spurgeon was not one to simply go with the flow. But he also understood the need for discipline and submission.

An example from his first months at New Park Street Chapel demonstrates this vividly. He was not truly ordained when he accepted the New Park Street pulpit. It was suggested there be a formal ordination service over which one of London's ordained ministers would preside. Spurgeon thoughtfully replied in a long letter to the deacons.

He opposed the ordination ceremony. His calling was from God, and he had already recognized his ministry. He objected to the concept of ministers passing on power from one to another and believed it was completely up to the local church. But, he was willing to submit to the church leadership if they felt his ceremonial ordination to be critically important: "It will be submission. I shall endure it as a self-mortification in order that you may all be pleased. I would rather please you than myself."

The ordination ceremony never took place.

Spurgeon also broke the mold of tradition by discouraging references to himself as "Reverend" or even "Pastor," and by discarding the long, black frock of ministers and wearing plain clothes. These changes were severely criticized by other ministers, who believed they ought to be set apart from the flock. Moreover, Spurgeon broke through the heavy academic style of preaching so in vogue. He chose instead to speak directly to his listeners in words that could not possibly be misunderstood.

But it was not the insistence on outward changes that brought people to hear Spurgeon; it was the message of Jesus Christ crucified and arisen, and the need for Him alone for salvation. And the people came and came. Soon, not only was the once nearly empty chapel filled, but the street outside was blocked on Sundays for the overflow crowd to listen to this very young man of God.

Soon it became evident that larger space was necessary. They turned to the Music Hall in the Royal Surrey Gardens. This was a huge step, because the building housed up to 12,000 people. Spurgeon and William Olney—the man who was instrumental in bringing Spurgeon to London—feared it might have been far too large and they would have looked silly. But where they were simply could not work any longer, so they pressed forward.

Terror, Flight, Disorder and Death

It was a disaster that first night in October 1856. The Music Hall was jammed to capacity, such as it never was with secular performances. But after a Scripture reading and prayer, the wicked had their planned moment. Someone shouted, "Fire!" and another shouted, "The balcony is giving way!" Several others shouted similar fears. A panic erupted among the people and as they pressed toward the doors, seven people were killed, trampled by others desperately trying to flee a perfectly safe building.

The British Banner wrote: "At the most solemn moment of the occasion, the wicked rose in their strength, like a whirlwind, sin entered, followed by terror, flight, disorder and death!" It seemed clear to everyone that it was a staged effort by evil-doers to wreck the work of God—everyone except Spurgeon, who to the end of his life wanted to "hope there was no concerted wickedness."

Spurgeon, only 22 years old, was devastated. The burden of it overwhelmed him. He became sick and was unable to preach for a couple of Sundays. But gradually his strength returned, and along with it his speaking became as powerful as ever. And the church was able to make good use of Music Hall afterward.

Eventually, however, a new building of their own was needed. In 1861, they built the Metropolitan Tabernacle, which still stands in London today. It was a huge structure that comfortably seated 3,700, with room for another 2,000 to squeeze in, which they normally did.

Charles in Love

Susannah Thompson was a "greatly privileged favourite" of William Olney, who was the lead Deacon and responsible for bringing Spurgeon to London. And so she saw Spurgeon preach his first three sermons at New Park Street Chapel.

Despite her Christian upbringing, she had never professed her faith in Christ, although she was very well aware of her need for the Saviour.

During a Sunday evening sermon about a year before Spurgeon arrived, the preacher spoke on "The word is nigh thee, even in thy mouth, and in thy heart," and the light dawned in Susannah's soul. She wrote:

> "The Lord said to me, through His servant, 'Give me thine heart,' and, constrained by His love, that night witnessed my solemn resolution of entire surrender to Himself."

But she records that she grew cold and indifferent to the things of God, and was in such a state when Spurgeon took the pulpit.

Some of their early connections are shrouded in personal privacy that eludes history. But she writes that quite unexpectedly, Spurgeon gave her an illustrated copy of *The Pilgrim's Progress*, the John Bunyan book that had meant so much to him since childhood. He inscribed it, "Miss Thompson, with desires for progress in the blessed pilgrimage, from C.H. Spurgeon, April 20, 1854."

In June 1854, the two were providentially seated next to each other at a party. Spurgeon handed a book written by Martin Tupper to Susannah and asked about a quotation in it: "Seek a good wife of Thy God, for she is the best gift of His Providence."

She blushed slightly, then heard him whisper the question, "Do you pray for him who is to be your husband?" There was a pause, and then Spurgeon asked her if she would take a walk with him. In August, they were engaged and they married on January 8, 1856.

The home they made was modest, and they took care to avoid any excessive displays. Their homes in town and later in Westwood were seemingly open to everyone: to missionaries, preachers and visitors from around the world. And they gave generously to those in need. The estimates from a review of their accounting books found that they gave away about five times as much as they kept for themselves. That's more than an 80 percent "tithe."

The Spurgeon's twin boys—Thomas and Charles—were born September 20, 1856. They were tremendous blessings to their parents and became preachers and leading men of God themselves. But the birth left Susannah an invalid in her home for 15 years. Yet her joy and that of her husband did not diminish.

"She was a fine example of the triumph of sanctified will over physical suffering," J.C. Carlile wrote in *Charles Spurgeon, The Great Orator*. "Even in pain, she dictated many letters to other sufferers and helped bear the burdens of ministries of all denominations who had fallen on evil times."

Out of the money she saved in frugal housekeeping, she began the Book Fund, which financed thousands of books of Bible study for pastors around the world. She also found money for soup kitchens, clothing for the children of poorly paid village ministers, and the individual needs of untold numbers of people.

Despite her fragile health, Susannah proved to be the ideal partner for Spurgeon, loving and serving the Lord first and sharing a spiritual intensity that helped buoy him when he needed it. Despite her extended illness, she did not seem to be a major burden on her husband. On the contrary, she was his helpmate.

Prince of Preachers

Spurgeon brought a whole new method to preaching. He did not strive for the flowery speech of the humanists or the rhetoric of the High Calvinists. Nor did he muddle through, as did many of the rural preachers. He spoke simply and from the depth of his heart and his intellect, but it was not to impress man. It was to impress upon man the glory of God, the fallen sinning state of each of us and the salvation of Christ.

"His ideal was that of the fisherman," wrote Carlile, who was a student under Spurgeon. "He lowered his net to catch fish; he baited his hook, not for decorative purposes but to secure souls."

Spurgeon never took his eye off the Word. God's great truths defined everything for him, and they informed his preaching. He wanted to make people clearly understand him. There would be no fogs in his preaching.

"Sermons should have real teaching in them, and their doctrine should be solid, substantial and abundant," Spurgeon wrote. "The world still needs to be told of its Saviour and of the way to reach Him."

Spurgeon did not do much on the spur of the moment. Occasionally he gave sermons without preparation—such as his first one. But most of the time he was intent on always finding just the right words and meanings to make his point clear. He wanted to use illustrations to make the points from ancient Scripture real to his listeners. He was very willing to quote other great men of God, from Bunyan to John Knox to Richard Baxter. And so he labored over every sermon, always starting at the beginning—with prayer. In speaking to students at his Pastors' College, he put it very clearly to them:

> "I frequently sit hour after hour praying and waiting for a subject, and this is the main part of my study; much hard labour have I spent in manipulating topics, ruminating upon points of doctrine, making skeletons out of verses and then burying every bone of them in the catacombs of oblivion, sailing on and on over leagues of broken water till I see the red lights and make sail direct to the desired haven.
>
> "Unstudied thoughts coming from the mind without previous research, without the subjects in hand having been investigated at all, must be of a very inferior quality, even from the most superior men, and as none of us would have the effrontery to glorify ourselves as men of genius or wonders of erudition, I fear that our unpremeditated thoughts upon most subjects would not be remarkably worthy of attention at all.
>
> "Our sermons should be our mental lifeblood—the outflow of our intellectual and spiritual vigor; or, to change the figure, they should be diamonds well cut and well set, precious intrinsically and bearing the marks of labour. God forbid that we should offer to the Lord that which costs us nothing."

And there you have the heart of C.H. Spurgeon on preaching. Notice that it does not include anything other than what is driving the preacher to preach. There is nothing on methods or deliveries or services. Where is the heart of the man expounding on the Word of God? That was the question for Spurgeon.

When asked once about how he attracted so many people while other churches were dormant or dwindling, he answered:

> "I did not seek them. They have always sought me. My concern has been to preach Christ and leave the rest to His keeping."

14

That was his heart.

Although it would not be his style, Spurgeon could certainly point to the results of preaching Christ first and Him crucified, preaching from deep study and prayer, and preaching for the glory of the Lord and not the preacher.

The Tabernacle For a Growing Congregation
The church needed a new home, and although the Music Hall worked for a while, the leadership knew that they needed to build. Spurgeon's vision was for a Greek structure. He felt there were no sacred languages other than ancient Greek and Hebrew. He believed that a Christian church should not be a Gothic structure, but should be Grecian.

The Metropolitan Tabernacle was completed in 1861—the largest church in the world at the time, holding nearly 6,000 people. Predictably, Spurgeon was criticized for building such a monumental edifice. He was charged with puffing himself up and being ostentatious. It was also said that the money could have been better spent on the poor. But the charges of egotism and ostentation evaporated when the church opened and filled up twice every Sunday. And as for helping the poor, Spurgeon's personal giving and books open for review shamed any critic. The couple's 80 percent tithe put to rest the lie that he was making himself rich through the Tabernacle.

At one point, an American lecture bureau invited him to come to America to tour all major cities and give 50 lectures. They offered to pay all expenses, plus $50,000—which would be a quarter million dollars today. Spurgeon wasn't interested. Ever keeping his eye on the Master's will, he quickly replied, "I can do better. I will stay in London and try to save 50 souls."

He was comfortable, but given his position of worldwide prominence and influence, and particularly the sales of millions of his books, his lifestyle was very modest. He could have lived as a king, but lived *for* the King and allowed his riches to be stored up in heaven rather than on earth.

Winning Souls From His Knees

Spurgeon did not desire to take church members from other congregations; he wanted to get the lost into the Tabernacle and into the Kingdom. By always preaching Christ and salvation, he knew he never missed the opportunity for a lost soul to hear the Gospel.

The soul-winning ways of Spurgeon began where everything began with him: in prayer. The Tabernacle was known as a church that prayed. Spurgeon may have set the example for many in later years, but the leadership had made the commitment before he arrived. The remnant that sought him out were on their knees, paving the way. That critical resolution was never lost.

No doubt many people came to hear Spurgeon out of curiosity, but saved or lost, they all heard a Christ preached that captured them.

Bob Ross wrote that Spurgeon "plainly preached the Word, pressing the Law and the Gospel upon his hearers—the Law to convict and break the hardened, and the Gospel to heal the broken."

He loved God and he loved his fellow men. Here is how he concluded one of his sermons:

> "He that believeth not shall be damned. Weary sinner, hellish sinner, thou who are at the devil's castaway, reprobate, profligate, harlot, robber, thief, adulterer, fornicator, drunkard, swearer … listen! I speak to thee as to the rest. I exempt no man. God hath said there is no exemption here. Whosoever believeth in the name of Jesus Christ shall be saved. Sin is no barrier. The guilt is no obstacle. Whosoever, though he were black as Satan, though he were guilty as a fiend—whosoever this night believes shall every sin forgiven, shall every crime effaced, shall every iniquity blotted out; shall be saved in the Lord Jesus Christ, and shall stand in heaven safe and secure. That is the glorious gospel. God apply it home to your hearts and give you faith in Jesus."

New Park Street went from 232 members when Spurgeon arrived to more than 5,000 about 10 years later. It was the largest independent congregation in the world—independent of denominations, but dependent on the King of kings. Prime Minister Gladstone, many members of the royal family, members of Parliament, and dignitaries from around the world visited the Tabernacle. But no matter who was in attendance, like Baxter and others before him, the message had to remain the same. All were sinners; all needed Christ or were condemned eternally. No one from the rag-tag orphan to the king escaped the equation. People swarmed to him to hear the Truth. No numbers were kept, because Spurgeon did not use the modern altar call. He did not request a public decision. He simply quoted Scripture to believe in Christ and be saved. But even without the numbers, the fruits were quite clear. The growth of the church was primarily new believers. He planted several other churches in the London area, offshoots of the Tabernacle.

"From the very early days of my ministry in London, the Lord gave such an abundant blessing upon the proclamation of His truth that whenever I was able to appoint a time for seeking converts and inquirers, it was seldom, if ever, that I waited in vain; and usually, so many came, that I was quite overwhelmed with gratitude and thanksgiving to God."

Spurgeon's Legacy of the Pen
Spurgeon always loved to write. As a child, he planned his own magazine and wrote articles for it. This gift carried on until his death, leaving a godly legacy to future generations through both his preaching and writings.

From early on, there was such demand for the words he gave that his sermons were printed and distributed in England and the United States. The first ones were bound up and 500 printed. They disappeared so fast, more were printed until about 6,000 were distributed. Later more than 200,000 booklets with his sermons were printed.

Probably the most popular books he wrote were a little series entitled *John Ploughman's Talk*. More than 300,000 volumes were printed and sold very quickly. Subsequent printings added greatly to that number.

His writings encouraged lay believers and instructed ministers. But mostly, they were meant for the average man.

There was more that Spurgeon accomplished. In 1856 he started the Pastor's College with only one student. It grew steadily until about 100 young men were enrolled to become ministers of the Gospel. The College also housed the Stockwell Orphanage with boys' and girls' schools overseen by Spurgeon and supported by funds he helped raise.

He published a monthly magazine called the *Sword and the Trowel*, beginning in 1865, in which he essentially continued preaching Christ, but also touched on issues of doctrine within the church.

His autobiography lists 78 books he wrote and published, in addition to the sermons and the magazine.

Calvinist Without Apology
Spurgeon was an unapologetic Calvinist, in that he believed what Calvin believed. But he disliked the term, because it took the focus off the Saviour. He simply agreed with Calvin's theology, and believed that the Puritan fathers had come closest to Scriptural truth.

> "We know nothing of the new ologies; we stand by the old ways ... Believing that the Puritanic school embodied more gospel truth in it than any other since the days of the apostles."

He defined Calvinism in its simplest terms this way:

> "If anyone should ask me what I mean by a Calvinist, I should reply, 'He is one who says, Salvation is of the Lord.' I cannot find in Scripture any other doctrine than this. It is the essence of the Bible. 'He only is my rock and my salvation.' Tell me anything contrary to this truth, and it will be heresy; tell me a heresy, and I shall find its essence here, that it has departed from

this great, this fundamental rock-truth, 'God is my rock and my salvation.'"

The Protestant pastors were generally evangelical, but they were weak in their doctrine. And the result was clear in the lives of church members. Spurgeon wanted to set the church back on the rock-hard path of strong doctrine. Spurgeon said,

> "My daily labor is to revive the old doctrines of Gill, Owen, Calvin, Augustine and Christ … The old truth that Calvin preached, that Augustine preached, is the truth that I preach today, or else I would be false to my conscience and my God. I cannot shape truth; I know of no such thing as paring off the rough edges of a doctrine. John Knox's gospel is my gospel. And that gospel which thundered through Scotland must thunder through England again."

In his day, however, not unlike today, there were elements from Hyper-Calvinists to Arminians who found fault with Spurgeon's doctrine. Knowing Scripture so well—he had much of it committed to memory—and knowing the writings of the church fathers intimately, he was able to aptly defend his doctrines.

But while willing to do it, he did not like the arena of battling other believers over issues of doctrine. He preferred the bottom line.

"If I am asked to say what my creed is, I think I must reply, 'It is Jesus Christ' … Jesus Christ, Who is the sum and the substance of the Gospel, Who is in Himself all theology, the Incarnation of every precious truth, the all-glorious embodiment of the way, the truth and the life."

He urged listeners, "Do not make minor doctrines main points," but stick with the theme of grace from God through Jesus. Yet he could discuss the most minute doctrines in great detail and earnestness, and they were apparently important to him.

Battling the Erosion and Corrosion of the Down-Grade

By the late 1880s, there was an insipid falling away from God's Truth that infected many churches, including the Baptists. Some ministers openly preached against the infallibility of the Bible, the deity of Christ and eternal salvation. Those few were censured by the Baptist Union. But many others did so more surreptitiously. In the light of great scientific discoveries, these learned men began to question portions of Scripture or elements of the Trinity. They cast themselves as progressive and modern. Some found a new understanding in the theories of Charles Darwin, and pointed to what they felt were contradictions between Scripture and science—choosing science as their guide. Their congregations followed.

Carlile wrote:

> "The pulpit was charged with silent surrender to the radical betrayal of the evangelical foundations of the Christian faith."

A blind eye was turned toward this apostasy within the Baptist Union and other denominations. It became known as the "Down-Grade" controversy.

Spurgeon at first thought it was an exception here and there. But he soon began to see a rapid spread of these ideas and was alarmed at the sudden infusion within his own denomination. Spurgeon was a very sick man by this point, and in fact, was only a few years from death. He likely knew it. And so there was no personal gain for him to enter into such a burgeoning fray at the end of his life. In fact, it probably taxed his failing strength.

Nonetheless, he felt compelled to defend the Gospel.

After a number of private conversations and correspondences with men he thought were reducing Scripture, and with S.H. Booth, the secretary of the Baptist Union, he brought the issue into the open in an 1887 *Sword and the Trowel* article. In the magazine, he issued a general warning to readers of the defection from the Truth that was riddling the Nonconformist churches.

Spurgeon laid out three charges: 1) The infallibility of Scripture from God was denied, 2) the way of salvation through

Christ was not preached, and 3) hell was denied, as was any eternal punishment for sin.

It went right to the heart of the Gospel.

Just how deeply the unbelief had ensnared the church became obvious with the response. Many in the camp of science vigorously attacked Spurgeon over religion. He was also attacked through Christian publications and even the pulpit. And shockingly, at the next annual meeting of the Baptist Union, the issue was ignored. There was complete silence.

After repeated attempts to get the Baptist Union to confront the issue, Spurgeon felt he had no choice. He withdrew from the union. By unanimous vote, the congregation of the Tabernacle followed him. This was a blow to the union, as Spurgeon was by far the best-known Baptist preacher, and his congregation many times larger than any other. After several private attempts to get Spurgeon to return, the union passed a motion of censure against him—almost unanimously.

Booth claimed that Spurgeon had never brought the matter up with him. Spurgeon was stunned and was ready to produce the written documentation between Booth and him as evidence that the matter had indeed been thoroughly explored. But Booth insisted that those were private correspondences. As easily as Spurgeon could have proved his position and Booth's hypocrisy, he honored his old friend, and in spite of the betrayal, never revealed the letters. Without the proof, he undermined his own credibility. He also lost a friend. This was a painful split, because Spurgeon and Booth had been close for many years. To Booth's credit, Spurgeon knew he was trying to keep the controversy from blowing up and dividing the union. But it was unacceptable compromise for Spurgeon.

The censure passed by the Baptist Union was a deep wound for Spurgeon. But he had set out his path of defense of Scripture and would not turn back. He was absolutely militant about God's Word. But however strong his heart was in the matter, his body was not up to the battle. The controversy wore down his feeble frame even further, hastening the inevitable.

Suffering with Christ

Like so many great men and women of God, Spurgeon tasted of immense physical suffering. And much of his suffering was brought on by his zeal to push himself to the brink and beyond to do God's good will.

Arnold Dallimore wrote of the schedule that took its toll on Spurgeon's body:

> "Although he began full of youthful vigor he labored to such an extent that his health soon was drained. He preached 10 times a week on the average, often in places that were far removed from London. He oversaw his Pastors' College, his orphanage and almshouses, and bore the responsibility of raising the funds to keep them all vibrant and healthy. Every Monday he edited a sermon preached the previous day to prepare it for the press and each month he produced his magazine. He was also constantly producing books."

By the age of 30, he was already showing the signs of the stress. The painful disease of gout developed. Over the years, he would be in such agony that he was bed-ridden and unable to move. Many of his sermons were preached through obvious pain. He would use his cane and, with the help of church members, mount the podium to preach. Frequently, once he embarked upon the word of God, the pain seemed to dissipate, and he became animated and energetic until he was finished.

Spurgeon's views on his physical suffering are not those of many Christians today. He saw suffering as a gift from God. Without his suffering, he never could have been the comforting and sympathetic man that he was to the sick and downtrodden.

His son, Charles Jr., wrote:

> "I know of no one who could, more sweetly than my dear father, impart comfort to bleeding hearts and sad spirits. As the crushing of the flower causes it to yield its aroma, so he, having endured in the long continued illness of my beloved mother, and also constant pains

himself, was able to sympathize most tenderly with all sufferers."

Spurgeon knew this truth intimately.

"In the matter of faith healing, health is set before us as if it were the great thing to be desired above all things. Is it so? I venture to say that the greatest earthly blessing that God can give to any of us is health, with the exception of sickness. Sickness has frequently been of more use to the saints of God than health has."

Spurgeon at Rest, at Last

In his last years, Spurgeon spent some wintertime in Menton, in South France, to help his ailing body. That is where he was in January 1892. He was very sick, yet he could not help but hold little services with just the handful of friends and family. He had spoken to the great throngs of thousands, but he would expound the word of God to any group, no matter how small.

Wilson Carlile was with Spurgeon in his last days, and it was clear that the Down-Grade issue was still on his heart.

"When he was dying at the East Bay, Menton, my wife and I went to his family prayers, which he took though in bed. He prayed for all the wandering sheep, concluding, 'Thou, Lord, seest the various labels upon them and rightly regardest them by the mark of the Cross in their hearts. They are all Thy one fold.'"

Spurgeon crossed the River Jordan January 31, 1892, and entered into the loving arms of the Master whom he served so diligently on this earth. Typical of his humility and understanding of man's heart, he had left the request: "Remember, a plain stone. 'C.H.S.' and no more; no fuss."

He knew that a monument would be to him, and not to his Saviour. On his casket was this inscription:

"In ever loving memory of Charles Haddon Spurgeon, born at Kelvedon, June 19, 1834, fell asleep in Jesus at Menton, January 31, 1892. I have fought a good fight, I have finished my course, I have kept the faith."

Indeed he did.

By Rod Thomson

Rod Thomson is an award-winning journalist and writer in Sarasota, Florida, and the administrator of Hand to the Plow Ministries.

Illustration Portfolio

THE BIRTHPLACE OF CHARLES H. SPURGEON
June 19, 1834 in Kelvedon, Essex, England

REV. JOHN SPURGEON
father of C.H. Spurgeon

ELIZA SPURGEON
mother of C.H. Spurgeon

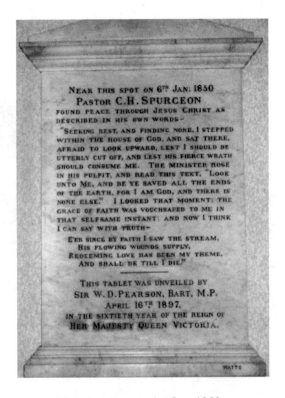

N<small>EAR THIS SPOT ON</small> 6<small>TH</small> J<small>AN.</small> 1950
P<small>ASTOR</small> C.H. S<small>PURGEON</small>
<small>FOUND PEACE THROUGH</small> J<small>ESUS</small> C<small>HRIST AS DESCRIBED IN HIS OWN WORDS</small> –
"S<small>EEKING REST, AND FINDING NONE,</small> I <small>STEPPED WITHIN THE</small> H<small>OUSE OF</small> G<small>OD,</small>
<small>AND SAT THERE, AFRAID TO LOOK UPWARD, LEST</small> I <small>SHOULD BE UTTERLY CUT</small>
<small>OFF, AND LEST</small> H<small>IS FIERCE WRATH SHOULD CONSUME ME.</small> T<small>HE MINISTER ROSE</small>
<small>IN HIS PULPIT, AND READ THIS TEXT,</small> "L<small>OOK UNTO</small> M<small>E, AND BE YE SAVED ALL</small>
<small>THE ENDS OF THE</small> E<small>ARTH, FOR</small> I <small>AM</small> G<small>OD, AND THERE IS NONE ELSE.</small>"
I <small>LOOKED THAT MOMENT: THE GRACE OF FAITH WAS VOUCHSAFED TO ME IN</small>
<small>THAT SELFSAME INSTATNT; AND NOW</small> I <small>THINK</small> I <small>CAN SAY WITH TRUTH</small> –
E'<small>ER SINCE BY FAITH</small> I <small>SAW THE STREAM,</small>
H<small>IS FLOWING WOUNDS SUPPLY,</small>
R<small>EDEEMING LOVE HAS BEEN MY THEME,</small>
A<small>ND SHALL BE TILL</small> I <small>DIE.</small>"

T<small>HIS TABLET WAS UNVEILED BY</small>
S<small>IR</small> W.D. P<small>EARSON,</small> B<small>ART,</small> M.P.
A<small>PRIL</small> 16<small>TH</small> 1897.
<small>IN THE SIXTIETH YEAR OF THE REIGN OF</small>
H<small>ER</small> M<small>AJESTY</small> Q<small>UEEN</small> V<small>ICTORIA</small>

Above: The cottage where Mr. Spurgeon preached his first sermon at age 16.

Left: Susannah Tompson became Mrs. Charles Spurgeon on January 8, 1856. Despite fragile health, she was a strong partner to her husband and his ministry. *Below:* The Spurgeons lived a comfortable but modest life at Westwood, and used the majority of their income to help ministers, the poor, and people in need.

WESTWOOD

THE NEW PARK STREET CHAPEL
Spurgeon accepted his first pastorate in December 1853,
at the age of 19.

MUSIC HALL IN THE ROYAL SURREY GARDENS
In spite of a disasterous beginning, the congregation used this
building as a meeting place for five years.

THE METROPOLITAN TABERNACLE
Above: Completed in 1861, the new home of the Park Street congregation was built in the Greek style. It was the largest church in the world at the time and held nearly 6,000 people. *Left*: Spurgeon sometimes needed to be helped into the pulpit because of the pain he suffered from gout.

STOCKWELL ORPHANAGE
Spurgeon oversaw and raised funds to support the Boy's
School and Girl's School at Stockwell Orphanage (*above*), as
well as the Pastor's College he founded (*bottom*).

THE PASTOR'S COLLEGE

THE SWORD AND THE TROWEL Spurgeon published this monthly magazine beginning in 1865, in which he essentially continued preaching Christ, but also touched on issues of doctrine within the church.

Spurgeon in his study at Westwood, his family home.

Spurgeon's study at Westwood (*above*) contained more than 12,000 volumes. Mr. Spurgeon's work was enormous. Besides editing and furnishing most of the matter for his monthly magazine, *The Sword and Trowel*, since January 1, 1865, he wrote *The Saint and His Saviour, The Treasury of David, an Exposition of the Psalms* in seven octavo volumes; *The New Park Street Pulpit* and the *Metropolitan Tabernacle Pulpit*, which contains about two thousand of his weekly sermons from 1855 to 1889, making thirty large volumes. Also *Lectures to My Students, Commenting and Commentaries, John Ploughman*, the *Cheque Book of the Bank of Faith*, and various other publications.

Mark XVI. 14.

This shows us the way in wh we must deal with unbelief in ourselves, + in others. It is a sin + should be treated as such. Jesus w'd not have upbraided had not this been the case.

In the case before us they had repeated testimonies, from their own brethren, + backed by his own word — but we have even more guilt for we know him to be risen + yet doubt.

__I. Let us consider its evil in itself__

Suppose some one doubted us.
Think of who he is + what he has done. —
Consider his near + dear relation to us.
The many times in wh we have doubled
And upon the same matter.
Where his promises forbade unbelief
Despite our own declarations.
What have we believed in preference?

__II. Let us observe the evils wh it causes__

It grieves the Spirit of God.
It causes distress in our own hearts
It weakens us for action or suffering.
It depresses others.
It leaves an ill impression con sinners
It cannot but gender to bondage.

__III. Let us reflect upon its sinfulness where it reigns__

It gives God the lie.
It argues hatred in the heart
It is the sign of utter moral death.
It is the essence of hell.

SERMON NOTES
This one page of handwritten notes is all Spurgeon took with him into the pulpit when he preached the sermon titled "Unbelievers Upbraided."

January

◢ January 1 ◣

*That year they ate of the produce of Canaan
(Joshua 5:12).*

Israel's weary wanderings were over. They had reached their promised rest. No more moving tents, fiery serpents, fierce Amalekites, and howling wildernesses. They came to the land that flowed with milk and honey,[1] and they ate the produce of the land.[2] Perhaps this year, this may be your case or mine. To be with Christ[3] in the rest waiting for the people of God[4] is a joyful hope indeed, and to expect this glory to come soon is double joy. Unbelief shudders at the Jordan that we must cross,[5] but rest assured that we've already experienced more ills than death at its worst can cause us. So let's banish every fearful thought, and rejoice with exceeding great joy that perhaps this year we will begin to be "with the LORD forever."[6] Many Christians, of course, will stay on earth this year to serve their LORD. But even if this is our case, our New Year's text is still true, for "we who have believed enter that rest."[7] The Holy Spirit is a deposit, guaranteeing our inheritance.[8] Those in heaven are secure, and we are preserved in Christ Jesus. They enjoy communion with their LORD, and so do we. They rest in His love,[9] and we have perfect peace in Him.[10] They sing His praise,[11] and so do we. This year we will gather heavenly fruits on earthly ground, where faith and hope make the desert a garden of the LORD. Long ago God's people ate angels' bread,[12] so why not now? Oh for grace to feed on Christ, and so eat of the produce of the land of Canaan[13] this year!

☙ January 2 ❧

Devote yourselves to prayer (Colossians 4:2).

Many of the Scriptures are occupied with the subject of prayer, either with providing examples, enforcing precepts, or pronouncing promises. We barely open the Bible before we read, "At that time men began to call on the name of the Lord."[14] And just as we finish the Bible, "Amen Come, Lord Jesus" greets our eyes.[15] Instances are plentiful. Here we find a wrestling Jacob—there a Daniel who prayed three times a day—and a David who called upon his God with all his heart. On the mountain we see Elias [Elijah]; in the dungeon Paul and Silas. We have multitudes of commands, and innumerable promises. What do these teach us?— the sacred importance and necessity of prayer. We can be certain that whatever God made prominent in His Word, He intended to be obvious in our lives. A prayerless soul is a Christless soul. Prayer is the lisping of the believing infant, the shout of the fighting believer, the requiem of the dying saint falling asleep in Christ.[16] It is the breath, the watchword, the comfort, the strength, the honor of a Christian. If you are a child of God, you will seek your Father's face, and live in your Father's love. Pray that this year you may be holy, humble, zealous, and patient; have closer communion with Christ, and enter oftener into the banqueting-house of His love. Pray that you may be an example and a blessing unto others, and that you may live more to the glory of your Master. The motto for this year must be: "Devote yourself to prayer."

≋ *January 3* ≋

I will ... make you to be a covenant for the people
(Isaiah 49:8).

Jesus Christ is Himself the sum and substance of the covenant, and as one of its gifts. He is the property of every believer. Believer, can you measure what you have gotten in Christ? "In Christ all the fullness of the Deity lives in bodily form."[17] Consider that word "God" and its infinity, and then meditate upon "perfect man" and all his beauty; for all that Christ, as God and man, ever had or has, is yours. Has he power? That power is yours to support and strengthen you, to overcome your enemies, and to preserve you even to the end. Has He love? Well, there is not a drop of love in His heart that is not yours; you may dive into the immense ocean of His love, and you may say of it all, "It is mine." Has He justice? Even that is yours, for He will by His justice see to it that all which is promised to you in the covenant of grace shall be secured to you. And all that He has as perfect man is yours. As a perfect man the Father's delight was upon Him. He stood accepted by the Most High. Oh, believer, God's acceptance of Christ is your acceptance; for don't you know that the love the Father set on a perfect Christ, He sets on you now? For all that Christ did is yours. That perfect righteousness that Jesus wrought out, when through His stainless life He kept the law and made it honorable, is yours, and is imputed to you.[18] Christ is in the covenant.

⊰ *January 4* ⊱

Grow in the grace and knowledge of our LORD *and Savior Jesus Christ (2 Peter 3:18).*

"Grow in the grace"—not in one grace only, but in *all* grace. Grow in that root-grace, *faith.* Believe the promises more firmly than you have done. Grow also in *love.* Ask that your love may become extended, more intense, more practical, influencing every thought, word, and deed. Grow in *humility.* Seek to lie very low, and know more of your own nothingness. As you grow *downward* in humility, seek also to grow *upward*—growing closer to God in prayer and having intimate fellowship with Christ. To know Him is "life eternal,"[19] and to advance in the knowledge of Him is to increase in happiness. Those who do not long to know more of Christ, know nothing of Him yet. If you know the love of Jesus Christ—as the deer pants for streams of water, so will you pant after deeper refreshments of His love. If you do not desire to know Him better, then you don't love Him, for love always cries, "Nearer, nearer." Absence from Christ is hell; but the presence of Christ is heaven. Seek to know more of Him in His divine nature, in His human relationship, in His finished work, in His death, in His resurrection, in His present glorious intercession, and in His future royal return. Abide hard by the Cross, and search the mystery of His wounds. An increase of love for Christ, and a more perfect apprehension of His love for us is one of the best tests of growth in grace.

*God saw that the light was good, and He separated
the light from the darkness (Genesis 1:4).*

Light is good because it sprang from that decree of goodness,
"Let there be light."[20] *Physical* light is sweet,[21] but *gospel*
light is infinitely sweeter, for it reveals eternal things, and
ministers to our immortal natures. When the Holy Spirit
gives us *spiritual* light and opens our eyes to behold the
glory of God in the face of Jesus Christ, we behold sin in
its true colors, and ourselves in our real condition. We see
the Most Holy God as He reveals Himself, the plan of
mercy as He propounds it, and the world to come as the
Word describes it. If the *spiritual* light we receive is good,
what must the *Essential* light be? Oh, LORD, since light
is so good, give us more of it, and more of Yourself, the
true light. No sooner is there a good thing in the world,
than *a division is necessary.* Light and darkness have no
communion. God has separated them, let us not confuse
them. Children of light must not have fellowship with
deeds, doctrines, or deceits of darkness. The children of the
day must be sober, honest, and bold in their LORD's work,
leaving the works of darkness to those who shall dwell in
it for ever. In judgment, in action, in hearing, in teaching,
in association, we must discern between the precious and
the vile, and maintain the great distinction that the LORD
made upon the world's first day. Oh, LORD Jesus, You be
our light throughout the whole of this day, for Your light
is the light of the world.

Cast all your anxiety on Him because
He cares for you (1 Peter 5:7).

It is a happy way of soothing sorrow when we can feel "He cares for me!" Don't dishonor Christianity by always wearing a worried brow. Cast your burden upon your LORD. You're staggering beneath a weight that He would not feel. What seems to you a crushing burden, would be to Him less than the smallest particle of dust. Child of suffering, be patient. God hasn't passed over you in His providence. Don't sit down in despair. *There is* One who cares for you. His eye is fixed on you, His heart beats with pity for your woe, and His hand omnipotent shall yet bring you the needed help. The darkest cloud shall scatter itself in showers of mercy. The blackest gloom shall give place to the morning. If you are one of His family, He will bind up your wounds, and heal your broken heart. Don't doubt His grace because of your tribulation, but believe that He loves you as much in seasons of trouble as in times of happiness. What a serene and quiet life you might lead if you would leave providing to the God of providence! With a little oil in the cruse, and a handful of meal in the barrel, Elijah outlived the famine,[22] and you will do the same. If God cares for you, why must you care, too? Can you trust Him for your soul, and not for your body? He never refuses to bear your burdens, or faints under their weight. Stop your worrying and leave all your concerns in the hand of a gracious God.

For to me, to live is Christ (Philippians 1:21).

As believers we did not always live to Christ. We began to do so when the Holy Spirit convinced us of sin, and when by grace we were brought to see the dying Savior making a propitiation for our guilt. From the moment of the new and heavenly birth we begin to live to Christ. He is the one pearl of great price, for whom we are willing to part with all that we have. He has so completely won our love, that it beats alone for Him. We would live to His glory and die in defense of His gospel. He is the pattern of our life, and the model after which we would sculpture our character. Paul's words mean more than most people think. They imply that the *aim and end of his life* was Christ — indeed, his life itself was Christ. Christ was his very breath, the soul of his soul, the heart of his heart, the life of his life. Can you say that you live up to this idea? Can you honestly say that for you to live is Christ? There are many who carry out this principle in some measure, but who dares say that they have lived wholly for Christ as the apostle did? Yet, this alone is the true life of a Christian—its source, its sustenance, its fashion, its end, all gathered up in one word—Christ. LORD, I present myself to live only in You and to You—to work or to be sacrificed, and ready for either.

◁ *January 8* ▷

The iniquity of the holy things (Exodus 28:38, KJV).

What a veil is lifted up by these words, and what a disclosure is made! It will be humbling and profitable for us to pause and see this sad sight. The iniquities of our public worship—its hypocrisy, lukewarmness, irreverence, wandering of heart. Our private devotions—their coldness, neglect, sleepiness, and vanity. Dr. Payson wrote to his brother, *"My parish, as well as my heart, very much resembles the garden of the sluggard; and what is worse, I find that very many of my desires for the melioration of both, proceed either from pride or vanity or indolence. I look at the weeds which overspread my garden, and breathe out an earnest wish that they were eradicated. But why? What prompts the wish? It may be that I may walk out and say to myself, 'In what fine order is my garden kept!' This is pride. Or, it may be that my neighbors may look over the wall and say, 'How finely your garden flourishes!' This is vanity. Or I may wish for the destruction of the weeds, because I am weary of pulling them up. This is indolence."* Even our desires after holiness may be polluted by ill motives—worms hide under the greenest sod. How cheering that when the High Priest bore the iniquity of the holy things, he wore upon his brow the words, "HOLINESS TO THE LORD."[23] Even so while Jesus bears our sin, He presents before His Father not our unholiness, but his own holiness. Oh for grace to view our great High Priest by the eye of faith!

✠ January 9 ✠

I will be their God (Jeremiah 31:33).

Christian, here is all you need. To make you happy you want something that will satisfy you—and isn't this promise enough? If you can pour this promise into your cup, you can say, "My cup runs over; I have more than my heart can wish!" When "I am your God" is fulfilled, you will possess all things. No one can measure the capacity of our wishes, but the immeasurable wealth of God can more than overflow it. Are you not complete when God is yours? Do you want anything but God? Isn't His all-sufficiency enough to satisfy you if all else should fail? But you want more than quiet satisfaction, you desire *rapturous delight*. Well here is music fit for heaven, for God is the maker of heaven. Not all the music blown from sweet instruments, or drawn from living strings, can yield such melody as the sweet promise, "I will be their God." Here is a deep sea of bliss, an endless ocean of delight. Swim forever and you'll find no shore. Dive throughout eternity and you'll find no bottom. "I will be their God." If this doesn't make your eyes sparkle, and your heart beat hard with bliss, then your soul is not in a healthy state. This is the masterpiece of all the promises. Its enjoyment makes a heaven below, and will make a heaven above. Dwell in the light of your LORD, and let your soul always be ravished with His love. Extract the marrow and fatness that your portion yields to you. Live up to your privileges, and rejoice with unspeakable joy.

Now there is in store for me the crown of
righteousness (2 Timothy 4:8).

Doubting one! you have sometimes said, "I'm afraid I will
never enter heaven." Don't be afraid, for all the people of
God will enter there. A dying person exclaimed, "I have
no fear of going home. I have sent all before me. God's
finger is on the latch of my door, and I am ready for Him
to enter." "But," said someone, "aren't you afraid that you
may miss your inheritance?" "No," the person replied.
"There's one crown in heaven that the angel Gabriel cannot
wear—it will fit no head but mine. There's one throne in
heaven that Paul cannot fill—it was made for me alone."
Oh, Christian, what a joyous thought—your portion is
secure. "But can't I forfeit it?" No, it's bestowed. If I'm
a child of God I will not lose it. It's mine as securely as if
I were there. Come, and let us sit upon the top of Nebo
and view the goodly land, even Canaan.[24] See that little
river of death glistening in the sunlight, and across it do
you see the pinnacles of the eternal city? Know, then, that
if you could fly across you would see written upon one of
its many mansions, "This remains for such a one—it is
preserved for you only." If you believe in the LORD Jesus,
if you've repented of sin, if you've been renewed in heart,
you're one of the LORD's people. There is a mansion and a
crown reserved for you, for there will be no vacant thrones
in glory when all the chosen are gathered in.

✎ *January 11* ✎

These have no root (Luke 8:13).

My soul, examine yourself by the light of this text. You have received the Word with joy, your feelings have been stirred, and a lively impression has been made. But to receive the word into the ear is one thing, and to receive Jesus into your soul is quite another. Superficial feeling is often joined to inward hardness of heart, and a lively impression of the Word is not always a lasting one. In the parable of our text, the seed in one case fell upon rock, perhaps covered over with a thin layer of earth. When the seed began to take root, its downward growth was hindered by the hard surface, and getting no water from its roots, it withered away. Is this our case? Have we been making a fair show in the flesh without having a corresponding inner life? Good growth takes place upwards and downwards at the same time. Am I rooted in sincere fidelity and love to Jesus? If my heart remains unsoftened and unfertilized by grace, the good seed may germinate for a season, but it must ultimately wither, for it cannot flourish on a rocky, unbroken, unsanctified heart. Let me dread a godliness that has no endurance. Let me count the cost of being a follower of Jesus, and above all let me feel the energy of His Holy Spirit—then I shall possess an abiding and enduring seed in my soul. Oh, heavenly Sower, plow me first, and then cast the truth into me, and let me produce a bounteous harvest for You.

ᴥ January 12 ᴥ

You are Christ's (1 Corinthians 3:23, NKJV).

You are Christ's." You are His by donation, for the Father gave you to His Son;[25] His by His blood, for He paid the price for your redemption;[26] His by dedication, for you have consecrated yourself to Him; His by relation, for you are named by His name, and made one of His family and joint-heirs.[27] When tempted to sin, reply, "I cannot do this thing, for I am Christ's." Immortal principles forbid the friend of Christ to sin. When money is before you to be gained by sin, say that you are Christ's, and don't touch it. Are you exposed to difficulties and dangers? Stand fast in the evil day,[28] remembering that you are Christ's. Are you placed where others are standing idly, doing nothing? Rise to the work with all your powers; and when the sweat stands upon your brow, and you are tempted to loiter, cry, "No, I cannot stop, for I am Christ's and cannot stand idly about." When the songs of pleasure would tempt you from the path of right, reply, "Your music cannot charm me, for I am Christ's." When the cause of God invites you, give your goods and yourself away, for you are Christ's. Always be one whose manners are Christian, whose speech is like Jesus of Nazareth, whose conduct and conversation are so suggestive of heaven that all who see you may know that you are the Savior's, recognizing in you His features of love and His countenance of holiness. Let your argument for holiness always be, "I am Christ's!"

☒ *January 13* ☒

Now Jehoshaphat built a fleet of trading ships to
go to Ophir for gold, but they never set sail—they
were wrecked at Ezion Geber (1 Kings 22:48).

Solomon's ships had returned in safety, but Jehoshaphat's vessels never reached the land of gold. Providence prospers one, and frustrates the desires of another, in the same business and at the same spot, yet the Great Ruler is as good and wise at one time as another. In remembrance of this text, may we have grace today to bless the LORD for ships wrecked at Ezion Geber, as well as for vessels loaded with temporal blessings. Let's not envy the more successful or murmur at our losses as though we were singularly and specially tried. Like Jehoshaphat, we may be precious in the LORD's sight even though our plans end in disappointment. The secret cause of Jehoshaphat's loss is worth noting, for it is the root of much of the suffering of the LORD's people. It was caused by his alliance with a sinful family, and fellowship with sinners. Second Chronicles. 20:37 says that the LORD sent a prophet to declare, "Because you have made an alliance with Ahaziah, the LORD will destroy what you have made." Would to God that Jehoshaphat's experience might be a warning to all of the LORD's people to avoid being unequally yoked together with unbelievers! A life of misery is usually the state of those who are united in marriage, or in any other way of their own choosing, with the unbelievers of the world. Oh that we had such love for Jesus that, like Him, we may be holy, harmless, undefiled, and separate from sinners.

Mighty to save (Isaiah 63:1).

By the words "to save" we understand the whole of the great work of salvation, from the first holy desire onward to complete sanctification. Christ is not only "mighty to save" those who repent, but He is able to make people repent. He will carry those to heaven who believe, and He is mighty to give people new hearts and to work faith in them. He is mighty to make the person who hates holiness love it, and to compel the despisers of His name to bend their knees before Him. The life of a believer is a series of miracles wrought by "the Mighty God."[29] He is mighty to keep His people holy after He has made them so, and to preserve them until He brings to completion their spiritual existence in heaven.[30] Christ's might doesn't lie in making believers and then leaving them to shift for themselves. He who imparts the first germ of life in the dead soul strengthens it until it's freed from the bondage of sin and leaps from earth, perfected in glory.[31] Believer, here is encouragement. Are you praying for some beloved one? Don't give up your prayers, for Christ is "mighty to save." You are powerless to reclaim the rebel, but your LORD is all powerful.[32] Lay hold on that mighty arm, and rouse it to put forth its strength. Does your own case trouble you? Fear not, for His strength is sufficient for you. Whether to begin with others, or to carry on the work in you, Jesus is "mighty to save." The best proof of this is the fact that He has saved *you.*

↠ *January 15* ↞

LORD God, do as You promised (2 Samuel 7:25).

God's promises were never meant to be thrown aside as waste paper. He intended them to be used. Nothing pleases our LORD better than to see His promises active in our lives. He loves to see His children bring them up to Him, and say, "LORD, do as You have promised." We glorify God when we plead His promises. Do you think that God will be any the poorer for giving you the riches He promised? Do you dream He will be any the less holy for giving holiness to you? Do you imagine He will be any the less pure for washing you from your sins? He has said, "Come now, let us reason together. Though your sins are like scarlet, they shall be as white as snow; though they are red as crimson, they shall be like wool."[33] Faith lays hold upon the promise of pardon, and goes straight to the throne with it, and pleads, "LORD, here is Your promise, 'Please, do as You promised.'" To which our LORD replies, "Your request is granted."[34] When you get hold of a promise, if you don't take it to God, you dishonor Him. Our heavenly Banker is delighted to cash His own promissory notes. God will not be troubled by your persistently reminding Him of His promises. It is His delight to bestow favors on His children. He is more ready to hear than you are to ask. It is God's nature to keep His promises. Go at once, therefore, to the throne with "Please do as You promised."[35]

⪯ *January 16* ⪰

"I myself will help you," declares the LORD
(Isaiah 41:14).

This morning let us hear the LORD speak to each one of us:
"I myself will *help* you." "It is a small thing for Me, your
LORD, to *help* you. Consider what I have done already.
What! not help you? Why, I bought you with My blood.
I have died for you—and if I have done the greater, will I
not do the less? It is the least thing I will ever do for you.
I *have* done more, and will do more. Before the world
began I chose you. I made the covenant for you. I laid
aside My glory and became a man for you. I gave up My
life for you. And if I did all this, I will surely help you
now. In helping you, I am giving you what I have bought
for you already. If you needed a thousand times as much
help, I would give it to you. You require little compared
with what I am ready to give. It's much for you to need,
but it is nothing for Me to give. If there were an ant at the
door of your granary[36] asking for help, it would not ruin
you to give him a handful of your wheat. And you are as
a tiny insect at the door of My all-sufficiency. 'I myself will
help you.'" Isn't this enough? Do you need more strength
than the omnipotence of the Godhead? Do you want more
wisdom, love, or power than there is in the Father, Son, and
Holy Spirit? Bring forth your empty container and fill it to
the brim! The river of God is full for your supply—what
more can you desire?

✠ *January 17* ✠

Then I looked, and there before me was the Lamb,
standing on Mount Zion (Revelation 14:1).

The apostle John was privileged to look within heaven, and in describing what he saw, he begins by saying, "I looked … and there was the Lamb!" This teaches us that the chief object of contemplation in the heavenly state is "the Lamb of God, who takes away the sin of the world!"[37] Nothing else attracted the apostle's attention so much as the person of that divine Being, who has redeemed us by His blood. Christian, here is joy for you—you have looked, and you have seen the Lamb. Through your tears your eyes have seen the Lamb of God taking away your sins. Rejoice, then. In a little while, when all the tears have been wiped from your eyes,[38] you will see the same Lamb *exalted on His throne.* It's the joy of your heart to hold daily fellowship with Christ—you will have the same joy to a higher degree in heaven, for there you will enjoy His constant presence, and will dwell with Him forever. That Lamb is heaven itself, for heaven and Christ are the same thing. To be with Christ is to be in heaven, and to be in heaven is to be with Christ. A prisoner of the LORD wrote: "Oh my LORD Jesus Christ, if I could be in heaven without You, it would be a hell. And if I could be in hell, and have You still, it would be a heaven to me, for You are all the heaven I want." It is true, Christian. All you need to be supremely blessed is "to be with Christ."

◁ *January 18* ▷

There remains, then, a Sabbath-rest for the
people of God (Hebrews 4:9).

How different the state of the believers will be in heaven from what it is here. Here we are born to toil and suffer weariness, but in the land of the immortal, fatigue is never known. Anxious to serve our Master, we find our strength unequal to our desire. If we are totally active, we will have much work—not too much for our will, but more than enough for our power. So much so, that we will cry out, "I am not tired *of* the work, but I am tired *in* it." Christian, the hot day of weariness doesn't last forever. The sun is nearing the horizon, and it will rise again with a brighter day than you have ever seen upon a land where we will serve God day and night, and yet rest from our labors. *Here*, rest is but partial. *There*, it is perfect. *Here*, we are always unsettled and feel that we haven't yet attained our goal. *There*, we will be at rest— we will have attained the summit of the mountain, and will have ascended to the bosom of our God. Higher we cannot go. Ah, toil-worn worker, think of when you will rest forever. Can you conceive it? It's a rest *eternal*—a rest that "remains." *Here*, everything is mortal and temporal—fading and filled with shadows and sorrows. *There*, everything is immortal and eternal—the eyes remain undimmed, the voice unfaltering, the heart unwavering, and the immortal being is wholly absorbed in infinite delight. What a happy day when mortality is swallowed up by life, and the eternal Sabbath-rest begins.

I looked for him but did not find him
(Song of Songs 3:1)

Tell me where you lost the company of Christ, and I will tell you the most likely place to find Him. Have you lost Christ in the closet by holding back in prayer? Then it is there you must seek and find Him. Did you lose Christ by sin? You will find Christ in no other way but by the giving up the sin and seeking by the Holy Spirit to mortify that part of you in which the sin lives. Did you lose Christ by neglecting the Scriptures? You must find Christ in the Scriptures. It's a true proverb: "Look for a thing where you dropped it, for it is there." So look for Christ where you lost Him, for He has not gone away. But it is hard work to go back for Christ. John Bunyan tells us that Pilgrim found that the piece of the road back to the Arbor of Ease, where he lost his roll, was the hardest he had ever traveled.[39] Twenty miles forward is easier than to go one mile back for the lost evidence. When you find your Master, be careful to cling close to Him. But why is it you lost Him? One would have thought you would never have parted with such a precious friend, whose presence is so sweet. How is it that you did not watch Him every moment for fear of losing sight of Him? Yet, since you have let Him go, what mercy from God that you are seeking Him. Go on seeking, for it is dangerous to be without your LORD.

⇜ *January 20* ⇝

Abel kept flocks (Genesis 4:2).

As a shepherd Abel *sanctified his work to the glory of God, and offered a sacrifice of blood upon his altar, and the* LORD *looked with favor on Abel and his offering.*[40] This early type of our LORD is exceedingly clear and distinct. Like the first streak of light that tinges the east at sunrise, it doesn't reveal everything, but it clearly reveals the fact that the sun is coming. As we see Abel, a shepherd and yet a priest, offering a sacrifice of sweet smell unto God, we discern our LORD, who brings before His Father a sacrifice to which Jehovah ever looks on with favor. Abel was hated by his brother—hated without a cause. And so was the Savior. The natural and carnal man hated the accepted man in whom the Spirit of grace was found, and did not rest until his blood was shed. Abel fell, and sprinkled his altar and sacrifice with his own blood, and therein shows forth the LORD Jesus slain by the hatred of people while serving as a priest before God. "The good shepherd lays down his life for the sheep." *Abel's blood speaks..* The LORD said to Cain, "Your brother's blood cries out to me from the ground." The blood of Jesus has a mighty voice, and its prevailing cry is not vengeance but mercy.[41] It's precious beyond all preciousness to stand at the altar of our good Shepherd, to see Him bleeding there as the slaughtered priest,[42] and to hear His blood speaking peace with God[43] to all His flock.

And so all Israel shall be saved (Romans 11:26).

When Moses sang at the Red Sea,[44] it was his joy to know that all Israel was safe. Not a drop of water fell from that solid wall until the last of God's Israel had safely set foot on the other side the flood. That done, immediately the waters returned to their proper place again, but not until then. Now safe, they sang a song of redemption, part of which said, "In your unfailing love you will lead the people you have redeemed." In the last time, when the elect will sing the song of Moses,[45] the servant of God, and of the Lamb, it will be the boast of Christ: "I have not lost one of those You gave me."[46] In heaven there will not be a vacant throne. As many as God has chosen, as many as Christ has redeemed, as many as the Spirit has called, as many as believe in Jesus Christ,[47] will safely cross the dividing sea. We are not all safely landed yet, but the vanguard of the army has already reached the shore. Let's be of good cheer—the rear-guard will soon be where the vanguard already is. The last of the chosen ones will soon have crossed the sea, and then will be heard the song of triumph, when all are secure. But oh! if one were absent—oh! if one of His chosen family should be cast away—it would make an everlasting discord in the song of the redeemed, and cut the strings of the harps of paradise, so that music could never be brought forth from them.[48]

"Son of man, how is the wood of a vine better than that of a branch on any of the trees in the forest?"
(Ezekiel 15:2)

These words were spoken to humble God's people. They are called God's vine, but what are they by nature more than others? By God's goodness, they have become fruitful, having been planted in a good soil. The LORD has trained them to grow upon the walls of the sanctuary, and they bring forth fruit to His glory—but what are they without their God? What are they without the continual influence of the Spirit producing fruitfulness in them? Oh, believer, learn to reject pride, seeing that you have no basis for it. Whatever you are, you have nothing to make you proud. The more you have, the more you're in debt to God—and you have no reason to be proud of what makes you a debtor. Consider where you came from, and look back to what you were. Consider what you would have been but for divine grace. Look at yourself as you are now. Doesn't your conscience reproach you? Don't your thousand wanderings stand before you, and tell you that you're unworthy to be called His child? And if He has made you anything, aren't you taught by it that it's grace that has made you different? Great believer, you would have been a great sinner if God hadn't changed you. Oh you who are valiant for truth, you would have been as valiant for error if grace hadn't gotten hold of you.[49] Therefore, don't be proud, even though you have a large estate—a wide domain of grace—for once you did not have a single thing to call your own except your sin and misery.

ᛜ January 23 ᛜ

*I have exalted one chosen out of the people
(Psalm 89:19).*

Why was Christ chosen out of the people? Speak, my heart, for thoughts from the heart are best. Wasn't it that He might be able to be *our brother*, in the blessed tie of kindred blood? Oh, what relationship there is between Christ and the believer. The believer can say, "I have a Brother in heaven. I may be poor, but I have a Brother who is rich, and is a King. Will He allow me to be in need while He's on His throne? Oh, no! He loves me—He's my Brother." Believer, wear this blessed thought like a necklace of diamonds around the neck of your memory. Put it on the finger of recollection like a golden ring, and use it as the King's own seal, stamping the petitions of your faith with confidence of success. He's a brother born for adversity, treat Him as such. Christ was also chosen out of the people that He might know our needs and sympathize with us. He "has been tempted in every way, just as we are—yet was without sin."[50] In all our sorrows we have His sympathy. He knows them all: temptation, pain, disappointment, weakness, weariness, poverty—for He has felt them all. Remember this, Christian, and let it comfort you. However difficult and painful your road, it's marked by the footsteps of your Savior. And even when you reach the dark valley of the shadow of death,[51] you'll find His footprints there. In whatever places we go, He has been our forerunner. Each burden we have to carry, was once laid on the shoulders of Immanuel.

≍ January 24 ≍

Surely He will save you from the fowler's snare
(Psalm 91:3).

God delivers His people from the fowler's snare in two ways: *from*, and *out of*. First, He delivers them *from* the snare—does not let them enter it. Second, if they should be caught in it, He delivers them *out of* it. The first promise is the most precious to some—the second is the best to others. "He will save you from the fowler's snare." How? Trouble is often the means by which God delivers us. God knows that our backsliding will soon end in our destruction, and in mercy He sends the rod. We say, "LORD, why is this?—not knowing that our trouble has been the means of delivering us from far greater evil. Many have been saved from ruin by their sorrows and their crosses, which have driven them *from* the net like frightened birds. At other times, God keeps His people *from* the fowler's snare by giving them great spiritual strength, so that when they are tempted they say, "How can I commit this sin against God?" But what a blessed thing it is that if we get caught in the snare in an evil hour, God will bring us *out* of it! Oh, backslider, be downcast, but don't despair. Though you have wandered away, hear what your Redeemer says: "Return, faithless people; I will cure you of backsliding."[52] But you say you cannot return, for you are a captive. Yet He has promised to bring you out of all evil into which you have fallen, and to give you joy and gladness. No bird of paradise will die in the fowler's snare.

*I will tell of the kindnesses of the LORD, the deeds
for which He is to be praised, according to all the
LORD has done for us (Isaiah 63:7).*

Can you do this? Are there mercies that you *have
experienced*? Even though you are gloomy now, can you
forget that blessed hour when Jesus met you and said,
"Come to me?"[53] Can you remember that rapturous
moment when He broke your slavery to sin,[54] and said, "I
came to break your bonds and set you free?" Or if you've
forgotten the love you felt when you were wedded to
Christ, there must surely be some precious milestone along
the road of life not quite grown over with moss, on which
you can read a happy memorial of His mercy towards you?
Were you ever sick before and He restored you? Were you
ever without before and He supplied your needs? Were
you ever in difficulties before and He delivered you? Get
up then and go to the river of your experience, and pull
up a few papyruses [bulrushes] and braid them into an
ark, in which your childlike faith may float safely on the
stream.[55] Don't forget what your God has done for you.
Look through the pages of your memory and think about
your past. Has God never helped you in time of need? I
know He has. Go back, then, a little ways to the choice
mercies of yesterday, and though all may be dark *now*,
light up the lamps of your past. They will shine through
the darkness, and you will trust in the LORD until the day
breaks and the shadows flee away. "Remember, O LORD,
Your great mercy and love, for they are from of old."[56]

≈ January 26 ≈

Your heavenly Father (Matthew 6:26).

God's people are doubly His children. They are His offspring by creation, and they are His children by adoption in Christ. Therefore they are privileged to call Him, "Our Father in heaven."[57] *Father*! Oh, what precious word that is. Here is *authority*: "If I am a father, where is the honor due Me?"[58] If you are sons and daughters, where is your obedience? Here is *affection* mingled with authority. It's an authority that doesn't provoke rebellion, but which demands an obedience that is cheerfully rendered, and that would not be withheld even if it might. The obedience that God's children yield to Him must be *loving* obedience. Don't serve God as slaves to a taskmaster's toil, but run in the way of His commands because it is your *Father's* way. Yield your bodies as instruments of righteousness,[59] because righteousness is your Father's will, and *His* will should be the will of His child. *Father*! Here is honor and love. How great is a father's love for his children! That which friendship cannot do, and mere benevolence will not attempt, a father's heart and hand must do for his sons and daughters. They are his children, he must be strong in their defense. If an earthly father watches over his children with unceasing love and care, how much more does our heavenly Father? *Abba, Father*![60] There is heaven in the depth of that word—*Father*! There is all I can ask, all my necessities can demand, and all my wishes can desire. I have all in all to all eternity when I can say to Almighty God, "*Father*."

And of His fullness we have all received
(John 1:16, NKJV).

These words tell us that there is a fullness in Christ. There is a fullness of essential Deity, for "in Christ all the fullness of the Deity [Godhead] lives in bodily form." There is a fullness of perfect manhood, for in Him that Godhead was revealed in bodily form. There is a fullness of atoning efficacy in His blood, for "the blood of Jesus, his Son, purifies us from all sin."[61] There is a fullness of justifying righteousness in His life, for "there is now no condemnation for those who are in Christ Jesus."[62] There is a fullness of divine prevalence in His plea, for "he is able to save completely those who come to God through him, because he always lives to intercede for them."[63] There is a fullness of victory in His death, for through death He destroyed "him who holds the power of death—that is, the devil."[64] There is a fullness of efficacy in His resurrection from the dead, for by it He "has given us new birth into a living hope."[65] There is a fullness of triumph in His ascension, for "when he ascended on high, he led captives in his train." There is a fullness of grace to pardon, grace to regenerate, grace to sanctify, grace to preserve, and grace to perfect. There is a fullness of comfort in affliction, and of guidance in prosperity. A fullness of divine wisdom, power, and love that is impossible to survey, much less to explore. Come, believer, and get all your need supplied—ask largely, and you will receive largely, for His fullness is inexhaustible.

◁ *January 28* ◁

Perfect in Christ (Colossians 1:28).

Don't you feel in your own soul that perfection is not in you? Doesn't every day teach you that? Every tear that trickles from your eye, weeps *imperfection*. Every harsh word that proceeds from your lip, mutters *imperfection*. You have too frequently had a view of your own heart to dream for a moment of any perfection *in yourself*. But in the midst of this sad consciousness of imperfection, here is comfort for you: you are "perfect *in Christ Jesus*."[66] In God's sight, you are "complete in Him."[67] *Even now* you are "accepted in the Beloved."[68] But there is a second perfection, yet to be realized, which is sure to all the seed. Isn't it wonderful to look forward to the time when every stain of sin will be removed from the believers, and we will be presented faultless before the throne, without spot, or wrinkle, or any such thing?[69] The Church then will be so pure, so holy and glorious, that not even the eye of Omniscience will see a spot or blemish in her. Then shall we know and feel the happiness of this vast but short sentence, "Complete in Christ." Not until then will we fully comprehend the heights and depths of the salvation of Jesus Christ. Oh, it is a marvelous salvation this. Christ takes a worm and transforms it into a saint. Christ takes a dirty and deformed thing and makes it clean and matchless in His glory, peerless in His beauty, and fit to be the companion of angels. Oh my soul, stand and admire this blessed truth of perfection in Christ.

❧ *January 29* ☙

What is unseen (2 Corinthians 4:18).

In our Christian pilgrimage it is well, for the most part, to be looking forward. Forward lies the crown, and onward is the goal. Whether it is for hope, for joy, for consolation, or for the inspiring of our love, the future must, after all, be the grand object of the eye of faith. Looking into the future we see sin cast out, the body of sin and death destroyed, the soul made perfect, and fit to be a partaker of the inheritance of the saints in light. Looking further yet, the believer's enlightened eye can see death's river passed,[70] the gloomy stream forded, and the hills of light attained on which stands the celestial city. There we see ourselves enter within the pearly gates, hailed as more than conquerors,[71] crowned by the hand of Christ, embraced in His arms, glorified with Him, and made to sit together with Him on His throne,[72] even as He overcame and sat down with the Father on His throne. The thought of this future may well relieve the darkness of the past and the gloom of the present. The joys of heaven will surely compensate for the sorrows of earth. Be still my doubts! Death is but a narrow stream, and you will soon have forded it. Time, how short—eternity, how long! Death, how brief—immortality, how endless! Even now I seem to be eating of Eshcol's clusters,[73] and sipping of the well that is within the gate.[74] The road is so, so short! I will soon be there.

◁ *January 30* ▷

*As soon as you hear the sound of marching in the
tops of the balsam trees, move quickly
(2 Samuel 5:24).*

The members of Christ's Church should be very prayerful,
always seeking the unction of the Holy One to rest upon
their hearts, that the kingdom of Christ may come, and that
His "will be done on earth as it is in heaven."[75] But there
are times when God seems especially to favor Zion,[76] and
such times should be to them like "the sound of marching in
the tops of the balsam trees." In those times, we should be
doubly prayerful, doubly earnest, and wrestling more at the
throne than has been our habit. Our actions then should be
prompt and vigorous. Oh, for Pentecostal outpourings and
Pentecostal labors. Christian, there are times in *yourself*
when you "hear the sound of marching in the tops of the
balsam trees." It is then that you have a peculiar power in
prayer, the Spirit of God gives you joy and gladness, the
Scriptures are open to you, the promises are forcefully
applied, you walk in the light of God's countenance, and
you have special freedom and liberty in devotion and a
closer communion with Christ than normal. Now, during
such joyous periods, is the time to bestir yourself—now is
the time to get rid of any evil habit, while the Holy Spirit
is helping your infirmities.[77] Seek God's help to be more
earnest in duty when made more strong in faith, to be
more constant in prayer when you have more liberty at the
throne, and to be more holy in your conversation while
you live more closely with Christ.

The LORD *Our Righteousness (Jeremiah 23:6).*

It always gives Christians the greatest calm and peace, to think of the perfect righteousness of Christ. Christians are often dejected and sad, but they would not be if they always saw their perfection in Christ. There are some who always talk about the depravity of the heart and innate evil of the soul. That's true, but go a little further and remember that we are "perfect in Christ."[78] It's no wonder that those who dwell upon their own corruption are dejected, but surely if we call to mind that "Christ Jesus ... has become for us ... righteousness,"[79] we will be cheerful. Though distresses afflict us, Satan assaults us, and there are many things we must experience before we get to heaven, those are done for us in the covenant of divine grace. Christ has done it all. On the Cross He said, "It is finished!"[80] If it is finished, then we are complete in Him, and can rejoice with joy unspeakable and full of glory—"not having a righteousness of my own that comes from the law, but that which is through faith in Christ—the righteousness that comes from God and is by faith."[81] When the believer says, "I rest solely on Christ for salvation—and I believe that, however unworthy, I am still saved in Jesus," then there rises up as a motive of gratitude this thought—"Shall I not live for Christ? Shall I not love Him and serve Him, seeing that I am saved by *His* merits?" If saved by imputed righteousness, we will greatly value imparted righteousness.

February

May they sing of the ways of the LORD, for the glory of the LORD is great (Psalm 138:5).

The time when Christians begin to sing in the ways of the LORD is when they first lose their burden at the foot of the Cross. Nothing is as sweet as the first song of rapture that gushes from the inmost soul of the forgiven sinner. John Bunyan wrote that when poor Pilgrim[82] lost his burden at the Cross, he gave three great leaps, and went on his way singing: "Blessed Cross! Blessed Sepulcher! Blessed rather be The Man that there was put to shame for me!" Believer, do you recollect the day when *your* burden fell off? Do you remember the place when Christ met you, and said, "I have swept away your offenses like a cloud, your sins like the morning mist. Return to me, for I have redeemed you."[83] When the LORD first pardoned my sin, I was so joyous that I could scarcely keep from dancing. I thought on my way home that I must tell the stones in the road the story of my deliverance. My soul was so full of joy that I wanted to tell every snow-flake that was falling from heaven of the wondrous love of Jesus Christ, who had blotted out the sins of one of the chief of rebels. But it's not only at the beginning of the Christian life that believers have reason to sing. As long as they live they discover reasons to sing about the LORD, and their experiences of His constant loving-kindness lead them to say, "I will extol the LORD at all times; His praise will always be on my lips."[84]

*Without the shedding of blood there is no
forgiveness (Hebrews 9:22).*

This is the voice of unalterable truth. In none of the Jewish
ceremonies were sins, even normal ones, removed without
blood-shedding. There is no way that sin can be pardoned
without atonement. It is clear, then, that there is no hope
for me out of Christ—for there is no other blood-shedding
that is worth a thought as an atonement for sin. Am I,
then, believing in Him? Is the blood of His atonement
truly applied to my soul? All of us are on the same level
concerning our need of Him. Whether we are moral,
generous, amiable, or patriotic, the rule will not be altered
to make an exception for us. Sin will yield to nothing less
potent than the blood of Him whom God has set forth as
a propitiation.[85] What a blessing that there is the one way
of pardon! Why should we seek another? Persons of merely
formal religion cannot understand how we can rejoice that
all our sins are forgiven us for Christ's sake. Their works,
prayers, and ceremonies give them little comfort; and well
may they be uneasy, for they are neglecting the one great
salvation, and endeavoring to get forgiveness without
blood. When conscience is aroused, it's useless to fly to
feelings and evidences for comfort. The only restorative
for a guilty conscience is the sight of Jesus suffering on the
Cross. "The blood is the life thereof," says the Levitical
law, and let us rest assured that it is the life of faith and
joy and every other holy grace. *"Oh, how sweet to view
the flowing of my Savior's precious blood."*

February 3

Therefore, brethren, we are debtors
(Romans 8:12, KJV).

As God's creatures, we are all debtors to Him—to obey Him with all our body, and soul, and strength. Having broken His commandments, as we all have, we are debtors to His justice, and we owe to Him a vast amount that we are not able to pay. But of the *Christian* it can be said that he does not owe God's *justice* anything, for Christ has paid the debt His people owed. I am a debtor to God's grace and forgiving mercy. But I am no debtor to His justice, for He will never accuse me of a debt already paid. Jesus cried, "It is finished!"[86] and by that He meant, that whatever His people owed was washed away forever. Christ satisfied divine justice completely[87]—the account is settled, the handwriting is nailed to the Cross,[88] and we are no longer debtors to God's justice. But we're now ten times more debtors to God than we would have been otherwise. Consider what a debtor you are to divine *sovereignty*! How much you owe to His love, for He gave His own Son to die for you. Consider how much you owe to His forgiving *grace*, that after ten thousand affronts He loves you as infinitely as ever. Consider what you owe to His *power*—He raised you from death,[89] preserved your spiritual life, and has kept you from falling. Consider what you owe to His *immutability*. You have changed a thousand times, He hasn't changed once. You're as deep in debt to God as you can be. You owe yourself and all you have to God.

February 4

As the LORD *loves (Hosea 3:1).*

Believer, *look back* through all your experiences and think of the way in which God led you in the wilderness, and how He fed and clothed you every day. Think of how He bore your ill manners, put up with your murmurings and longings after the meat-pots of Egypt,[90] opened the rock to refresh you,[91] and fed you with heavenly food. Think of how His grace has been sufficient for you in all your troubles,[92] how Jesus' blood has continually washed your sins,[93] and how His rod and His staff have comforted you.[94] When you look back at the love of the LORD in this way, then let faith survey His love *in the future*, for He who has loved you and pardoned you will never cease to love and pardon. He is the Alpha and the Omega, the first the last.[95] Therefore, when you pass through the valley of the shadow of death, don't be afraid, for He is with you.[96] When you stand in the cold floods of Jordan,[97] don't be afraid, for death cannot separate you from His love. And when you come into the mysteries of eternity, don't tremble, "For I am convinced that neither death nor life, neither angels nor demons, neither the present nor the future, nor any powers, neither height nor depth, nor anything else in all creation, will be able to separate us from the love of God that is in Christ Jesus our LORD."[98] Surely as we meditate on "the love of the LORD," our hearts burn within us, and we long to love Him more.

⊲ *February 5* ⊳

The Father has sent His Son to be the Savior of the world (1 John 4:14).

It's comforting to know that Jesus Christ did not come without His Father's authority and assistance. He was sent by the Father that He might be the Savior of humanity.[99] Though there are distinctions as to the *persons* in the Trinity, there are no distinctions of *honor*. We too frequently ascribe the honor of our salvation more to Jesus Christ than we do the Father. This is a very great mistake. What if Jesus came? Didn't His Father send Him? If He spoke wondrously, didn't His Father pour grace into His lips so He might be an able minister of the new covenant? Christians who know the Father, and the Son, and the Holy Ghost as they should know them, never set one before another in their love. They see them at Bethlehem, at Gethsemane, and on Calvary, all equally engaged in the work of salvation. Christian, have you put your confidence in the man Christ Jesus?[100] Have you placed your reliance solely on Him? Are you united with Him? If so, then in Him you are linked with God the Eternal, and "the Ancient of Days"[101] is your Father and your friend. Did you ever consider the depth of love in the heart of Jehovah, when God equipped His Son for the great enterprise of mercy? If not, let this be today's meditation—the *Father* sent Him! Contemplate that fact. Think how Jesus works what the *Father* wills. In the wounds of the dying Savior see the love of the great "I AM."[102] Let every thought of Christ link you to the eternal, ever-blessed, God the Father.

⚄ *February 6* ⚄

Always keep on praying (Ephesians 6:18).

What a great number of prayers we've said from the first moment we learned to pray. Our first prayer was for ourselves—we asked God to have mercy on us and forgive our sins.[103] He heard us. But after He swept away our sins like the morning mist, we had more prayers for ourselves—prayers for sanctifying grace, for constraining and restraining grace, for a fresh gift of faith,[104] for deliverance in the hour of temptation, for help in the time of duty, and for assistance in the day of trial. We've been compelled to go to God for all the needs of our souls. Bear witness, Christian, you've never been able to get anything for your soul elsewhere. All the bread your soul has eaten has come down from heaven, and all the water it drank has flowed from the living rock—Christ Jesus the LORD. Your soul has never grown rich in itself, it has always been dependent upon the daily riches of God,[105] and so your prayers have ascended to heaven for a variety of spiritual mercies. Your needs were innumerable, and so your prayers have been as varied as the mercies have been countless.[106] Your prayers have been many, so also have been God's answers to them. He heard you in the day of trouble, and helped you even when you dishonored Him by your doubts at the mercy seat. Remember this, and let it fill your heart with gratitude to God, who has graciously heard your poor, weak, prayers. "Bless the LORD, O my soul, and forget not all His benefits."[107]

✄ February 7 ✄

Get up, go away! (Micah 2:10)

The hour is approaching when the message will come to us, as it comes to all: "Get up, and leave the home in which you have lived, the city in which you have worked, your family that you love, and your friends. Get up, and take your last journey." And what do we know of the journey, and of the country to which we are going? We've read a little about it, and some of it has been revealed to us by the Spirit; but we really know little of the realms of the future. We know there's a stormy river called "Death." God bids us cross it, promising to be with us. And after death, what wonder-world will open upon our astonished sight? What scene of glory will be unfolded to our view? No traveler has ever returned to tell. But we know enough of the heavenly land to make us welcome our summons to it with joy and gladness. The journey of death may be uncertain, but we can go forth on it fearlessly, knowing that God is with us as we walk through the valley.[108] We will be leaving all we have known and loved here, but we will be going to our Father's house where Jesus is—"to the city with foundations, whose architect and builder is God."[109] Christian, meditate much on heaven, it will help you to press on, and to forget the labors of the journey. This vale of tears is but the pathway to the better country—this world of trouble is but the stepping-stone to a world of joy.

☙ *February 8* ☙

You are to give Him the name Jesus
(Matthew 1:21).

When someone is dear to us, everything connected with them becomes dear for their sake. In the estimation of all true believers, the LORD Jesus is so precious that they consider everything about Him to be far beyond all price. "All your robes are fragrant with myrrh and aloes and cassia,"[110] said David, as if the very garments of the Savior were so sweetened by His person that he could not but love them. Certainly there isn't a spot where His feet have walked, not a word that His lips have spoken, and not a thought that His Word has revealed, that isn't precious to us beyond all price. This is true of the *names* of Christ— they are all sweet to the believer's ear. Whether He is called the Husband of the Church, her Bridegroom, the Lamb slain from the foundation of the world, King of kings, our High Priest, our Master, Shiloh, Emmanuel, Wonderful, or the Mighty Counselor, it matters not. Every name is like a honeycomb dripping with honey. But if there is one name sweeter than another to us, it is *Jesu*s. Jesus!—the life of all our joys. If there is one name more charming, more precious than another, it is this name. Many of our hymns begin with it, and scarcely any, that are good for anything, end without it. It's the sum total of all delights. It's the music with which the bells of heaven ring, a song in a word, a universe for meditation, and a gathering up of the hallelujahs of eternity in five letters.

David inquired of the LORD *(2 Samuel 5:23).*

When David made this inquiry, he had just fought the Philistines and won a notable victory. The Philistines came in large numbers, but by the help of God David easily defeated them. Note, however, that when they came a second time, David did not go up to fight them without inquiring of the LORD. Having been victorious once, he might have said, as many have, "I will be victorious again. I can be certain that if I have conquered once I will conquer again. Why then should I wait to seek the LORD's help?" Not David. He had won one battle by the LORD's strength, and he would not begin another until he was certain of the same. So he asked, "Shall I go up against them?" and waited until God answered. Learn from David to take no step without God. Christian, if you would know the path of duty, take God for your compass. If you would steer your ship through the stormy sea, put the tiller into the hand of the Almighty. A Puritan said, "As sure as can be, if Christians carve for themselves, they'll cut their own fingers." Said another, "Those who go before the cloud of God's providence go on a fool's errand." We must see God's providence leading us—and if providence delays, wait until providence comes. "I will instruct you and teach you in the way you should go,"[111] is God's promise to His people. So take all your uncertainties to Him, and say, "LORD, what do you want me to do?" Don't leave your room this morning without asking Him.

I know what it is to have plenty (Philippians 4:12).

There are many who know "how to be in need" who have not learned "how to have plenty." When they are set upon a pinnacle their heads grow dizzy and they are ready to fall. Christians far more often disgrace their profession of faith in prosperity than in adversity. It's a dangerous thing to be prosperous. The crucible of adversity is a less severe trial to a Christian than the refining-pot of prosperity. Oh, what leanness of soul and neglect of spiritual things have often been brought on through the very mercies and bounties of God! Yet this isn't necessary, for the apostle tells us that he knew how to have plenty. When he had much he knew how to use it. Abundant grace enabled him to bear abundant prosperity. It needs more than human skill to carry the brimming cup of mortal joy with a steady hand, yet Paul had learned that skill, for he declares, "I have learned the secret of being content in any and every situation, whether well fed or hungry." It's a divine lesson to know how to have plenty. When we have much of God's providential grace, it often happens that we have but little gratitude for the bounties we received. We are full and we forget God[112]—satisfied with earth, we're content to do without heaven. It's harder to know how to have plenty than it is to know how to be in need—we tend always toward pride and forgetfulness of God. Take care that you ask in your prayers that God will teach you "how to have plenty."[113]

*They took note that these men had been with Jesus
(Acts 4:13).*

A Christian should have a striking resemblance to Jesus
Christ. The best biography of Jesus is His life written out
in the words and actions of His people. If we were what
we profess to be and should be, we would be pictures of
Jesus. We would be such striking likenesses of Him, that
the world wouldn't have to examine us for hours just
to say, "Well, you're somewhat of a likeness." Instead,
once seeing us they would exclaim, "They're what Jesus
of Nazareth must have been like—truly good and holy
people." Christians should be like Christ in their *boldness*.
Never be ashamed to acknowledge your faith.[114] Your
profession of faith in Christ will never disgrace you—take
care you never disgrace it. Be valiant for God like Jesus
was. Be like Him in your *loving* spirit—think kindly, speak
kindly, and do kindly. Be like Him in His *holiness*. Was
He zealous for God? You be also. Was He self-denying,
never looking to His own interest? Be the same. Was He
devout? Be fervent in your prayers. Did He submit Himself
to His Father's will? So submit your will to Him. Was He
patient? Learn to be the same. Best of all, as the highest
portrait of Jesus, forgive your enemies as He did. Let the
words of your Master, "Father, forgive them, for they do
not know what they are doing," be yours. Forgive, as you
have been forgiven.[115] Return good for evil.[116] Be like Jesus
in all your ways, so that all may say of you, "That person
has been with Jesus."

◁ February 12 ▷

For just as the sufferings of Christ flow over into our lives, so also through Christ our comfort overflows (2 Corinthians 1:5).

There is a blessed balance. The Ruler of providence bears a pair of balancing scales. On one side He puts His people's trials, and on the other He puts their comfort. When the scale of trial is nearly empty, you will always find the scale of comfort to still be full. When the scale of trial is full, you will find the scale of comfort to be overflowing. When the black clouds gather most, the light is most brightly revealed to us. It's a blessed thing that when we're most cast down, it's then that we're most lifted up by the comfort of the Spirit. One reason is that *trials make more room for consolation.* Great hearts are only made by great troubles. The more humble we are, the more comfort we'll always get, because we're more prepared to receive it. Another reason why we're often most happy in our troubles, is that it is then that *we have the closest dealings with God.* When the pantry is full, we can live without God. When the money is plentiful, we can do without prayer. But take our *food and money* away, and we want *God.* "Out of the depths I cry to you, O LORD!"[117] There's no cry like that which comes from the deep valley. No prayer like that which comes up from the depths of the afflicted and desperate soul. They bring us to God, and we are happier, for nearness to God is happiness. Troubled Christian, don't fret over your heavy troubles, they are the pathways to great comfort from "the God of all comfort."[118]

≈ February 13 ≈

How great is the love the Father has lavished on us, that
we should be called children of God! And that is what
we are! The reason the world does not know us is that
it did not know Him. Dear friends, now we are
children of God (1 John 3:1-2).

Consider who we were, and what we feel ourselves to
be even now when sin is powerful in us, and you will
wonder at our adoption. Yet we are called *"the children*
of God."[119] What a high relationship is that of a child,
and what privileges it brings! What care and tenderness
the child expects from the father, and what love the father
feels towards the child. But all *that*, and more than that, we
now have through Christ. As for the temporary drawback
of suffering with our elder Brother, we accept it as an
honor: "The reason the world does not know us is that it
did not know him." We are content to be unknown with
Him in His humiliation, for we are to be exalted with Him.
"Dear friends, now we are children of God." That's easy
to read, but it's not so easy to feel. How is it with your
heart this morning? Are you in deep sorrow? Does sin rise
within you, and grace seem like a weak spark trampled
under foot? Does your faith almost fail you? Fear not, it's
neither your perceptions nor feelings on which you are to
live—you must live simply by faith in Christ. With all these
things against us, *now*—in the very depths of our sorrow,
wherever we may be—"Dear friends, *now* we are children
of God." And what is to come is greater still: *"what we*
will be has not yet been made known. But we know that
when He appears, we shall be like Him, for we shall see
Him as He is."

Day by day the king gave Jehoiachin a regular allowance as long as he lived (2 Kings 25:30).

Jehoiachin wasn't sent away from the king's palace with provisions to last him for months, his provisions were given to him every day. In this is pictured the happy position of all the LORD's people. A daily portion is *all that a person really needs*. We don't need tomorrow's supplies—that day hasn't come yet. The hunger we may feel in June doesn't need to be fed in February. If we have enough for each day as the days arrive we will never know want. What is sufficient for the day is *all that we can enjoy*.[120] We cannot eat or drink or wear more than the day's supply of food and clothing. Enough is not only as good as a feast, but is all that even an absolute glutton can truly enjoy. This is *all that we should expect*; a craving for more than this is ungrateful. When our Father doesn't give us more, we should be content with His daily allowance. Jehoiachin's situation is ours—we have a sure portion, a portion *given us by the King*, a *gracious* portion, and a *perpetual portion*. This is surely basis for thankfulness. Dear Christian, in matters of grace *you need a daily supply*. You have no store of strength. Day by day you must seek help from above. It's a great comfort to know that *a daily portion is provided for you*. In God's "glorious riches in Christ Jesus,"[121] everything you need is laid up for you. So *enjoy your continual allowance*. Never go hungry while the daily bread of grace is on the table of mercy.[122]

⊰ *February 15* ⊱

To Him be glory both now and forever!
(2 Peter 3:18)

Heaven will be full of the ceaseless praises of Jesus. Eternally! Forever He is the King of kings and LORD of lords, the everlasting Father! "To Him be glory *forever.*" His praises will never cease. The glory of the Cross will never be eclipsed, the luster of the grave and of the resurrection will never be dimmed. O Jesus! you will be praised forever. So long as immortal spirits live, so long as the Father's throne endures—forever, forever, to You will be glory. Believer, you are anticipating the time when you will join the saints above in ascribing all glory to Jesus, but are you glorifying Him *now?* The apostle's words are, "To Him be glory both *now* and forever." Pray this day: "LORD, help me to glorify You. I am poor—help me to glorify You by contentment. I am sick—help me to give you honor by patience. I have talents—help me to extol you by using them for You. I have time—help me to use it to serve You. I have a mind to think—help me to think *of* You and *for* You. You have put me in this world for something, LORD, show me what that is, and help me to work out my life-purpose. I cannot do much, but as the widow put in her two mites, which were all her living, so I cast myself into Your treasury. I am all Yours. Take me and enable me to glorify You now in all that I say, in all that I do, and with all that I have."

I have learned to be content whatever the
circumstances (Philippians 4:11).

These words show us that contentment is not a natural
disposition of people. Covetousness, discontent, and
murmuring are as natural to people as thorns are to soil.
We don't need to sow weeds, they come up naturally
because they live in the soil. Even so, we don't need to teach
people to complain, they complain fast enough without any
training. The precious things of the soil, however, must be
cultivated. If we want wheat, we must plow and sow. If we
want flowers, there must be a garden, and all the gardener's
care. Contentment is one of the flowers of heaven, and if
we would have it, we must cultivate it—it will not grow
in us naturally. Only the new nature can produce it, and
even then we must be especially careful and watchful that
we maintain and cultivate the grace that God has sown in
us. Paul says, "I have *learne*d to be content;" which means
at one time he didn't know how. It cost him some pains
to attain to the mystery of that great truth. No doubt he
sometimes thought he had learned, and then broke down.
And when at last he had attained to it, and could say, "I
have learned to be content," he was an old man in prison.
Don't think that you can be content without *learning*,
or learn without discipline. It's not a power that comes
naturally, but a science that is acquired gradually. We know
this from experience. So Christian, stop that complaining,
natural though it is, and continue as a diligent student in
the College of Content.

⊰ *February 17* ⊱

Isaac ... lived near Beer Lahai Roi (Genesis 25:11).

Hagar had once found deliverance there, and Ishmael had drank from the water so graciously revealed by the God who lives and sees the human race. But these were merely passing visits, such as worldly people pay to the LORD in times of need, when it serves their purpose. They cry to Him in trouble, but forsake Him in prosperity. Isaac *lived* there, and made the well of the living and all-seeing God[123] his *constant* source of supply. The usual course of a person's life, where their soul lives, is the true test of their condition. Apparently the providential visitation experienced by Hagar stuck in Isaac's mind and led him to revere the place, and its mystical name endeared it to him.[124] Also, his frequent meditations by its brim at evening made him familiar with the well, and his meeting Rebecca there made his spirit feel at home near the spot. Most of all, however, the fact that he there enjoyed fellowship with the living God made him select that hallowed ground for his dwelling. Let *us* learn to live in the presence of the living God.[125] May the LORD be as a well to us, delightful, comforting, unfailing, springing up unto eternal life. The well of our Creator never fails—blessed is the person who lives at the well, and so has abundant and constant supplies near at hand. God is All-sufficient, and through Him our soul has found the LORD Jesus. "In Him," Paul said, "we live and move and have our being." Let us, then, always live by the well of the living God.[126]

♔ February 18 ♔

Tell me what charges You have against me
(Job 10:2).

Perhaps you are being tried by the Lord to develop your Christian virtues. There are some of your virtues that would never be *discovered* if it weren't for your trials. Don't you know that your faith never looks so grand in good times as it does in bad? Love is too often like a glow-worm, showing only a little light except when surrounded by darkness. Hope itself is like a star—not found during the day of prosperity but during the night of adversity. Afflictions are often the black foils on which God places the jewels of His children's virtues to make them shine better. Perhaps you recently prayed, "Lord, I'm not certain I have any faith. Please let me know that I do have." If so, wasn't this really, though perhaps unconsciously, praying for trials?—for how can you know that you have the virtue of faith until your faith is exercised? Depend upon it, God often sends us trials so we may discover our virtues and be certain of their existence. Besides, it isn't merely discovery, *real growth* in Christian virtues is the result of sanctified trials. God often takes away our comforts and our privileges to make us better Christians. He doesn't train His soldiers in tents of ease and luxury, but by turning them out and using them in forced marches and hard service. He makes them ford through streams, swim through rivers, climb mountains, and walk long miles with heavy burdens on their backs.[127] Perhaps this accounts for the troubles you're passing through. The Lord is developing your Christian virtues.

☜ *February 19* ☞

"This is what the Sovereign LORD says: Once again I will yield to the plea of the house of Israel and do this for them" (Ezekiel 36:37).

Prayer is the forerunner of mercy. Turn to sacred history, and you will find that scarcely ever did a great mercy come to this world unheralded by supplication. You've found this true in your own personal experience. God has given you many unsolicited favors, but still great prayer has always been the prelude of great mercy with you. When you first found peace through the blood of the Cross, it was because you had been praying much for deliverance from your sinful state, or because others had been praying much for you. Either way, your assurance of forgiveness and eternal life was the result of prayer. When you've had high and rapturous joys, you've been obliged to look upon them as answers to your prayers. When you've had great deliverance out of severe troubles, you've had to say, "I sought the LORD, and He answered me; He delivered me from all my fears."[128] Prayer is always the prelude to blessing. It goes before the blessing *as the blessing's shadow.* When the sunlight of God's mercies rises upon our necessities, it casts the shadow of prayer far down upon the plain. Thus we may be certain, if we are earnestly in prayer, that our pleadings are the shadows of God's mercy. Prayer is connected to the blessing *to show us the value of it.* If we had the blessings without asking for them, we would consider them common things. Prayer makes God's mercies more precious than diamonds. The things we ask for are precious, but we do not realize their preciousness until we have sought for them earnestly.

God, who comforts the downcast
(2 Corinthians 7:6).

Who comforts like Him? Go to some poor, melancholy, distressed child of God, tell sweet promises, whisper choice words of comfort, and it will be like trying to comfort a wall that cannot hear. Comfort the despairing child of God as you may, you will get only a note or two of mournful resignation—but no psalms of praise, no hallelujahs, no joyful sonnets. But let *God* come to His child, let Him lift up the person's countenance, and the despairing eyes will sparkle with hope.[129] *You* could not cheer the person, but the LORD has done it. He is "the God of all comfort." There's no balm in Gilead, but there's balm in God.[130] There's no physician among the creatures, but the Creator is Jehovah-rophi.[131] It's marvelous how one sweet word of God will make whole songs for Christians. One word of God is like a piece of gold, and the Christian who beats it into gold leaf can hammer that promise out for whole weeks. Christian, you needn't sit down in despair. Go to the Comforter, and ask Him to give you comfort. When a well's hand-pump is dry, you must first pour water into the pump to prime it, and then you'll get water from the well. So when you're dry, go to God and ask Him to pour His joy into your heart, and then your joy will be full.[132] Don't go to earthly acquaintances, for you'll find them Job's comforters after all. Go first to God, and you'll soon say, "When anxiety was great within me, your consolation brought joy to my soul."

God has said (Hebrews 13:5).

If we can grasp these words by faith, we have an all-conquering weapon in our hand. All doubts will be slain by this two-edged sword. Fear will be pierced with a fatal wound by this arrow from the bow of God's covenant. The distresses of life and the pangs of death, the corruptions within and the snares without, the trials from above and the temptations from below, will all seem like light afflictions when we stand by faith in the strength of "God has said." Whether for delight in our tranquility, or for strength in our conflict, "He has said" must be our daily resort. This may teach us the extreme value of *searching* the Scriptures. There may be a promise in the Word that would exactly fit your case, but you may not know of it, and therefore you miss its comfort. There may be a potent medicine in the great pharmacy of Scripture, and yet you may remain sick unless you examine and search the Scriptures to discover what "God has said." Besides reading the Bible, shouldn't you store in your memory the rich promises of God? If you can recall the sayings of great people, and quote the words of popular songs, shouldn't your knowledge of the words of God be extensive, so that you can quote them readily when you need to solve a difficulty or overthrow a doubt? Since "God has said" is the source of all wisdom and the fountain of all comfort,[133] let it dwell in you richly, as "a spring of water welling up to eternal life."[134]

❧ *February 22* ☙

The arms of his hands were made strong By the hands of the Mighty God of Jacob (Genesis 49:24, NKJV).

That strength that God gives to His people is *real* strength. It's not a boasted valor, a fiction, a thing of which people talk, but which ends in smoke—it's true *divine strength*. Why does Joseph stand against temptation? Because God gives him aid. There's nothing that we can do without the power of God. All true strength comes from "the Mighty God of Jacob." Notice in what a *blessedly familiar way* God gives this strength to Joseph: "The arms of his hands were made strong by the hands of the Mighty God of Jacob." Thus God is represented as putting His hands on Joseph's hands, placing His arms on Joseph's arms. Like as a father teaches his children, so the LORD teaches them that fear Him. The strength given to Joseph was also covenant strength, for it's ascribed to "the Mighty *God of Jacob*." Now, wherever you read of the God of Jacob in the Bible, you should remember the covenant with Jacob. Christians love to think of God's covenant. All the power, grace, blessings, mercies, comforts, everything we have, flow to us through the New Covenant.[135] If there were no New Covenant, then we would fail indeed, for all grace proceeds from it, just as light from the sun. In the Old Covenant, no angels ascend or descend, except upon that ladder that Jacob saw, at the top of which stood a covenant LORD.[136] Christian, it may be that the fiery darts have painfully wounded you, but still you are strong be sure, then, to give all the glory to "the Mighty God of Jacob."

☙ February 23 ☙

Never will I leave you (Hebrews 13:5).

No promise is for private interpretation. Whatever God has said to any one saint, He has said to all. When He opens a well for one, it is so all may drink. When He opens a granary door to give out food [grain], there may be one starving person who is the reason for its being opened, but all hungry saints may come and eat. Whether He gave the word to Abraham or to Moses, doesn't matter. He's given it to you also as one of the covenanted seed.[137] There is not a blessing too high for you, or a mercy too great for you. Lift up your eyes to the north and to the south, to the east and to the west, for all this and more is yours.[138] Climb to Pisgah's top, and view the utmost limit of the Promise Land, for the land is all yours. There is not a brook of living water of which you may not drink. If the land flows with milk and honey, eat the honey and drink the milk, for both are yours. But be bold to believe, for He has said, "Never will I leave *you*; never will I forsake *you*." In this promise, God gives to His people everything. "Never will *I* leave you." Then no attribute of God can cease to be active on our behalf. Is He mighty? He will show Himself strong on the behalf of them that trust Him. Is He love? Then with loving kindness He will have mercy upon us—always! "Never will I leave you; never will I forsake you."

"I will send down showers in season; there will be showers of blessing" (Ezekiel 34:26).

Here is *sovereign mercy:* "I will send down showers in season." Isn't that sovereign, *divine,* mercy—for who can say, "I will send down showers," except God? There's only one voice that can speak to the clouds and command them to give rain. Who sends down the rain upon the earth? Who scatters the showers upon the green plant? Do not I, the LORD? So grace is the gift of God,[139] and is not to be created by people. It's also *needed* grace. What can the ground do without showers? You may till the ground, you may sow your seeds, but what can you do without the rain? As absolutely needful is the divine blessing of grace. Note also that it's *plenteous grace.* "I will send them *showers.*" Not "drops," but "showers." So it is with grace. If God gives a blessing, He usually gives it in such a measure that there isn't room enough to receive it.[140] We cannot do without saturating showers of grace. Again, it is *seasonable grace.* "I will send down showers in *season.*" What is your season this morning? Is it the season of drought? Then this is the season for showers. Is it a season of great heaviness? Then this is the season for showers. And it is a *varied* blessing. "I will give you *showers* of blessing." The word is plural. God will send *all kinds of blessings.* If He gives converting grace, He will also give comforting grace. He will send "*showers* of blessing." Look up today, O parched plant, and open your leaves and flowers for a heavenly watering.

≥ *February 25* ≤

The coming wrath (Matthew 3:7).

It's pleasant to travel through the country after a rainstorm, to smell the freshness of the grass, and to see how the raindrops glisten like diamonds in the sunlight. That's the position of Christians. We're traveling through a land where the storm has spent itself upon our Savior's head, and if there are a few drops of sorrow falling, they come from clouds of mercy, and Jesus cheers us by His assurance that they're not for our destruction. But how terrible it is to witness the approach of a violent storm and note the sign of its coming—the sky filling with dark and angry clouds until the sun no longer shines. How terrible to await the dread approach of a hurricane or thunder storm that may birth tornados—to wait in terrible apprehension for the storm's fury to break upon you and all you possess. And yet, sinner, this is your present position. No burning drops have yet fallen, but a shower of fire is coming upon you. No terrible winds howl around you, but God's tempest is gathering its dread fury. The floodwaters are still dammed up by mercy, but the floodgates will soon be opened. How awful will that moment be when God, robed in vengeance, will march forth in wrath. Where, O sinner, will you then hide your head, or to what place will you flee? O that God's mercy may lead you now to Christ. You cannot escape God's vengeance upon your sins without Christ—so believe in Him, cast yourself upon Him, and the fury will pass over you forever.

Salvation is of the LORD *(Jonah 2:9, KJV).*

Salvation is the work of God. It is He alone who rouses the soul "dead in trespasses and sins,"[141] and it is He who maintains the soul in its spiritual life. He is both "Alpha and Omega."[142] If I am prayerful, God makes me prayerful. If I have virtues, they are God's gifts to me. If I hold on in a consistent life, it is because He upholds me with His hand. I do nothing whatever toward my own preservation, except what God Himself first does in me. Whatever I have, I received from the LORD.[143] Sinning is my own doing; living righteously is of God, wholly and completely. Do I live a consecrated life before people? It is not I, but Christ who lives in me.[144] Am I sanctified? I don't purify myself—I am sanctified through the sacrifice of Christ and the Holy Spirit.[145] Am I separated from the world?[146] I am separated by *God's* chastisements, which are sanctified to my good.[147] Do I grow in knowledge? The great Instructor teaches me. Do I feed on the Word? That Word would be no food for me unless the LORD made it food for my soul, and helped me to feed upon it. Do I daily receive fresh strength to endure? Where do I get my strength? "My help comes from the LORD,"[148] for without Jesus I can do nothing. No branch can bear fruit unless it remains in the vine,[149] and neither can I, except I abide in Him. What Jonah learned in the great deep, let me learn this morning: "Salvation is of the LORD."

✑ *February 27* ✑

You make the Most High your dwelling even the
LORD, who is my refuge (Psalm 91:9).

The Israelites in the wilderness *were continually exposed*
to change. Whenever the pillar of cloud stopped, the
tents were pitched. But often early the next morning
the trumpets would sound and the ark would be carried
forth by the priests as the pillar of cloud began to move
and once more lead them through the vast wilderness.[150]
They scarcely had time to rest before they heard the cry of
"Arise! This is not your place of rest. You must continue
forward toward Canaan!" They were never long in one
place. Even refreshing wells and shaded palm trees could
not detain them. Yet they had an abiding home in their
God. His pillar of cloud was their shade by day and their
warming fire at night. They must go onward from place to
place, continually changing, never having time to stay and
rest. "Yet," says Moses, "though we are always changing,
LORD, you have been our dwelling place throughout all
generations."[151] Christians know no change with regard to
God. We may be rich today and poor tomorrow, sick today
and well tomorrow, happy today and sad tomorrow—but
there is no change with regard to our relationship to God.[152]
If He loved us yesterday, He loves us today. Our unmoving
mansion of rest is our blessed LORD. Let our prospects be
blighted, our hopes blasted, our joys withered, and our
possessions destroyed—we still have lost nothing of what
we have in God. We are pilgrims in the world, but at home
in our God. In the earth we wander, but in God we dwell
in a quiet habitation.[153]

February 28

My hope comes from Him (Psalm 62:5).

As Christians it is our privilege to use this language. If we are looking for anything from the world, it is a poor hope indeed. But if we look to God to supply our needs,[154] whether temporal or spiritual, our hope will not be in vain. We may draw from the bank of faith and get our needs supplied out of God's glorious riches in Christ Jesus. I know this—I'd rather have God for my banker than all the Rothschilds.[155] My LORD never fails to honor His promises. When we bring them to His throne,[156] He never sends them back unanswered. Therefore, I will wait only at His door, for He always opens it with the hand of grace. But we have hope beyond this life.[157] We will die soon, and then our "hope comes from Him." Don't we hope that when we die He will send angels to carry us to His bosom?[158] We believe that when our heart begins to fail, some angelic messenger will whisper, "Redeemed of Christ, come away!"[159] As we approach the heavenly gate, we expect to hear the welcome invitation, "Come, you who are blessed by my Father; take your inheritance, the kingdom prepared for you since the creation of the world."[160] We are looking forward and longing for the time when we will be like our glorious LORD—for "we shall see Him as He is."[161] If these are your hopes, then live with the desire to glorify Him whose grace in your election, redemption, and calling is the only reason that you have any hope of coming glory.[162]

⇥ *February 29* ⇤

I have drawn you with loving-kindness
(Jeremiah 31:3).

The thunders of the law and the terrors of judgment are all used to bring us to Christ,[163] but the final victory is brought about by loving-kindness.[164] The Prodigal Son returned to his father's house from a sense of need, but his father saw him a great way off, and ran to meet him.[165] So that the last steps he took toward his father's house were with the kiss still warm upon his cheek, and the welcome still joyous in his ears. The Master came one night to the door, and knocked with the iron hand of the law. The door shook and trembled upon its hinges, but the person within piled everything possible against the door and declared, "I will not admit the Man." The Master turned away, but after awhile He came back, and with that part of His hand where the blood had flowed from the piercing nail, He knocked again—softly and tenderly. This time the door did not shake, but, strange to say, it opened, and there on bended knees the once unwilling occupant was found eager to receive the LORD. "Come in, come in. You have so knocked that my heart is open to You. I couldn't think of Your pierced hand leaving its blood-mark on my door, and of Your going away homeless. I yield, I yield. Your love has won my heart."[166] So it is in every case—loving-kindness wins the day. What Moses with the tablets of stone could never do, Christ does with His pierced hand. This is the way God effectually calls lost sinners to His Son.[167]

March

Awake, north wind, and come, south wind! Blow on my garden, that its fragrance may spread abroad (Song of Songs 4:16).

Anything is better than the dead calm of indifference. The spouse in this verse humbly submitted herself to the reproofs of her Beloved, only entreating Him to send forth His grace in some form, and making no stipulation as to the peculiar manner in which it should come. Like we often do, she became so utterly weary of deadness and unholy calm that she sighed for any visitation that would stimulate her to action. Yet she also desires the warm south wind of comfort, the smiles of divine love, and the joy of the Redeemer's presence. These are often greatly effective in arousing our sluggish life. She desires either one or the other, or both, so that she may but be able to delight her Beloved with the fragrance of her garden. She cannot endure to be unprofitable, nor should we. How cheering a thought that Christ can find comfort in our poor feeble virtues. It seems far too good to be true. We may well court trial or even death itself if we will thereby bring joy to Immanuel's heart. O that our heart were crushed to atoms if only by such bruising our sweet LORD Jesus could be glorified. Unexercised virtues are like sweet perfumes slumbering in the heart of the flowers. To produce the one desired result, the great Husbandman overrules seemingly diverse and opposite things.[168] Thus He makes both affliction and consolation draw forth the grateful fragrances of faith, love, patience, hope, resignation, joy, and the other fair flowers of the garden. May we know by sweet experience, what this means.

March 2

So all Israel went down to the Philistines to have their plowshares, mattocks, axes and sickles sharpened (1 Samuel 13:20).

We're engaged in a great war with the Philistines of evil. *Every weapon within our reach must be used.* Preaching, teaching, praying, giving, all must be brought into action. Any talents that have been thought too inferior for service, must now be employed. Each moment of time, each fragment of ability, each opportunity must be used, for we have many spiritual enemies and not many laborers.[169] *Most of our weapons need preparation.*[170] We need quickness of perception, tact, energy, promptness—in a word, complete adaptation for the LORD's work. Practical common sense is a very scarce thing among those who lead Christian enterprises. We might learn from our enemies if we would, and so *make the Philistines sharpen our weapons.* This morning let us note enough to sharpen our zeal during this day by the aid of the Holy Spirit. See the energy of the Eastern religions, how they now compass sea and land to make one proselyte—are they to monopolize all the earnestness? Mark the heathen devotees, what tortures they endure in the service of their idols—are they alone to exhibit patience and self-sacrifice? Observe the prince of darkness, how persevering in his endeavors, how unabashed in his attempts, how daring in his plans, how thoughtful in his plots, how energetic in all.[171] The devils are united as one creature in their infamous rebellion, while we believers in Jesus Christ are divided in our service of God, and scarcely ever work in one accord.[172] O that from Satan's infernal industry we may learn to go about like good Samaritans, seeking whom we may bless!

⊲ March 3 ⊳

See, I have refined you ... I have tested you in the furnace of affliction (Isaiah 48:10).

Comfort yourself, tested believer, with this thought: God says, "I have tested you in the furnace of affliction." Doesn't the word come like a soft shower, assuaging the fury of the flame? Isn't it like an insulated armor against which the heat has no power? Let affliction come—God has already tested and refined me.[173] Poverty, you may stride in at my door, but God is in the house already, and He has tested me. Sickness, you may intrude, but I have a balm ready—God has tested me. Whatever happens to me in this vale of tears, I know that He has tested me. Believer, if you require still greater comfort, remember *that you have the Son of Man with you in the furnace.* In that silent chamber of yours, there sits by your side One whom you have not seen, but whom you love. And often when you don't know it, He makes a bed for you in your affliction and smoothes your pillow for you. Though you may be poor, in that lovely house of yours the LORD of life and glory is a frequent visitor. He loves to visit those in difficult places. You cannot see Him, but you may feel the pressure of His hands. Don't you hear His voice? Even in the valley of the shadow of death He says, "Fear not, I am with you; be not dismayed, for I am your God."[174] "Fear not, for I am with you,"[175] is His sure word of promise to His chosen ones who are tested and refined in the "furnace of affliction."

My grace is sufficient for you (2 Corinthians 12:9).

If none of God's saints were poor and tried, we wouldn't know half so well the consolations of divine grace. When we find a homeless wanderer with nowhere to stay who still trusts in the LORD; when we see a destitute person going hungry who still glories in Jesus; or when we see a bereaved widow overwhelmed in affliction who still has faith in Christ—oh! what honor it gives to the Gospel. God's grace is illustrated and magnified in the afflictions and trials of believers. Saints bear up under every discouragement, believing that all things work together for their good.[176] They believe that out of apparent evils a real blessing will ultimately spring—that their God will either work a deliverance for them speedily, or most assuredly support them in it. This patience of the saints proves the power of divine grace. When everything is calm I can't tell how strong a house is built—a storm must rage and beat against it before I'll know it's strength.[177] So it is with the Spirit's work. If it wasn't on many occasions surrounded by a storm, we wouldn't know that it was true and strong. If the winds didn't blow upon it, we wouldn't know how firm and secure it was. The masterworks of God are those saints who stand steadfast and unmovable in the midst of difficulties. Those who would glorify God must expect many trials. There are no great victories without great battles. So if your life is full of trials, rejoice, because you will all the more experience the all-sufficient grace and power of the LORD.[178]

⊰ *March 5* ⊱

Let us not be like others, who are asleep
(1 Thessalonians 5:6).

There are many ways of promoting Christian wakefulness. Among others, Christians should talk together about the ways of the LORD. In the *Pilgrim's Progress*, as Christian and Hopeful journeyed towards the Celestial City, Christian said to Hopeful, "Now then, to prevent drowsiness in this place, let's have a good discussion." "Gladly," said Hopeful.[179] Then Christian asked, "Where shall we begin?" "Where God began with us," answered Hopeful. Christians who isolate themselves and walk alone are very liable to grow drowsy. By meeting together with other Christians[180] you will remain alert, and be refreshed and encouraged to make quicker progress along the road to heaven. But when you fellowship with others about the ways of God, make certain the theme of your conversation is the LORD Jesus. Keep the eyes of your faith constantly looking to Him, your heart full of Him, and your lips speaking of His worth. Live near to the Cross, and you'll never get spiritually drowsy. *Labor to impress yourself with a deep sense of the value of the place to which you're going.* If you remember that you're going to heaven, you won't sleep on the road. If you know the devil is pursuing you like a roaring lion, you won't loiter.[181] Would the person who has killed someone sleep with the avenger close behind, and the city of refuge ahead?[182] Christian, will you sleep while the pearly gates are open, the LORD is waiting for you to join Him, and a gold crown is ready for you?[183] No! So in holy fellowship continue to watch and pray that you enter not into temptation.[184]

⋈ *March 6* ⋈

You must be born again (John 3:7).

Regeneration is a subject that lies at the very basis of salvation, and we should be very diligent to make certain that we really are "born again"—for there are many who believe they are but are not. Be assured that the *name* of a Christian is not the *nature* of a Christian, and that being born in a Christian land, belonging to a Christian church, and being recognized as professing the Christian religion is of no use whatever, unless there is something more added to it—the being "born again" is a matter so *mysterious,* that human words cannot describe it. Jesus said, "The wind blows wherever it pleases. You hear its sound, but you cannot tell where it comes from or where it is going. So it is with everyone born of the Spirit." Nevertheless, it's a change that is *felt* and *known*—felt by a definite experience, and known by increasing works of holiness.[185] This great work is *supernatural.* God infuses a new principle that works in the heart, renews the soul, and affects the entire person. It's not a change of your name, but a renewal of your nature, so that you are not the person you used to be, but a new creation in Christ Jesus.[186] If you have been truly "born again," your heart cries "Abba, Father!"[187] Though you don't know how you know it, you know that everything is all right between you and Almighty God.[188] May God assure us on this vital point,[189] for if we are not "born again," we are yet unsaved, unpardoned, without hope, and without God.[190]

◁ *March 7* ▷

Have faith in God (Mark 11:22).

Faith is that which enables the soul to march victoriously along the road of the commandments. Love can make the soul move more swiftly, but it's faith that carries it. With faith you can do all things,[191] without faith you will neither have the inclination nor the power to do anything in the service of God. If you would find the people who serve God the best, you must look for those with the most faith.[192] Little faith will save a person, but little faith cannot do great things for God.[193] In *Pilgrim's Progress,* Poor Little-faith couldn't have fought Apollyon, it needed Christian to do that. Poor Little-faith couldn't have slain Giant Despair, it required Great-heart's arm to knock that monster down. Little faith will go to heaven most certainly, but it often has to hide itself in a nutshell, and it frequently loses most of what it has. Little faith says, "It's a rough road, beset with sharp thorns, and full of dangers. I'm afraid to go on." But great faith[194] remembers the promise, "The bolts of your gates will be iron and bronze, and your strength will equal your days," and boldly goes on. Little faith stands fearful, weeping at every river of adversity. But great faith sings, "When you pass through the waters, I will be with you; and when you pass through the rivers, they will not sweep over you," and fords the stream at once. Would you be comfortable and happy? Would you enjoy Christianity? Would you be a cheerful Christian and not a gloomy one? Then "have faith in God."[195]

*"We must go through many hardships to enter the
kingdom of God" (Acts 14:22).*

God's people have their trials. It was never designed by
God that His chosen people should be an untried people.
Freedom from afflictions and pain was never promised
them. Trials are a part of our lot—they were predestinated
for us in Christ's last legacy. So surely as the stars are
fashioned by his hands, and their orbits fixed by Him, so
surely are our trials allotted to us. He has ordained their
season and their place, their intensity and the effect they
will have upon us. Good people must never expect to escape
troubles.[196] If they do, they will be disappointed, for none
of their predecessors have been without them. Remember
Abraham, for he had his trials, and by his faith under
them[197] he became the "Father of the faithful." Note well
the biographies of all the patriarchs, prophets, apostles,
and martyrs, and you will find that there were none whom
God made vessels of mercy who were not made to pass
through the fire of affliction. It's ordained of old that the
cross of trouble should be engraved on every vessel of
mercy, as the royal mark whereby the King's vessels of
honor are distinguished.[198] But although the path of God's
children are strewn with hardships, they have the comfort
of knowing that their Master traveled it before them. And
so they have His presence and sympathy to cheer them,[199]
His grace to support them,[200] and His example to teach
them how to endure. Remember also what Paul said: "our
present sufferings are not worth comparing with the glory
that will be revealed in us."[201]

He is altogether lovely (Song of Songs 5:16).

The superlative beauty of Jesus is all-attracting—it is not so much to be admired as to be loved. He is more than pleasant and fair, He is *lovely*. Surely the people of God can fully justify the use of this golden word, for He is the object of their warmest love, a love founded on the intrinsic excellence of His person, the complete perfection of His charms. Don't His words cause your hearts to burn within you as He talks with you on the way?[202] Isn't your adoration sweetened with affection as you humbly bow before that countenance that is like Lebanon, choice as its cedars?[203] Is there one member of His glorious person that isn't attractive? There is charm in His every feature, and His whole person is fragrant with a savor of His good ointments.[204] Our love isn't as a seal set upon His heart of love alone, it's fastened upon His arm of power also, and there isn't a single part of Him upon which it doesn't fix itself. His whole life we would imitate. His whole character we would transcribe. In all other beings we see some lack, in Him there is all perfection. The best even of His favored saints have had blots upon their garments and wrinkles upon their brows—He is nothing but loveliness. All earthly suns have their spots. The fair world itself has its wilderness. And we cannot love the whole of the most lovely thing. But Christ Jesus is gold without impurity, light without darkness, glory without cloud. "Yes, He is *altogether* lovely."

When I felt secure, I said, "I will never be shaken"
(Psalm 30:6).

"Moab has been at rest from youth, like wine left on its dregs."[205] Give us great wealth. Let our ships continually bring home rich cargos. Let our lands yield abundant crops. Let uninterrupted success be ours. Let us stand among others as successful business people. Let us enjoy continual health. Let us march through the world with strong nerves and sharp eyes. Give us buoyant spirits, a song perpetually on our lips, and our eyes always sparkling with joy. And the natural consequences of such an easy state for any person, even the best Christian who ever lived, will be *presumption*. Even David said, "I will never be shaken," and we are not better than David—not half as good. Christian, if you're walking in a smooth place, beware of it. If your way is rough, thank God for it. If God always rocked us in the cradle of prosperity, if there were not a few clouds in the sky; if we had not some bitter drops in the wine of this life, we would become intoxicated with pleasure, and would dream "we stand." And stand we would, but it would be as upon the edge of a cliff. Like a sailor asleep at the top of a ship's mast, each moment of our lives would be in danger. We bless God, then, for our afflictions, we thank Him for our changes, and we extol His name for losses of property. For we feel that had He not chastened us in this way, we might have become too secure. Continued worldly prosperity is a fiery trial.

Sin ... utterly sinful (Romans 7:13).

Beware of thinking lightly of sin. When we were first converted, our conscience was so tender we were afraid of the slightest sin. Young converts have a sensitivity to sin and fear of offending God. But soon the sensitivity is dulled by the rough handling of the surrounding world—the sensitive plant of young piety turns into a willow that bends and yields too easily. It's sadly true that even Christians may grow so callous by degrees that sins that once repulsed them don't alarm them in the least. By small degrees we get familiar with sin. The ear that constantly listens to the roar of artillery won't notice slight sounds. At first a little sin startles us, but soon we say, "It's just a little one." Then there comes another, larger, and then another, until by degrees we begin to regard sin as nothing *really* serious. Soon after there comes an unholy presumption: "I haven't fallen into *open* sin. True, I stumbled a *little*, but most of the time I've walked upright. I may have uttered an unholy word or two, but most of my conversation has been righteous." Christian, beware of thinking lightly of sin—thinking of it as only a *little* thing. Great trees can be toppled by continual small strokes. Water dripping on a stone can wear it away. Sin, a *little* thing? It drove nails into Jesus' hands and feet. If you want to see how grievous sin truly is, look at the Cross on Calvary's hill.[206] Consider carefully that sin crucified your Savior,[207] and you will see it to be "utterly sinful."

❧ *March 12* ❧

Love your neighbor (Matthew 5:43).

Perhaps your neighbors are rich and you're poor—they live in an estate and you live in a cottage—they have lavish banquets and you barely survive. It's God who has given them those things, so don't covet their wealth[208] or think harshly of them. If you cannot do better, be content with what you have.[209] But don't look upon your neighbors and wish they were as you are. Love them and you won't envy them. Perhaps, however, you're rich and your neighbors are poor. Don't be too proud to call them neighbors. You're commanded to love them. Now the world may call them your inferiors, but in what way are they inferior? They're far more your equals than your inferiors, for God made all the people on the earth of one blood (man).[210] God did not create you as something superior to them. So take heed that you love your neighbors no matter what their economical or social level. But, perhaps, you say, "I cannot love my neighbors, because they're ungrateful and contemptuous of everything I do for them." So much the more opportunity for love.[211] Those who dare the most, win the most. If your path of love is rough, walk it boldly and love your neighbors through thick and thin. If they're hard to please, don't seek to please *them*, but to please your *Master*. Even if *they* spurn your love, your Master hasn't spurned it, and your deed is as acceptable to Him as if it had been acceptable to them. Love your neighbor, for in so doing you're following the footsteps of Christ.[212]

"Why stay here until we die?"(2 Kings 7:3)

This book was mainly intended for the edification of believers, but if you're yet unsaved, our heart yearns over you, and we would like to say a word that may be a blessing to you. Open a Bible, and read the story of the lepers,[213] and note their condition, which was much like yours. If you remain where you are you'll spiritually perish, if you go to Jesus you can only physically die. None escape who refuse to go to Jesus for eternal life.[214] Surely you know some who are saved who believe in Him—so why not you? The Ninevites said, "Who can tell?"[215] Act upon the same hope, and with the same good sense, and try the LORD's mercy. To perish is so awful that, if there were only a straw to grab hold of, the instinct of self-preservation should make you stretch out your hand. To this point we've been talking to you on your own unbelieving ground. Now we assure you that if you seek the LORD you will find Him.[216] Jesus casts out no one who comes to Him.[217] You won't perish if you trust Him.[218] On the contrary, you'll find treasure far richer than the lepers gathered in Syria's deserted camp.[219] May the Holy Spirit encourage you to go to Jesus at once. When you're saved, tell others the good news. Don't keep it to yourself. Tell Christians first, and unite with them in fellowship. Inform the pastor of your eternal life in Christ, and proclaim the good news everywhere. May the LORD save you before the sun goes down this day.

⊰ *March 14* ⊱

If you think you are standing firm, be careful that you don't fall! (1 Corinthians 10:12)

It's a curious fact, that there is such a thing as being proud of grace. A person says, "I have great faith, I won't fall—poor little faith may, but I'll never." Another says, "I have fervent love. I can stand, there's no danger of my going astray." Those who boast of grace have little grace to boast of. Some who do this imagine that the graces they've received[220] can keep them, not knowing that the stream must flow constantly from the fountainhead, or else the brook will soon be dry. If a continuous stream of oil doesn't come to the lamp, even though it burns brightly today, it will smoke tomorrow and give out a noxious odor. Take heed that you don't glory in your graces, but let all your glorying and confidence be in Christ and His strength, for only that way can you be kept from falling. Be much more in prayer and worship. Read the Scriptures more earnestly and constantly. Watch your life more carefully. Live nearer to God. Take the best examples for your pattern. Let your conversation be perfumed with heaven. Let your heart be filled with affection for souls. So live that people will know that you have been with Jesus,[221] and have learned of Him. Forward, Christian, with care and caution! Forward, with holy fear and trembling! Forward, with faith and confidence in Jesus alone, and let your constant petition be, "Sustain me according to Your promise."[222] He alone is able "to keep you from falling and to present you before His glorious presence without fault and with great joy."

*Be strong in the grace that is in Christ Jesus
(2 Timothy 2:1).*

Christ has grace without measure in Himself, but He has not retained it for Himself. As the reservoir empties itself into the pipes, so has Christ emptied out His grace for His people. "From the fullness of His grace we have all received one blessing after another." He seems to have only in order to dispense to us. He stands like the fountain, always flowing, but only running in order to supply the empty pitchers and the thirsty lips that draw near to it. Like a tree, He bears sweet fruit not for Himself but to be gathered by those who need. Grace is always available from Him freely and without price.[223] As the blood of the body flowing from the heart belongs equally to every member, so the influences of grace are the inheritance of every saint united to the Lamb—both Christ and His Church receive the same grace.[224] Christ is the head upon which the oil is first poured; but the same oil runs to the very skirts of the garments,[225] so that the lowest saint has an unction of the same costly moisture as that which fell upon the head. As we day by day receive grace from Christ, and constantly recognize it as coming from Him, we will behold Him in communion with us, and enjoy the happiness of communion with Him. Let us make daily use of our riches, and always go to Him as to our own LORD in covenant, taking from Him the supply of all we need with as much boldness as taking money from our own bank accounts.

I dwell with you as ... a stranger (Psalm 39:12).

Yes, O Lord, *with* You, but I am not a stranger *to* You. Your grace has effectually removed all my natural alienation from you. Now I walk in fellowship with You through this sinful world as a pilgrim in a foreign country. *You* are a stranger in Your own world. Humankind forgets You, dishonors You, sets up new laws and alien customs, and doesn't know You. You dear Son "was in the world, and though the world was made through him, the world did not recognize Him."[226] Never was foreigner so strange a bird among the animals of any land as Your beloved Son among His mother's family.[227] It's no marvel, then, if I who live the life of Jesus should be unknown and a stranger here below. Lord, I would not be a citizen where Jesus was an alien. His pierced hand has loosened the cords that once bound my soul to earth, and now I find myself a stranger in the land. My speech seems like an outlandish tongue to these Babylonians among whom I dwell—to them my manners are different and my actions are strange. A Tartar[228] would be more at home in Cheapside[229] than I could ever be in the haunts of sinners. But here is the sweetness of my lot—I am a stranger *with* You. You are my co-sufferer, my co-pilgrim. Oh, what joy to wander in such blessed society! My heart burns within me on the way when you speak to me, and though I'm a sojourner in a strange land,[230] I'm far more blessed than those who sit on thrones.

✠ *March 17* ✠

Remember the poor (Galatians 2:10).

Why does God allow so many of His children to be poor? He could make them all rich if He pleased. He could lay bags of gold at their doors. He could send them a large annual income, or He could provide them with an abundance of provisions. There's no need them for to be poor, except that He sees it to be spiritually best for them. "The cattle on a thousand hills are His,"[231] and if it was best for His children He could make the richest, the greatest, and the mightiest bring all their power and riches to them, for everyone's heart is in His control. But He doesn't choose to do so. Why is this? There are many reasons—one is to give those who are favored with enough an opportunity to show their love to Jesus. We show our love to Christ when we sing of Him and when we pray to Him. But if there were no needy people in the world we would lose the privilege of showing our love by ministering in giving to the poorer members of His body.[232] If we truly love Christ, we will care for those who are loved by Him. Those who are dear to Him will be dear to us. It's not a duty but a privilege to relieve the poor of the LORD's flock—remembering the words of the LORD Jesus, "whatever you did for one of the least of these brothers of mine, you did for Me."[233] Surely this is a strong enough motive for us to willingly and lovingly help others.

You are all sons of God through faith in Christ Jesus (Galatians 3:26).

The fatherhood of God is common to all His children. Ah! Little-faith,[234] you have often said, "Oh that I had the courage of Great-heart,[235] that I could wield his sword and be as valiant as he! But, alas, I stumble at every straw, and a shadow makes me afraid." Listen, Little-faith, Great-heart is God's child, and you are God's child. Great-heart is not one bit more God's child than you are. Peter and Paul, the highly-favored apostles, were of the family of the Most High, and so are you. The weak Christian is as much a child of God as the strong one.[236] All the names are in the same family register. One may have more grace than another, but God our heavenly Father has the same tender heart toward all. One may do more mighty works, and may bring more glory to God, but those whose names are the least in the kingdom of heaven are as much God's children as those who stand among the King's mighty people. Let this cheer and comfort us, when we draw near to God and say, "Our Father."[237] Yet, while we are comforted by knowing this, don't be content with weak faith, but ask to have it increased.[238] However feeble our faith may be, if it's real faith in Christ we will reach heaven at last, but we won't honor Christ much, or have abundant joy and peace here on earth. If you want to glorify Christ and be happy in His service, seek to be filled with the spirit of adoption more completely,[239] until perfect love casts out fear.[240]

Strengthened in ... faith (Romans 4:20).

Faith is the only way by which you can obtain blessings. If we want blessings from God, nothing can bring them to us but faith. Prayer cannot bring answers from God's throne unless it's the earnest prayer of the person who believes. Faith is the telephone wire that links earth and heaven—on which God's messages of love fly so fast, that before we call He answers, and while we are yet speaking He hears us.[241] But if that telephone wire of faith be snapped, how can we receive the promise?[242] Am I in trouble? I can obtain help for trouble by faith.[243] Am I beaten about by the enemy? My soul leans by faith on God who is my refuge.[244] But take faith away, and in vain I call to God. There is no road between my soul and heaven except faith, on which the chariots of prayer may travel even in the bitterest wintertime. But close the road, and how can I communicate with the Most High?[245] Faith links me with divinity. Faith clothes me with the power of God. Faith ensures every attribute of God in my defense. It helps me to defy the hosts of Satan. It matches me triumphant over the necks of my enemies.[246] But without faith how can I receive anything of the LORD? Let not those who doubt think they will receive anything from the LORD.[247] Christian, watch well your faith, for with it you can win all things, but without it you can obtain nothing. "If thou canst believe, all things are possible to him that believeth."[248]

ᴁ *March 20* ᴁ

My beloved (Song of Songs 2:8, KJV).

This was a golden name that the ancient Church in her most joyous moments gave to the Anointed of the LORD.[249] She sang, "*My beloved* is mine and I am His: He feedeth among the lilies."[250] Always in her song of songs she calls Him by that delightful name, "My beloved!" Even in the long winter of God's people, when idolatry had withered the garden of the LORD, the prophets found space to lay aside the burden of the LORD for a little season, and to say, as Isaiah did, "Now will I sing to my well-beloved a song of my beloved touching His vineyard."[251] Though the saints had never seen His face—and though as yet He was not made flesh, and had not lived among us, and no one had beheld His glory—yet He was the consolation of Israel, the hope and joy of all the chosen, and the "beloved" of all those who were upright before the Most High. We, in the summer days of the Church, are also accustomed to speaking of Christ as the best beloved of our soul, and to feel that He is very precious, the "chiefest among ten thousand," and "altogether lovely."[252] So true is it that the Church loves Jesus Christ, and claims Him as her beloved, that the apostle dares to defy the whole universe to separate her from the love of Christ, and declares that neither persecutions, distress, affliction, peril, or sword have been able to do it. And then joyously boasts, "In all these things we are more than conquerors through Him that loved us."[253]

❧ *March 21* ❧

You will be scattered, each to his own home. You will leave Me all alone (John 16:32).

Few had fellowship with the sorrows of Gethsemane. The majority of the disciples weren't sufficiently advanced in grace to be admitted to behold the mysteries of the "agony."[254] Occupied with the Passover feast at their own houses, they represent the many who live according to the letter, but are mere babes concerning the spirit of the gospel.[255] Only eleven were given the privilege to enter Gethsemane and see "this great sight."[256] Out of the eleven, eight were left at a distance. They had fellowship, but not that intimate sort to which those greatly beloved are admitted. Only three highly favored ones could approach the veil of our LORD's mysterious sorrow. But within that veil even these must not intrude, and so a stone's throw distance must be left between them and Jesus. He must tread the wine-press *alon*e, and none of the people there must be with Him. Peter and the two sons of Zebedee,[257] represent the few eminent, experienced, saints who can to some degree measure the depth of their Redeemer's passion. To strengthen them for future conflicts, it is given to some selected spirits to enter the inner circle and hear the pleadings of the suffering High Priest. They fellowship with Him in His sufferings, and are made conformable unto His death.[258] Yet even these cannot penetrate the secret places of the Savior's woe. There was an inner chamber in our Master's grief, shut out from human knowledge and fellowship, where His sufferings were known only to Him and to God. There Jesus was "left alone,"[259] that He might become more than ever an "unspeakable gift."[260]

*Going a little farther, He fell with His face to the
ground and prayed (Matthew 26:39).*

There are several instructive features in our Savior's prayer
in His hour of trial. It was *lonely prayer*. He withdrew
even from His three favored disciples. Believer, be much in
solitary prayer, especially in times of trial. Family prayer,
social prayer, prayer in the church, will not suffice, these
are very precious, but the best incense will smoke in your
censer in your private devotions,[261] where no ear hears
but God's. It was *humble prayer*. Luke says He knelt,[262]
but Matthew says "He fell with His face to the ground."
Humility gives us a good foothold in prayer. There's no
hope of prevailing with God[263] unless we humble ourselves
that He may exalt us in due time.[264] It was *filial prayer*.
"Abba, Father."[265] You will find it a stronghold in the day
of trial to plead your adoption.[266] Nothing can forfeit a
child's right to a father's protection. Don't be afraid to say,
"My Father, hear my cry."[267] It was *persevering prayer*. He
prayed three times. Cease not until you prevail.[268] Be as the
importunate widow, whose continual coming earned what
her first supplication did not.[269] Continue in prayer, and
watch in the same with thanksgiving.[270] It was a *prayer of
resignation*. "Nevertheless, not as I will, but as you will."[271]
Yield, and God yields. Let it be as God wills, and God will
determine for the best. Be content to leave your prayer in
His hands, who knows when to give, how to give, what
to give, and what to withhold. So pleading earnestly and
importunately, yet with humility and resignation, you will
surely prevail.

His sweat was like drops of blood falling to the ground (Luke 22:44).

The mental pressure arising from our LORD's struggle with temptation forced His body into such an unnatural condition that great drops of blood seeped out of His pores and fell to the ground. This proves *how tremendous must have been the weight of sin* when it was able to crush the Savior so that he oozed great drops of blood. This demonstrates *the mighty power of His love.* This sets forth the *voluntariness of Christ's sufferings*, since the blood flowed freely without a wound. No need to apply the knife, it flows spontaneously. No need for to cry, "Spring up, O well."[272] The blood flows in crimson torrents by itself. If people suffer great emotional pain, apparently the blood rushes to the heart. The cheeks become pale, the person feels faint—the blood goes inward as if to nourish the inner person while passing through its trial. But see our Savior in His agony; He is so utterly oblivious of self, that instead of His agony driving His blood to the heart to nourish Him, it drives it outward to wet the earth with crimson dew. The agony of Jesus, inasmuch as it pours Him out upon the ground, pictures the fullness of the offering that He made for humankind. Do we understand how intense must have been the wrestling through which He passed, and do we hear its voice *to u*s? "You have not yet resisted to the point of shedding your blood." "Consider the Apostle and High Priest of our profession, Christ Jesus,"[273] and sweat even blood rather than yield to the tempter of your souls.

✒ *March 24* ✒

He was heard in that He feared (Hebrews 5:7, KJV).

Did this fear arise from the infernal suggestion *that He was utterly forsaken*. There may be sterner trials than this, but surely it is *one* of the worst to be utterly forsaken? "See," said Satan, "You don't have a friend anywhere! Your Father has closed His heart of compassion to You. Not an angel in His courts will stretch out a hand to help You. All heaven is alienated from You. You've been left alone. See the sons of Zebedee, James and Your beloved John, and Your bold apostle Peter—how the cowards sleep when Your suffering so much![275] You have no friend left in heaven or earth. All my forces are against You. I have sent messengers throughout all regions summoning every prince of darkness to set upon You this night. We will spare no arrows.[276] We will use all our infernal power to overwhelm You.[277] And what will You do, You are all alone?" Possibly this was the temptation. We think it was, because of the angel from heaven appearing to Him, strengthening Him and removing that fear.[278] He was heard in that He feared. He was no more alone—heaven was with Him. When He came to His disciples He found it true that everyone had forsaken Him—they were all asleep. But perhaps He gained some faint comfort from the thought that they weren't sleeping from treachery, but from sorrow. The spirit indeed was willing, but the flesh was weak.[279] At any rate, He was heard in that He feared. Jesus was heard in His deepest woe. My soul, *you* will be heard also.

ᴧ *March 25* ᴇ

"Are you betraying the Son of Man with a kiss?"
(Luke 22:48)

Be on guard when the world puts on a loving face, for if possible it will betray you with a kiss as it did Jesus.[280] Whenever people are about to stab Christianity, they usually profess great reverence for it. So beware of the sleek-faced hypocrisy that is armor bearer to heresy and infidelity. Knowing the deceivableness of unrighteousness, be wise as a serpent to detect and avoid the designs of the enemy.[281] The young man, void of understanding, was led astray by the kiss of the strange woman.[282] May your soul be so graciously instructed all this day that "the persuasive words"[283] of the world have no effect upon you. Holy Spirit, keep us from being betrayed with a kiss. But what if you should be guilty of the same sin as Judas? You've been baptized into the name of the LORD Jesus, you're a member of a church, you sit at the communion table—all these are so many kisses of your lips. Are you sincere in them? If not, you're a base traitor. Do you live in the world as carelessly as others do, and yet make a profession of being a follower of Christ? Then you expose Christianity to ridicule, and lead people to speak evil of the holy name by which you're called. Such acts make you a Judas, and it would be better for you if you had never been born.[284] LORD, preserve us from every false way. Never let us betray our Savior. We do love You, Jesus, and though we often grieve You, we do desire to abide faithful even to death.

Jesus answered. "If you are looking for Me, then let these men go" (John 18:8).

Notice, my soul, the concern Jesus showed for His sheep even in His hour of trial. He resigns Himself to the enemy, but He interjects a word of power to set His disciples free. As to Himself, like a sheep before her shearers He is silent and does not open His mouth.[285] But for His disciples' sake He speaks with Almighty energy. This is love—constant, self-forgetting, faithful love. But there is far more here than is found upon the surface. We have the very soul and spirit of the atonement in these words. The Good Shepherd lays down His life for the sheep,[286] and pleads that they must therefore go free. The Surety is bound,[287] and justice demands that those for whom He is a substitute should go their way. In the midst of Egypt's bondage, that voice rings as a word of power, "Let these go." Out of slavery of sin and Satan the redeemed must come. In every cell of the dungeons of Despair, the sound is echoed, "Let these go," and Despondency and Much-afraid come forth.[289] Satan hears the well-known voice, and lifts his foot from the necks of the fallen. Death hears it, and "the dead in Christ" arise.[290] Go the way of holiness, triumph, glory, and none will dare to keep you from it. The thunder-cloud has burst over the Cross of Calvary, and the pilgrims of Zion will never be struck by the bolts of vengeance.[291] Come, my heart, rejoice in the immunity that your Redeemer has secured for you, and bless His name all the day, and every day.

Then all the disciples deserted Him and fled
(Matthew 26:56).

He never deserted them, but in cowardly fear of their lives they fled from Him in the very beginning of His sufferings. This is just one instructive instance of the frailty of all believers if left to themselves—they are but sheep at best, and they flee when the wolf comes. They had all been warned of the danger, and had promised to die rather than leave their Master,[292] and yet they were seized with sudden panic and took to their heels. It may be that this morning I prepared my mind to bear a trial for the LORD's sake, and I imagined that I'll be certain to exhibit perfect faithfulness. But let me be very watchful of myself, lest having the same evil heart of unbelief I desert my LORD as the apostles did. It's one thing to promise, and quite another to perform. It would have been to their eternal honor to have stood faithfully at Jesus' side—instead, they fled from honor. LORD, keep me from imitating them. Where else would they have been so safe as near their Master, who could have called for twelve legions of angels?[293] They fled from their true safety. Divine grace can make the coward brave. These very apostles who were timid as rabbits, became bold as lions after the Spirit descended upon them. Even so, the Holy Spirit can make my cowardly spirit brave to confess my LORD and witness for His truth. If I forsake my LORD, I crucify Him afresh and put Him to open shame.[294] Keep me, blessed Spirit, from so shameful an end.

⊰ *March 28* ⊱

The love of Christ ... that surpasses knowledge
(Ephesians 3:19).

The love of Christ passes all human understanding. Where can language be found that is able to describe His matchless, unparalleled, love toward all humanity? It's so vast and boundless that all descriptive words just touch the surface, while immeasurable depths lie beneath. Christ's love is so measureless and fathomless that no human can achieve it. Before we can have any right idea of the love of Jesus, we must understand His previous glory in its height of majesty,[295] and His incarnation upon the earth in all its depths of shame. But who can tell us the majesty of Christ? When He was enthroned in the highest heavens He was very God of very God. The heavens and all that is in them were made by Him.[296] His own mighty arm upheld the stars and planets. The praises of cherubim and seraphim perpetually surrounded Him. The full chorus of the hallelujahs of the universe unceasingly flowed to the foot of His throne. He reigned supreme above all His creatures. Who can tell His height of glory then? And who can tell how low He descended? To be a man was something, to be a man of sorrows and acquainted with grief was far more.[297] To bleed and die and suffer—these were much for Him who was the Son of God.[298] But to suffer such unparalleled agony, and to endure a death of shame and desertion by His Father,[299] this is a depth of condescending love that even the most inspired mind must utterly fail to understand.[300] This is love—and truly it is love that "surpasses knowledge."

Although He was a son, He learned obedience from what he suffered (Hebrews 5:8).

We are told that the Captain of our salvation was made perfect through suffering.[301] Therefore, we who are sinful and far from being perfect must not wonder if we're called to pass through suffering, too. Shall the head be crowned with thorns and the other members of the body be rocked upon the dainty lap of ease? Must Christ pass through seas of His own blood to win the crown, while we walk to heaven with dry feet in silver slippers? No, our Master's experience teaches us that suffering is necessary for perfection. But there is one very comforting thought in the fact of Christ's being made perfect through suffering—He can have complete sympathy with us. "We do not have a high priest who is unable to sympathize with our weaknesses [infirmities, KJV]."[302] In this sympathy of Christ we find a sustaining power. One of the early martyrs said, "I can bear it all, for Jesus suffered, and He suffers in me now. He sympathizes with me, and this makes me strong." Believer, lay hold of this thought in all times of agony. Let the thought of Jesus strengthen you as you follow in His steps. Find a strong support in His sympathy. And remember, to suffer patiently is honorable, but to suffer for Christ is glory. The apostles rejoiced that they were counted worthy to suffer beatings and shame for His name.[303] The LORD will give us grace to suffer *for* Christ and to suffer *with* Christ. The jewels in the crowns of Christians are their afflictions.[304] "If we suffer, we shall also reign with Him."[305]

*He ... was numbered with the transgressors
(Isaiah 53:12).*

Why did Jesus allow Himself to be enrolled with sinners? This wonderful condescension was justified by many powerful reasons. *In such a character He could the better become their advocate.* In some trials there is an identification of the lawyer with the client, and they are seldom looked upon as separate from one another. Now, when the sinner is brought into court, Jesus appears there Himself. *He* stands to answer the accusation. He points to His side, His hands, His feet, and challenges Justice to bring anything against the sinners whom He represents. He pleads His blood, and pleads so triumphantly, being numbered with them and having a part with them, that the Judge proclaims, "Let them go their way; deliver them from going down into the pit, for we have a ransom."[306] Our LORD Jesus was numbered with the transgressors so they might *feel their hearts drawn toward Hi*m. Who can be afraid of one who is written in the same list with us? He who is numbered with us cannot condemn us. Wasn't He put down in the transgressor's list so we might *be written in the red roll of the saint*s? He was holy, we were guilty. His name was transferred from the holy list to the guilty list, and our names were transferred from the guilty to the holy, for there is a complete transfer made between Christ and His people.[307] Rejoice, believer, in your union to Him who was numbered among the transgressors; and prove that you are truly saved by being clearly numbered with those who are new creatures in Him.

By His wounds we are healed (Isaiah 53:5).

Pilate delivered our LORD to the Roman soldiers to be scourged.[308] The Roman scourge was a most dreadful instrument of torture. It was made of the tendons of oxen, and sharp bones were intertwined in several places among the tendons. As a result, every time the lash struck the body these pieces of bone inflicted fearful cuts that tore the flesh open down to the bone. Without doubt, the Savior was bound face forward to a post, stripped naked, and lashed forty times minus one,[309] which was the usual number of lashes. He had previously been beaten about the face,[310] but this scourging by the Roman soldiers was the most severe of His torments. My soul, stand here and weep over His poor torn body. Believer in Jesus, can you gaze upon Him without tears as He stands before you the very image of agonizing love? He is at once fair as the lily for innocence, and red as the rose with the crimson of His own blood. As we feel the sure and blessed healing that His stripes have accomplished in us, don't our hearts melt at once with love and grief? If ever we've loved our LORD Jesus, surely we must feel that affection glowing now within our hearts. We would prefer to go to our rooms and weep, but since our work calls us away, we'll first ask our Beloved to print the image of His bleeding body upon the tablets of our hearts all day long. Then this night we'll return to talk with Him, and grieve that our sins cost Him so much.

April

◁ *April 1* ▷

Let Him kiss me with the kisses of His mouth
(Song of Songs 1:2).

For several days we've been dwelling upon the Savior's passion, and we will linger there awhile longer. In beginning a new month, let's seek the same desires after our LORD as those that glowed in the heart of the elect spouse. See how she leaps at once to *Him*. She doesn't even mention His name. She's in the heart of her theme at once, for she speaks of *Him* who was the only Him in the world to her. How bold is her love! It was much condescension that permitted the woman to anoint Jesus' feet with spikenard.[311] It was rich love that allowed Mary to sit at His feet and learn of Him.[312] Esther was uncertain about going uncalled to King Ahasuerus,[313] but the elect spouse in joyful liberty of perfect love knows no fear.[314] If we've received the same free spirit, we also may ask the same. By kisses we suppose is meant those varied manifestations of affection by which the believer enjoys the love of Christ. The kiss of *reconciliation* we enjoyed at our conversion. The kiss of *acceptance* assures us He has accepted our persons and our works through rich grace. The kiss of daily *communion* we desire to have repeated daily until it's changed into the kiss of *reception*, which removes the soul from earth—and then the kiss of *consummation* that fills the soul with the joy of heaven. Faith is our walk,[315] but fellowship felt by our senses is our rest. Faith is the road, but communion with Jesus is the well of living water from which the thirsty pilgrim drinks.[316]

But Jesus made no reply, not even to a single charge
(Matthew 27:14).

He had never been slow of speech when He could bless others, but He wouldn't say a single word for Himself. "No one ever spoke the way this man does,"[317] and never was anyone silent like Him. Was this unusual silence *a sign of His perfect self-sacrifice*? Did it show that He wouldn't say a word to stop His crucifixion? Had He so entirely surrendered Himself that He would not interfere in His own behalf, even in the smallest degree, but be bound and slain an unstruggling, uncomplaining, victim? Was this silence *a type of the defenselessness of sin*? Nothing can be said to ease or excuse human guilt, and so He who bore its whole weight stood silent before His judge. Isn't patient silence *the best reply to an opposing world*? Calm endurance answers some questions infinitely better than the loftiest eloquence. The best apologists[318] for Christianity have always been its martyrs. The anvil breaks a host of hammers by quietly bearing their blows. The silent Lamb of God gives us *a grand example of wisdo*m. And by His silence, our LORD gave *a remarkable fulfillment of prophecy*. A long defense of Himself would have been contrary to Isaiah's prediction: "He was led like a lamb to the slaughter, and as a sheep before her shearers is silent, so he did not open his mouth."[319] By His silence He conclusively proved Himself to be the true Lamb of God.[320] As such we salute Him this morning. Be with us, Christ Jesus, and in the silence of our heart, let us hear the voice of Your love.

They took Jesus, and led Him away" (John 19:16).

He had been all night in agony. He had spent the early morning at the hall of Caiaphas, and then was hurried from Caiaphas to Pilate, from Pilate to Herod, and from Herod back again to Pilate. He therefore had little strength left, and yet He was given neither refreshment nor rest. They were eager for His blood, and so loaded the Cross on Him and led Him out to die. In this we see the shadow of the high-priest bringing forth the scapegoat, putting both his hands upon its head, confessing over him all the transgressions, thereby putting them upon the head of the goat. The goat was then led away into the wilderness, bearing upon itself all the iniquities of the people.[321] Now we see Jesus brought before the priests and rulers, who pronounce Him guilty. God Himself imputes our sins *to Him*: "the LORD has laid on Him the iniquity *of us all*."[322] "He was made sin *for us*."[323] As the substitute for our guilt, we see the great Scapegoat led away, bearing the Cross of our sins. Do you feel assured that He carried *your* sin? As you look at the Cross He bore, does it represent *your* sin? There is one way by which you can be certain. Have you repented of your sins and trusted in Him?[324] Then your sin lies not on you. It has all been transferred by blessed imputation to Christ. Let not the picture of your Sin Bearer fade until you have rejoiced in your own deliverance, and adored your loving Redeemer upon whom your iniquities were laid.

God made Him who had no sin to be sin for us, so that in Him we might become the righteousness of God (2 Corinthians 5:21).

Christian, why are you weeping? Are you mourning over your own corruptions? Look to your perfect LORD, and remember you are complete in Him.[325] In God's sight you are as perfect as if you had never sinned.[326] More than that, the LORD our Righteousness[327] has put a divine garment upon you, so that you have more than the righteousness of man—you have the righteousness of God. You who are mourning by reason of inbred sin and depravity, remember, none of your sins can condemn you. You've learned to hate sin, but you've learned also to know that sin is not yours—it was laid upon Christ's head. Your standing is not in yourself, it's in Christ. Your acceptance is not in yourself, it's in your LORD. You're as much accepted of God today, with all your sinfulness, as you'll be when you stand before His throne, free from all corruption. Take hold of this precious thought, *perfection in Christ*! For you are "complete in Him." With your Savior's garment on, you're holy as the Holy One. "Who is he that condemns? Christ Jesus, who died—more than that, who was raised to life—is at the right hand of God and is also interceding for us." Christian, let your heart rejoice, for God made you "accepted in the Beloved."[328] So what do you have to fear? Let your face always wear a smile. Live near your Master. Live in the suburbs of that celestial city, New Jerusalem.[329] For soon, when your time has come, you'll rise up where your LORD sits, and reign at His right hand.[330]

*They … put the cross on him and made him carry it
behind Jesus (Luke 23:26).*

We see in Simon's carrying the cross a picture of Christians
throughout all generations. Christian, Jesus' suffering
doesn't exclude your suffering. Christ exempts you from
sin, but not from sorrow. But let's comfort ourselves with
this thought—in our case, as in Simon's, *it's not our cross
but Christ's cross that we carry.* When you're ill-treated
for your piety, when you're mocked for your Christianity,
remember it's not *your* cross, it's *His* cross. And it's
delightful to carry the cross of our LORD! You carry the
cross *after* Him. Your path is marked with the footprints
of Jesus. The mark of His blood-red shoulder is upon that
heavy burden. It's *His* cross, and He goes before you as a
shepherd goes before his sheep. Take up your cross daily,
and follow Him.[331] Don't forget, also, *that you bear this
cross in partnership.* Some say Simon carried only one end
of the cross, not all of it. If so, Jesus would have carried
the heavier part, against the transverse beam, and Simon
would have carried the lighter end. It's so with you—you
only have to carry the light end of the cross, Christ carries
the heavy end. Simon had to bear the cross for a very little
while, yet it gave him lasting honor. Even so the cross we
carry is only for a little while at most, and then we will
receive the crown, the glory. Surely we should love the
cross and, instead of shrinking from it, *count it very dear,*
while it works out for us "a far more exceeding and eternal
weight of glory."[332]

April 6

Let us, then, go to Him outside the camp
(Hebrews 13:13).

Bearing His cross, Jesus went to suffer outside the camp. As Christians, our reason for leaving the camp of the world's sin and religion is not because we love to be different, but because *Jesus did so*, and we must follow our Master. Christ was "not of the world," and neither are we.[333] His life and His testimony were a constant protest against conformity with the world. He loved people, but still He was separate from sinners. In like manner Christ's people must "go to Him." They must take their position "outside the camp," as witness-bearers for the truth. They must be prepared to tread the straight and narrow road.[334] They must have bold, unflinching, lion-like hearts, loving Christ first, His truth next, and Christ and His truth beyond all the world. Christ would have His people "go outside the camp" *for their own sanctification.* You cannot grow in grace to any high degree while you're conformed to the world. The life of separation may be a path of afflictions, but it's the highway of safety. And though the separated life may cost you many pangs, and make every day a battle, yet it's a happy life after all. No joy can excel that of the soldier of Christ. Jesus reveals Himself so graciously, and gives such sweet refreshment, that the warrior feels more calm and peace in the daily battles than others in their hours of rest. The highway of holiness is the highway of communion. It's the way we hope *to win the crown,*[335] if divine grace enables us to faithfully follow Christ "outside the camp."

How long ... will you turn my glory into shame?
(Psalm 4:2)

What honors did the blinded people of Israel award to their long-expected King. (1.) They gave Him *a procession of honor*, in which Roman legionaries, Jewish priests, men and women, took a part, and He carried His cross. This is the triumph that the world awards to Him who comes to overthrow our worst enemies. Derisive shouts are His only acclamations, and cruel taunts His only praise. (2.) They presented Him with *the wine of honor*. Instead of a golden cup of generous wine they offered Him the condemned person's stupefying drink,[336] which He refused because He would suffer our sins to the fullest. Afterwards when He cried, "I thirst,"[337] they gave Him vinegar mixed with gall, thrust to His mouth upon a sponge.[338] (3.) He was provided with *a guard of honor*, who showed their esteem of Him by gambling over His garments, which they had seized as their booty. (4.) *A throne of honor* was found for Him upon the bloody tree. No easier place of rest would they give to the One who made them.[339] The Cross was, in fact, the full expression of the world's feeling towards Him. It was as if they said, "You Son of God, this is how we would treat God Himself, if we could reach Him." (5.) *The title of honor* was nominally "King of the Jews,"[340] but that they repudiated by preferring the murderer Barabbas,[341] and by placing Jesus in the place of highest shame between two thieves.[342] The world thereby turned His glory into shame, but it will yet gladden the eyes of saints and angels forever.[343]

For if men do these things when the tree is green,
what will happen when it is dry?" (Luke 23:31)

When God saw Jesus in the sinner's place, He did not spare Him, and when He finds the unregenerate without Christ, He won't spare them. Sinner, Jesus was led away by His enemies, and so will you be taken away to the place appointed for you.[344] Jesus was forsaken by God—and if He to whom sin was only imputed was forsaken, how much more will you be? *"Eloi, Eloi, lama sabachthani?"*[345] What an awful shriek! But what will be your cry when you say, "O God! O God! why have You forsaken me?" and the answer comes back, "since you ignored all my advice and would not accept my rebuke, I in turn will laugh at your disaster; I will mock when calamity overtakes you."[346] If God spared not His own Son, how much less will He spare you![347] What whips of burning wire will be yours when conscience smites you with all its terrors. Self-righteous sinner, who will stand in your place when God says, "Awake, O sword, against those who rejected Me—smite them, and let them feel the pain forever"? The Son of God was mocked and spit upon—sinner, your shame will be merciless! We cannot estimate the suffering that rained upon Jesus who died for us, therefore it's impossible for us to tell you what torrents of grief will pour upon you if you die as you are now. You may die soon, even this day. In the name of Jesus Christ, do not bring upon yourself the wrath to come! Trust in the Son of God, and you will not perish.[348]

A large number of people followed Him, including women who mourned and wailed for Him (Luke 23:27).

Amid the rabble rousers who hounded the Redeemer to His doom, there were some gracious souls whose bitter anguish sought relief in wailing and mourning—fit music to accompany that march of woe. When my soul can, in imagination, see the Savior bearing His Cross to Calvary, it joins the godly women and weeps with them. For, indeed, there is true cause for grief—lying deeper than those mourning women thought. They bewailed innocence maltreated, goodness persecuted, love bleeding, meekness about to die, but my heart has a deeper and more bitter cause to mourn. *My* sins were the scourges that lacerated His blessed shoulders, and crowned with thorns His bleeding head.[349] *My* sins cried "Crucify Him! Crucify Him!"[350] and laid the Cross upon His gracious shoulders. His being led forth to die is sorrow enough for one eternity, but my having been His murderer is more, infinitely more, grief than one poor fountain of tears can express. Why those women loved and wept it isn't hard to guess, but they could not have had greater reasons for love and grief than my heart has. Nain's widow saw her son restored,[351] but I myself have been raised to newness of life. Peter's mother-in-law was cured of a fever,[352] but I of the greater plague of sin. Seven demons were cast out of Magdalene,[353] but a whole legion out of me. Mary and Martha were favored with visits,[354] but He's always with me.[355] His mother bore His body, but He lives in me. I am not behind them in debt, let me not be behind them in gratitude.

⨳ *April 10* ⨳

The place which is called Calvary (Luke 23:33, KJV).

The hill of comfort is the hill of Calvary. The house of consolation is built with the wood of the Cross. The temple of heavenly blessing is founded upon the riven rock—riven by the spear that pierced His side.[356] No scene in sacred history ever gladdens the soul like Calvary's tragedy. Light springs from the midday-midnight of Golgotha, and every herb of the field blooms sweetly beneath the shadow of the once accursed tree. In that place of thirst, grace has dug a fountain that ever gushes with waters pure as crystal, each drop capable of relieving the woes of humanity. You who have had your seasons of conflict will confess that it was not at Olivet[357] that you ever found comfort, or on Sinai[358] or Tabor, but Gethsemane, Gabbatha,[359] and Golgotha have been a means of comfort to you. The bitter herbs of Gethsemane have often taken away the bitters of your life, the scourge of Gabbatha has often scourged away your cares, and the groans of Calvary yields us comfort rare and rich. We never should have known Christ's love in all its heights and depths if He hadn't died, nor could we guess the Father's deep affection if He hadn't given His Son to die. The common mercies we enjoy all sing of love, just as when we put a sea-shell to our ears it whispers of the deep sea from which it came. But if we desire to hear the ocean itself and see the depth of love, we mustn't look at everyday blessings—we must go to Calvary and watch Jesus die.

I am poured out like water, and all my bones are out of joint (Psalm 22:14).

Did earth or heaven ever behold a sadder spectacle! In soul and body, our LORD felt weak as water poured upon the ground. Over the long six hours on the Cross as His weight sagged against the nails, every ligament was stretched beyond endurance, every joint in His arms and shoulders was dislocated, and every nerve screamed in pain. His thirst was nearly unbearable, and His body was a mass of sickness and suffering. When Daniel saw his great vision, he wrote, "I had no strength left, my face turned deathly pale and I was helpless."[360] How much more faint must have been our LORD when He saw the dread vision of the wrath of God and felt it tearing through His body and soul. To us, what our LORD endured would have been unendurable, and kind unconsciousness would have come to our rescue. But in His case, He was wounded for our transgressions[361] and must endure the sword of God's wrath,[362] and drain the cup to its bitter dregs.[363] As we kneel before our Savior's throne, let us remember well the way by which He prepared it as a throne of grace for us.[364] Let us in spirit drink of His cup,[365] that we may be strengthened for our hour of heaviness whenever it may come. In His natural body every member suffered, and so must it be in the spiritual.[366] Out of His sufferings His body came forth uninjured to glory and power, even so will His mystical body come through the furnace with not so much as the smell of fire upon it.[367]

✦ April 12 ✦

*My heart has turned to wax; it has melted away
within me (Psalm 22:14).*

Our blessed LORD experienced a terrible sinking and melting of soul. "A man's spirit sustains him in sickness, but a crushed spirit who can bear?"[368] Deep depression of spirit is the most grievous of all trials—nothing compares with it. Believer, come near the Cross this morning, and humbly adore the King of glory[369] as having once been brought far lower in mental distress and inward anguish than we've ever been. By such sufferings He became a faithful High Priest who can be touched with a feeling of our infirmities.[370] Especially let those of us whose sadness springs directly from the withdrawal of a present sense of our Father's love,[371] enter into near and intimate communion with Christ. Let's not give way to despair, since the Master passed through this dark room before us. Our souls may sometimes long and faint, and thirst unbearably, to behold the light of the LORD's countenance.[372] At such times, let's remember our great High Priest who sympathizes with us. O strong and deep love of Christ, come in like a flood and cover all my faculties, drown all my sins, wash out all my cares, lift up my earth-bound soul, and float it up to my LORD's feet. There let me lie, a poor broken shell, washed up by His love, having no virtue or value. Only venturing to whisper to Him that if He will put His ear against my chest, He will hear within my heart faint echoes of the vast waves of His own love that have brought me where I delight to lie at His feet forever.[373]

*My lover is to me a sachet of myrrh
(Song of Songs 1:13).*

Myrrh may well be chosen as the type of Jesus on account of its preciousness; its perfume; its pleasantness; its healing, preserving, disinfecting qualities; and its connection with sacrifice. But why is He compared to "a *sachet* of myrrh"? First, for plenty. He's not a drop of it, He's a treasure chest full. He's not a sprig or flower of it, but a whole bundle. There's enough in Christ for all my necessities, so let me not be slow to avail myself of Him. He's also compared to a sachet for *variety*, for there is in Christ not only the one thing needful, but "in Christ all the fullness of the Deity lives in bodily form"[374]—everything needful is in Him. Take Jesus in His different characters, and you will see a marvelous variety—Prophet, Priest, King, Friend, Shepherd. Consider Him in His life, death, resurrection, ascension, second advent. View Him in His virtue, gentleness, courage, self-denial, love, faithfulness, truth, righteousness—everywhere He is a bundle of preciousness. He is a "sachet of myrrh" for *preservation*— not loose myrrh tied up, myrrh to be stored in a treasure chest. We must value Him as our best treasure, prize His words and commandments,[375] and keep our thoughts and knowledge of Him under lock and key, lest the devil should steal anything from us.[376] Also, Jesus is a "sachet of myrrh" *for speciality*. The emblem suggests the idea of distinguishing, discriminating, grace. From before the foundation of the world, He was set apart for His people,[377] and He gives forth His perfume only to those who are close to Him.

*All who see Me mock Me; they hurl insults, shaking
their heads (Psalm 22:7).*

Mockery was a great ingredient in our LORD's woe. At times
the very ones He was helping laughed at Him,[378] Herod and
his soldiers ridiculed him;[379] soldiers clothed Him in purple,
crowned Him with thorns, beat Him on the head with a
reed, spit on Him, and mockingly knelt to worship Him;[380]
and on the Cross all sorts of horrid jests and hideous taunts
were hurled at Him.[381] Ridicule is always hard to bear, but
when we're in intense pain it's so heartless, so cruel, that it
cuts us to the quick. Imagine the Savior crucified, racked
with anguish far beyond human understanding, and then
picture that motley multitude, all shaking their heads and
hurling insults in bitterest contempt of one poor suffering
victim! Surely there must have been something more in
the crucified One than they could see, or else such a great
and mingled crowd would not unanimously have honored
Him with such contempt. Was it not evil confessing, in the
very moment of its greatest apparent triumph, that after
all it could do nothing more than mock at that victorious
goodness that was then reigning on the Cross? O Jesus,
"despised and rejected of men,"[382] how could You die for
people who treated You so badly? Here is amazing love,
divine love, love beyond measure. We, too, have despised
You in the days of our unregeneracy, and even since our
new birth we have set the world above You in our hearts.
Yet even though You knew we would sin against You, You
bled to heal our wounds and died to give us life.[383]

My God, my God, why have You forsaken Me?
(Psalm 22:1)

Here we behold the Savior in the depth of His sorrows. No other place so well shows the griefs of Christ as Calvary, and no other moment at Calvary is so full of agony as that in which His cry rends the air: "My God, my God, why have You forsaken Me?" At this moment physical weakness was united with acute mental torture from the shame and humiliation through which He had to pass, and to make His grief climax with emphasis, He suffered spiritual agony surpassing all expression, resulting from the departure of His Father's presence. This was the black midnight of His horror. It was then that He descended into an abyss of suffering. No one can fathom the full meaning of His anguished cry. At times some of us feel like crying, "My God, my God, why have You forsaken me?" There are seasons when the brightness of our Father's smile is eclipsed by dark clouds, but let's remember that God never does forsake us—it's only a *seeming* forsaking. But in Christ's case it was a *real* forsaking. We grieve at a little withdrawal of our Father's love, but who can calculate how deep Jesus' agony was at the real turning away of God's face from Him? Our cry is often dictated by unbelief. But His was the statement of a dreadful fact, for God had really turned away from Him for a season. Since even the *thought* that He has forsaken us causes us anxiety, what must have been Jesus' horror when He cried, "My God, my God, why have You forsaken Me?"

The precious blood of Christ (1 Peter 1:19).

Standing at the foot of the Cross, we see head, hands, feet, and side, all pouring forth crimson streams of precious blood. It's "precious" because of its *redeeming* and *atoning power*. By it the sins of Christ's people are atoned for[384]—they are redeemed from under the law,[385] reconciled to God[386] and made one with Him.[387] Christ's blood is also "precious" in its *purifying power*—it "purifies us from all sin."[388] "Though your sins are like scarlet, they shall be as white as snow."[389] Through Jesus' blood there is not a spot left upon any believer,[390] no wrinkle nor any such thing remains.[391] The blood of Christ is likewise "precious" in its *preserving power*. We are safe from the destroying angel under the sprinkled blood. Remember it is *God's seeing* the blood that is the true reason for our being spared.[392] Here is comfort for us when the eye of faith is dim, for God's eye is still the same. The blood of Christ is "precious" also in its *sanctifying influence*. The same blood that justifies by taking away sin, does in its after-action, vitalize the new nature and lead it onward to holiness. There is no motive for holiness so great as that which streams from the veins of Christ.[393] And "precious," unspeakably precious, is this blood, because it has an *overcoming power*. "They overcame him by the blood of the Lamb."[394] How could they do otherwise? Those who fight with the precious blood of Jesus Christ, fight with a weapon that cannot know defeat. By trusting the power of Jesus' blood, we will always conquer!

You have come ... to the sprinkled blood that
speaks a better word than the blood of Abel
(Hebrews 12:24).

Reader, have *you* come to the sprinkled blood? The question isn't whether you've come to a knowledge of doctrine, or an observance of ceremonies, or to a certain kind of experience, but *have you come to the blood of Jesus?* The blood of Jesus is the life of all vital godliness. If you've truly come to Jesus, we know how you came—the Holy Spirit drew you there. You came to the sprinkled blood with no merits of your own. Guilty, lost, and helpless, you came to take that blood, and that blood alone, as your everlasting hope.[396] You came to the Cross of Christ with a trembling and an aching heart, and, what a precious sound it was to you to hear the voice of the blood of Jesus! The dropping of His blood is as the music of heaven to the repentant people of earth.[397] We're full of sin, but as we gaze upon Christ's streaming wounds, each drop of blood cries as it falls, "It is finished![398] I've made an end of sin, I've brought in everlasting righteousness." Oh! sweet words of the precious blood of Jesus! If you've come to that blood once, you'll come to it constantly. Your life will be "Looking unto Jesus."[399] If you've ever come to the sprinkling blood, you'll feel your need of coming to it every day. Those who don't desire to wash in it *every day*, have never washed in it at all. This morning let's sprinkle our doorpost with fresh blood, and then feast upon the Lamb, assured that the destroying angel must pass us by.[400]

✒ *April 18* ✒

She tied the scarlet cord in the window
(Joshua 2:21).

Rahab depended upon the promise of the spies for her preservation. She saw them as the representatives of the God of Israel. Her faith was simple and firm, but it was very obedient. Tying the scarlet cord in the window was a very trivial act in itself, but she dared not run the risk of omitting it. Come, my soul, isn't there here a lesson for you? Have you been attentive to all your LORD's will, even though some of His commands might seem non-essential? This act of Rahab sets forth a solemn lesson. Have I implicitly trusted in the precious blood of Jesus? Have I tied the scarlet cord, as with a Gordian Knot,[401] in my window, so that my trust can never be removed? Or can I look out towards the Dead Sea of my sins, or the Jerusalem of my hopes, without seeing the blood and all things in connection with its blessed power? A passerby can easily see a cord of so conspicuous a color—if it hangs from the window. It will be well for me if my life makes the power of the atonement conspicuous to all onlookers. What is there to be ashamed of?[402] Let people or demons stare if they want to, the blood is my boast and my song. My soul, there is One who will see that scarlet cord even when you can not see it yourself because of weakness of faith. The LORD will see it and pass over you.[403] My soul, tie the scarlet cord in the window afresh, and rest in peace.

At that moment the curtain of the temple was torn in two from top to bottom (Matthew 27:51).

The tearing of such a strong and thick a curtain[404] was not intended merely as a display of power, but to teach us many lessons. *The old law of ordinances* was put away, and like a worn-out robe, it was torn and laid aside. When Jesus died, the blood sacrifices required by the law were all finished, because all the law was fulfilled in Him. That tear also *revealed all the hidden things of the Old Covenant*—the mercy seat could now be seen.[405] In the tabernacle in the wilderness, God communed with Moses "from above the mercy seat, from between the two cherubims."[406] By the death of our LORD Jesus, life and immortality were brought to light, and things hidden since the foundation of the world are now manifest in Him.[407] *The annual ceremony of atonement was thus abolished. The atoning blood* that was sprinkled within the veil once every year was now offered once for all by the great High Priest. No blood of bullocks or of lambs is needed now, for Jesus has entered within the veil with His own blood.[408] Hence *access to God is now permitte*d, and is the privilege of every believer in Christ Jesus.[409] We may come boldly to the throne of the heavenly grace.[410] Are we mistaken if we say that the opening of the Most Holy Place in this marvelous manner was *the type of the opening of the gates of paradise* to all the saints by virtue of Jesus' Passion? Christ Jesus alone is the way to heaven[411]—so let us enter with Him into that eternal place.

≤ *April 20* ≥

*So that by His death He might destroy him who
holds the power of death—that is, the devil
(Hebrews 2:14).*

Child of God, death has lost its sting,[412] because the devil's
power over it is destroyed. So stop being afraid of dying.
Ask God for grace so that by an intimate knowledge
and a firm belief of your Redeemer's death, you may be
strengthened for that coming hour. Living near the Cross
of Calvary you may even think of death with pleasure, and
welcome it with intense delight when it comes. It's sweet
to die in the LORD It's a covenant blessing to sleep in Jesus.
Death is no longer banishment, it's a return from exile, a
going home to the many mansions where His loved ones
already dwell.[413] The distance between glorified spirits in
heaven and blessed saints on earth seems great; but it isn't.
We're not far from home—a moment will take us there.
Listen to Paul, "Absent from the body … present with the
LORD."[414] Your ship just departed, but it's already at its
haven. It just spread its sail and it was there. Like that ship
of old upon the Lake of Galilee, a storm had tossed it, and
then Jesus walked across the rough waters to His disciples
and said, "It is I; don't be afraid," and *immediately* the
ship was at land.[415] Don't think there's a long time between
the instant of death and the eternity of glory. When the
eyes close on earth they open in heaven. So, child of God,
there's nothing for you to fear in death, for through the
death of your LORD its curse and sting were destroyed.
Sleep in peace, awake in joy.

I know that my Redeemer lives (Job 19:25).

The marrow of Job's comfort lies in that little word *My*—
My Redeemer, and in the fact that his Redeemer lives. Oh,
to get hold of a living Christ. We must get Him before we
can enjoy Him. What good to me is gold in a mine? It's
gold in my purse that will purchase the things I need. So
a Redeemer who doesn't redeem *me* is of no use to me.
Don't be content until by faith you can say "Yes, I cast
myself upon the living Christ, and He is mine." You may
hold Him with a weak hand, and think it's presumption
to say, "He lives as *my* Redeemer;" but if you've faith as
a grain of mustard seed,[416] that little faith *entitles* you to
say it. But there's also another word here that expresses
Job's strong confidence, "*I know*." To say, "I hope so, I
trust so" is comfortable, and there are thousands in the
body of Christ who hardly ever get much further. But to
reach the essence of consolation you *must* say, "I know."
Ifs, buts, and maybes, are murderers of peace and comfort.
Doubts are dreary things in times of sorrow. If I have any
thought that Christ isn't mine, then there's apprehension
and fear of the coming night. But if I know that Christ
lives for me, then darkness is not dark and even the night
is light about me.[417] If in those ages before the coming
and advent of Christ, Job could say, "I *know*," *we* should
not be less certain. A living Redeemer, truly mine, is joy
unspeakable.

God exalted Him (Acts 5:31).

Jesus, our LORD, once crucified, dead, and buried, now sits upon the throne of glory. The highest place that heaven affords is His by undisputed right. It's wonderful to remember that the exaltation of Christ in heaven is a *representative exaltation*. As mediator and head of the New Covenant, the honors that Jesus wears in heaven are the heritage of all the saints. It's delightful to reflect how close Christ's union is with His people. We're actually one with Him—we are members of His body,[418] and His exaltation is our exaltation. We who overcome will sit upon His throne, even as He overcame and sat down with His Father on His throne.[419] He has a crown, and He gives us crowns, too.[420] Look up to Christ now. Let the eye of your faith behold Him with many crowns upon His head.[421] One day you will be like Him, when you will see Him as He is. You will not be so great as He is,[422] you will not be so divine, but still you will, in a large measure, share the same honors, and enjoy the same happiness and dignity that He possesses. Be content to live unknown for a little while, and to walk your weary way through this difficult world, for sooner than you think you will reign with Christ—forever and ever. What a wonderful thought for the children of God! We have Christ for our glorious representative in heaven's *courts* now, and soon He will come and take us to be with Him,[423] to behold His glory, and to share His joy.

No, in all these things we are more than conquerors through Him who loved us (Romans 8:37).

We go to Christ for forgiveness, and then too often look to the law for power to fight our sins. For this, Paul rebukes us, "You foolish Galatians! Who has bewitched you? Before your very eyes Jesus Christ was clearly portrayed as crucified. I would like to learn just one thing from you: Did you receive the Spirit by observing the law, or by believing what you heard? Are you so foolish? After beginning with the Spirit, are you now trying to attain your goal by human effort?" Take your sins to Christ's Cross, for the old self can only be crucified there—we are crucified *with Him*.[424] The only weapon to fight sin with is the spear that pierced Jesus' side. For instance, you have a bad temper, how do you get rid of it? You've probably never tried the right way of going to Jesus with it.[425] How did you get salvation? You came to Jesus just as you were and trusted Him to save you. You must kill your temper in the same way. You must go to the Cross with it and say to Jesus, "LORD, I trust You to deliver me from it." That's the only way to give it a death-blow. Are you covetous? You can struggle against this evil for as long as you please, but only the blood of Jesus will deliver you from it. Take it to Christ. Your prayers, your repentances, and your tears—all of them together—are worth nothing apart from Him.[426] Only through Him can you conquer your sins[427]—there is no other way.

*And because of all this we make a sure covenant
(Nehemiah 9:38, KJV).*[428]

There are many occasions when we may beneficially renew
our covenant with God. After *recovery from sickness* when,
like Hezekiah, we have had more years added to our life,
we may properly do it. After any *deliverance from trouble*,
when our joys spring forth again, we should perhaps
visit the foot of the Cross and renew our consecration.
Especially, let us do this after any *sin that has grieved
the Holy Spirit*, or brought dishonor upon the name of
Jesus and the cause of God. Further, we should not only
confirm our dedication to God during our troubles, but
also during *our prosperity*. If we ever have occasions that
could be called "crowning mercies," then we should also
crown God anew in our heart. If we would learn to profit
by our prosperity, we wouldn't need so much adversity. If
we would gather from a kiss all the good it might confer
upon us, we wouldn't so often smart under the rod. Have
we recently received some blessing that we little expected?
Has the LORD put our feet in a large room? Can we sing of
mercies multiplied? Then this is the day to put our hand
upon the horns of the altar, and say, "Bind me here, my
God; bind me here with cords, even forever."[429] Inasmuch
as we need the fulfillment of new promises from God, let
us offer renewed prayers that our old vows may not be
dishonored.[430] Let us this morning make with Him a sure
covenant because of the sufferings of Jesus, which for the
last month we have been considering with gratitude.

❧ April 25 ❧

Rise up, my love, my fair one, and come away
(Song of Songs 2:10).[431]

I hear the voice of my Beloved! He speaks to *me*! Fair weather is smiling upon the face of the earth, and He would not have me spiritually asleep while nature all around me is waking from her winter's rest. He bids me "Rise up," and well He may, for I have long enough been lying among worldly things. He is risen, I am risen in Him, why then should I cleave unto the dust? From lower loves, desires, pursuits, and aspirations, I will rise toward Him. He calls me by the sweet title of "My love," and counts me beautiful. If He has exalted me, and thinks I am beautiful, how can I stay among worldly people? He bids me "Come away."—further and further from everything selfish, worldly, and sinful.[432] "Come away" doesn't have a harsh sound to me, for what is there to hold me in this wilderness of vanity and sin? O my LORD, I would come away if it were possible, but I'm caught among the thorns and cannot free myself from them as I want to. To come away is to come to land out of the raging storm, to come to rest after long labor, to come to the goal of my desires and the summit of my wishes. But LORD, how can a lump of clay come away from the horrible pit? Only Your grace can do it.[433] Send forth Your Holy Spirit to kindle flames of love in my heart, and I'll continue to rise until I leave life and time behind me, and indeed come away.

Do this in remembrance of Me
(1 Corinthians 11:24).

It seems then, that Christians may forget Christ! There would be no need for this loving exhortation, if there weren't a fearful supposition that our memories might prove treacherous. It appears almost impossible that those who have been redeemed by the blood of the dying Lamb,[434] and loved with an everlasting love by the eternal Son of God, would forget that gracious Savior. But there's too much evidence for us to deny the crime. Forget Him who never forgot us! Forget Him who poured His blood forth for our sins! Forget Him who loved us even to the death! Can it be possible? Yes, it's not only possible, but conscience confesses that it's too sadly a fault with all of us. He whom we should make the abiding tenant of our memories is too often treated as only a visitor. The Cross where one would think that memory would linger, and unmindfulness would be an unknown intruder, is desecrated by the feet of forgetfulness. Doesn't your conscience say that this is true? Don't you find yourself sometimes forgetting Jesus—at least for awhile? Some creature steals away your heart, and you are unmindful of Him upon whom your affection should be set. Some earthly business engrosses your attention when you should fix your eye steadily upon the Cross. It's the incessant turmoil of the world, the constant attraction of earthly things that takes the soul away from Jesus Christ. It should not be. Let's determine to bind a heavenly forget-me-not about our hearts for Jesus our beloved and, whatever else we let slip, let's hold fast to Him.

⊰ *April 27* ⊱

God, our God (Psalm 67:6).

It's strange how little use we make of the spiritual blessings that God gives us, but it's stranger still how little use we make of God Himself. Though He's "*our* God," we devote ourselves very little to Him, ask little of Him, and seldom seek counsel from Him. We often conduct our business without seeking His guidance, In our troubles, we constantly try to bear our burdens ourselves, instead of casting them upon the LORD.[435] It's our own fault if we don't freely take of the riches of our God. Never be lacking while you have a God to go to. Never fear or faint while you have God to help you. Go to God's riches[436] and take whatever you need—there is all that you can want. Learn the divine skill of making God all things to you. He can supply you with everything, or, better still, He Himself can be everything to you.[437] Let me urge you, then, to make use of your God. Make use of Him *in prayer*. Go to Him often, because He is *your* God. Don't fail to use so great a privilege. Run to Him, tell Him all your needs. Use Him constantly *by faith* at all times. If some dark providence has clouded your way, use your God as a "sun"—if some strong enemy has troubled you, find in Him a "shield," for He is a sun and shield to His people.[438] Whatever you are, and wherever you are, remember God is just *what* you need, and just *where* you need, and that He can do *all* you need.

ᴥ *April 28* ᴥ

Remember Your word to Your servant, for You
have given me hope (Psalm 119:49).

Whatever your need may be, you'll readily find a promise
in the Bible suited to it. Are you faint and feeble because
your way is rough and you're weary? Here is the promise:
"He gives strength to the weary."[439] When you read such a
promise, lift it to the great Promiser, and ask Him to fulfill
His Word. Are you seeking after Christ, and thirsting for
closer communion with Him? This promise shines like a
star upon you: "Blessed are those who hunger and thirst for
righteousness, for they will be filled."[440] Take that promise
to the throne continually. Don't plead anything else, but go
to God over and over again with this: "LORD, You have said
it. Do as You promised."[441] Are you distressed because of
sin, and burdened with the heavy load of your iniquities?
Listen to these words: "I, even I, am He who blots out your
transgressions, for My own sake, and remembers your sins
no more."[442] You have no merit of your own to plead why
He should pardon you, but plead His written promises and
He will perform them.[443] Are you afraid that you may not
be able to hold on to the end? If that is your state, take
this word of grace to the throne and plead it: "Though
the mountains be shaken and the hills be removed, yet My
unfailing love for you will not be shaken."[444] Feed your
faith upon God's Word, and whatever your fears or needs,
go to the bank of faith with your Father's promise in your
hand, saying, "Remember Your Word to Your servant."

≼ April 29 ≽

*You are my refuge in the day of disaster
(Jeremiah 17:17).*

The path of the Christian isn't always bright with sunshine—there are seasons of darkness and storm. True, it's written in God's Word, "Her ways are pleasant ways, and all her paths are peace." It's also a great truth that Christianity is calculated to give a person happiness below as well as bliss above. But experience tells us that although the course of the just is "like the first gleam of dawn, shining ever brighter till the full light of day,"[445] sometimes that light is eclipsed. Sometimes clouds cover our sun and we walk in darkness without light. There are many who basked in sunshine in the earlier stages of their Christian career, and walked along the "green pastures" by the side of the "still waters."[446] Then suddenly the green pastures dry up and wither and the sweet waters turn bitter.[447] It's then they say, "Surely, if I were a child of God, this wouldn't happen." Don't say that just because you're walking in darkness. The best of God's saints must drink bitter waters, and the dearest of His children must bear the cross. No Christian ever enjoyed perpetual prosperity. Perhaps the LORD gave you a smooth and unclouded path at first because you were weak and timid. But now that you're stronger in the spiritual life, you must enter into the rougher experience of God's full-grown children. We need winds and storms to exercise our faith, to tear off the rotten branches of self-dependence, and to root us more firmly in Christ. The day of evil reveals to us the value of our glorious hope.[448]

All the Israelites grumbled (Numbers 14:2).

There are grumblers among Christians now, as there were among the Israelites. When the chastening rod falls, there are those who cry out against it. They ask, "Why am I afflicted? What have I done to be chastened in this manner?" A word with you, grumbler! Why should you murmur against the chastening of your heavenly Father?[449] Does He treat you more harshly than you deserve? Consider what a rebel you were once, but He has pardoned you! Surely, if He in His wisdom sees fit now to chasten you, you shouldn't complain. After all, are you chastened more harshly than your sins deserve? Considering the corruption that is in your heart, why do you wonder that there needs to be so much of the rod to bring it out? Doesn't that proud rebellious spirit of yours prove that your heart is not thoroughly sanctified? Aren't those grumbling words contrary to the holy submissive nature of God's children? Isn't the correction needed? But if you *will* grumble against the chastening, be careful, for it will go hard with grumblers. God always chastises His children twice if they don't bear the first stroke patiently. But know this: "He does not willingly bring affliction or grief to the children of men.[450] All His corrections are sent in love, to purify you, and to draw you nearer to Himself.[451] It will help you to bear the chastening with resignation if you recognize your *Father's* hand. For "the LORD disciplines those He loves, and He punishes everyone he accepts as a son. Endure hardship as discipline; God is treating you as sons."[452]

May

✍ *May 1* ✍

His cheeks are like beds of spice yielding perfume
(Song of Songs 5:13).

The flowery month is here! March winds and April showers have done their work, and the earth is clothed with beauty. Come my soul, put on your holiday attire and go forth to gather wreaths of heavenly thoughts. You know where to go, for "the beds of spices" are well known to you, and you have often smelled the perfume of "the sweet flowers." Go at once to your beloved and find all loveliness and all joy in Him. That cheek once so rudely struck with cruel hands,[453] often wet with tears of sympathy[454] and then defiled with spittle—that cheek as it smiles with mercy is a fragrant aroma to my heart. You did not hide Your face from shame and spitting,[455] O LORD Jesus, and therefore I will find my dearest delight in praising You. Those cheeks were furrowed by grief, and crimsoned with lines of blood from Your thorn-crowned head.[456] Such marks of unlimited love charms my soul far more than anything on earth. In Jesus I find not only fragrance, but a bed of spices. Not one flower, but all manner of sweet flowers. He is my rose and my lily, the sweetest flower ever known. When He is with me it is May all year long, and my soul goes forth to wash its happy face in the morning-dew of His grace, and to comfort itself with the singing of the birds of His promises. Precious LORD Jesus, let me know in everything that I do every day the blessedness that dwells in abiding, unbroken, fellowship with You.

"My prayer is not that You take them out of the world" (John 17:15).

It's a sweet and blessed event that will happen to all believers in God's own time—the going home to be with Jesus. In a few more years the LORD's soldiers, who are now fighting "the good fight of the faith,"[457] will be finished with conflict and enter into the joy of their LORD.[458] But although Christ prays that His people may eventually be with Him where He is,[459] He doesn't ask that they be taken immediately away from this world to heaven. He wishes them to stay here. Yet how often the wearied pilgrim prays, "Oh, that I had the wings of a dove! I would fly away and be at rest."[460] But Christ doesn't pray like that, He leaves us in His Father's hands until, like fully-ripened shocks of grain, we'll each be gathered into our Master's granary. Jesus doesn't plead for our instant removal by death because our remaining here is necessary for others, and beneficial to us. He asks that we may be kept from evil, but He never asks for us to be admitted to the inheritance in glory until we're of full age. When they have trouble, Christians often want to die. Ask them why, and they tell you, "Because we would be with the LORD."[461] We fear, however, it's not so much they're longing to be with the LORD as it is their desire to get rid of their troubles. Rather than trying to escape from your troubles, however, glorify God by your life here as long as He pleases, and leave it to Him to say when "it is finished."[462]

⊰ *May 3* ⊱

"In this world you will have trouble" (John 16:33).

Are you asking the reason for this, believer? Look *upward* to your heavenly Father, and behold Him pure and holy. Do you know that one day you are to be like Him? Will you easily be conformed to His image? Won't you require much refining to purify you?[463] Will it be an easy thing to get rid of your corruptions, and make you perfect even as your Father in heaven is perfect?[464] Next, turn your eyes *downward*. Do you know what foes you have beneath your feet? You were once a servant of Satan, and no prince will willingly lose his subjects.[465] Do you think that Satan will leave you alone? No, he will always be at you, for he "prowls around like a roaring lion looking for someone to devour."[466] Expect trouble, therefore, Christian. Then look *around* you. Where are you? You're in enemy country, a stranger, and a sojourner.[467] The world isn't your friend. If it is, then you're not God's friend, for the one who is a friend of the world is an enemy of God.[468] Be assured that you will find enemies everywhere. Lastly, look *within you*, into your own heart, and observe what's there. *Sin* and *self* are still within. If you had no devil to tempt you, no enemies to fight you, and no world to ensnare you, you'd still find in yourself enough evil to trouble you: "The heart is deceitful above all things and beyond cure."[469] Expect trouble but don't despair over it. God has said, "I will be with you in trouble, I will deliver you and honor you."[470]

"Do men make their own gods? Yes, but they are not gods!" (Jeremiah 16:20)

The continual sin of ancient Israel was idolatry, and spiritual Israel, which we are, has the same problem. Though the ancient idols are now dust, mammon still intrudes its golden calf, and the shrines of pride are not forsaken. Self in various forms struggles to subdue the chosen ones under its dominion, and the flesh sets up its altars wherever it's allowed a place for them. Favorite children are often the cause of sin in believers, and the LORD is grieved when He sees us doting upon them above measure. They'll live to be as great a curse to us as Absalom was to David, or they'll be taken from us to leave our homes desolate. If Christians desire to grow thorns to stuff their sleepless pillows, let them dote on their dear ones. It is truly said, "they are not gods," for the objects of our foolish love are sometimes doubtful blessings. The solace they yield us now is dangerous, and the help they can give us in our troubles is small indeed. Why, then, are we so bewitched with vanities? We pity the heathen who adores a God of stone, and yet worship a God of gold. The principle and the sin are the same in both cases. In our case, however, the sin is worse because we have more light and yet we still sin. The heathen bows to a false deity, but has never known the true God. We commit two evils—we forsake the living God and turn to idols. May the LORD purge us all from this grievous iniquity.

*I will be their God, and they will be My people
(2 Corinthians 6:16).*

What a blessed title: "My people!" What a cheering
revelation: "their God!" How much meaning is contained
in those two words, "My people!" Here is *speciality.*
The whole world is God'— the heaven, even the heaven
of heavens is the LORD's, and He reigns among all of
humanity. But of those whom He has chosen, whom He has
purchased for Himself, He says what He doesn't say about
others—"My people" In these words there is *ownership.*
All the nations upon earth are His, and the whole world
is in His power. But His chosen ones are more especially
His possession, for more was done for them than for
others—they were purchased with the blood of Christ.[471]
He brought them near to Himself. He set His great heart
upon them. He loves them with an everlasting love that
many waters cannot quench, and time itself will never
diminish in the least degree. Dear friends, can you, by faith,
see yourselves in that number? Can you look up to heaven
and say, "My LORD and my God."[472] Can you read the
Bible and find there the cost and contract of your salvation?
Can you read your title written in precious blood? Can
you, by humble faith, lay hold of Jesus' garments, and say,
"my Savior, my Christ"? If you can, then God says of you,
and of others like you, "My people." For if God is *your*
God, and Christ is *your* Savior and Christ, the LORD has
done you a special, peculiar, favor—*you* are the object of
His choice, accepted in His beloved Son.

We live in Him (1 John 4:13).

Do you want a house for your soul? Do you ask, "What is the price?" It's something less than proud human nature will like to give. It's without money and without price. But you want to pay a respectable rent. You want to do something to win Christ. Then you cannot have the house, for it's without price. Will you take my Master's house on a lease for all eternity, with nothing to pay for it, nothing but the cost of loving and serving Him forever? Will you take Jesus and "live in Him?" See, this house is furnished with all you need, and filled with more riches than you'll spend in your lifetime. Here you can have intimate communion with Christ and feast on His love. Here you can find rest with Jesus. And from this house you can look out and see heaven itself. Will you have the house? If you're houseless, you'll say, "I'd like to have the house. May I have the key?" Yes—the key is, "Come to Jesus." "But," you say, "I'm too shabby for such a house." Never mind, there are garments inside. If you feel guilty and condemned, come. Christ will make you good enough for the house. He'll wash you and cleanse you, and you'll be able to sing, "We live in Him." Believer, you're greatly privileged to have a "strong habitation"[473] in which you're always safe, and which is an *everlasting* one. When this world melts like a dream, your house will live—more solid than granite, self-existent as God, for your house is God Himself.

⊰ *May 7* ⊱

Many followed Him, and He healed all their sick
(Matthew 12:15).

What a mass of ancient diseases must have been brought to Jesus. Yet we don't read that He was disgusted, but patiently waited on every case. What a variety of evils must have met at His feet. What sickening ulcers and putrefying sores. Yet He was ready for every form of health shattering evil, and was victor over it every time. Let the arrow fly from what quarter it might, He quenched its fiery power. Whatever it was—fever,[474] epilepsy,[475] madness,[476] leprosy,[477] blindness[478]—all felt the power of His Word and fled at His command.[479] In every corner of the field He was triumphant over evil, and received the homage of delivered captives. He came, He saw, He conquered everywhere. It's even so this morning. Whatever my own case may be, the beloved Physician can heal me.[480] And whatever may be the state of others whom I remember in prayer, I have hope in Jesus that He will heal them also. My child, my friend, my dearest one, I can have hope for each, for all, when I remember the healing power of my LORD. He who on earth walked among the diseased and sick[481] still dispenses His grace and works wonders among the children of God. Let me go to Him at once in earnest. Let me praise Him this morning as I remember how He wrought His divine cures by taking our sicknesses upon Himself:[482] "By His wounds we are healed."[483] The Church on earth is full of souls healed by our beloved Physician, and the inhabitants of heaven itself confess that "He healed them all."[484]

☙ *May 8* ☙

The man who was healed had no idea who it was
(1 John 5:13).

Years are short to the happy and healthy, but thirty-eight years of disease must have been a long time for the poor invalid man. So when Jesus healed him while he lay at the pool of Bethesda, he was delightfully aware of a change. In the same way, the sinner who has for weeks and months been paralyzed with despair, and has wearily sighed for salvation, is very conscious of the change when the LORD Jesus gives joy and peace. The evil removed is too great to be removed without our discerning it, the life imparted is too remarkable to be possessed and not be active, and the change brought about is too marvelous not to be felt.[485] Yet the poor man was ignorant of the author of his cure. He did not know the sacredness of Jesus or the purpose that brought Him into the world.[486] Great ignorance of Jesus may remain in hearts that yet feel the power of His blood. The Holy Spirit makes people penitent[487] long before He makes them divine, and those who believe what they know, will soon know more clearly what they believe. Ignorance is, however, an evil. This poor man was questioned by the Pharisees and was unable to answer them. It's good to be able to answer disputers, but we can't do so if we don't know the LORD Jesus clearly and with understanding. The man's ignorance was soon cured, however, for he was visited by the LORD in the temple. After that gracious manifestation, he was found testifying that "it was Jesus who had made him well."[488]

✠ *May 9* ✠

Who has blessed us in the heavenly realms with every spiritual blessing in Christ (Ephesians 1:3).

All the goodness of the past, the present, and the future, Christ gives to His people. In the mysterious ages of the past the LORD Jesus was God's first elect, and in His election He gave us an interest, for we were chosen in Him from before the foundation of the world.[489] He had from all eternity the prerogatives of Sonship, and by adoption[490] and regeneration He elevated us to sonship[491] also, and gave us "the right to become children of God."[492] The eternal covenant,[493] based upon suretyship[494] and confirmed by oath,[495] is ours, for our strong comfort[496] and security. In the eternal covenant of predestinating wisdom,[497] and omnipotent decree,[498] the eye of the LORD Jesus was always on us. In the writings of destiny there's not a line that militates against His redeemed.[499] The marvelous incarnation of the God of heaven, with all the condescension and humiliation that attended it, is ours. The bloody sweat, the scourge, the Cross, are ours forever. Whatever blissful consequences flow from perfect obedience, finished atonement, resurrection, all are ours by His own gift. Upon His breastplate He bears our names. In His authoritative pleadings at the throne He remembers who we are and pleads our cause.[500] His dominion over principalities and powers[501] and His absolute majesty in heaven are used for the benefit of those who trust in Him. His high estate is as much at our service as was His condition of abasement. He who gave Himself for us in the depths of woe and death, does not withdraw the grant now that He is enthroned in the highest heavens.

⊲ *May 10* ⊳

*But Christ has indeed been raised from the dead
(1 Corinthians 15:20).*

The whole system of Christianity rests upon the fact that "Christ has been raised from the dead." For "if Christ has not been raised, our preaching is useless and so is your faith … you are still in your sins."[502] Christ's *divinity* is proved by His resurrection: He "was declared with power to be the Son of God by His resurrection from the dead."[503] Christ's *sovereignty* depends upon His resurrection: "For this very reason, Christ died and returned to life so that He might be the LORD of both the dead and the living."[504] Our *justification*, that choice blessing of the covenant, is linked with Christ's triumphant victory over death and the grave: "He was delivered over to death for our sins and was raised to life for our justification."[505] Our *regeneration* is connected with His resurrection: "In His great mercy He has given us new birth into a living hope through the resurrection of Jesus Christ from the dead."[506] And most certainly our *ultimate resurrection* rests here: "if the Spirit of Him who raised Jesus from the dead is living in you, He who raised Christ from the dead will also give life to your mortal bodies through His Spirit, who lives in you."[507] If Christ has not risen, we will not rise. But if He has risen, then they who are asleep in Christ have not perished,[508] and they will surely see their God. The gold thread of resurrection runs through all our blessings, from our regeneration to our eternal glory, and binds them together. Praise God for His glorious truth: "Christ has risen!"

Surely I am with you always (Matthew 28:20).

It's good there's One who is always the same and always with us. It's good there's one stable Rock in the middle of storms on the sea of life.[509] O, my soul, don't set your affections upon rusting, moth-eaten, decaying treasures, but set your heart upon Him who is always faithful to you. Don't build your house upon the moving quicksands of a deceitful world, but base your hopes on this Rock that stands immovably secure during the rain and roaring floods.[510] Put everything in Christ. Set all your affections on His person, all your hope in His merit, all your trust in His effective blood, and all your joy in His presence. By so doing, you can laugh at loss and defy destruction. The day is coming when nothing will be left but the black, cold, earth. Death's extinguisher must soon put out your candle. But how sweet to have sunlight when the candle is gone! The dark flood must soon roll between you and all you have, so wed your heart to Him who will never leave you. Trust yourself to Him who will go with you through the dark and surging current of death's stream. He will land you safely on the celestial shore, and make you sit with Him in heavenly places forever. Trust all your concerns to Him who never can be taken from you, who will never leave you, and who will never let you leave Him: Jesus Christ ... the same yesterday and today and forever.[511] "I am with you always" is enough for my soul to live on.

☙ *May 12* ❧

"And show Myself to him" (John 14:21).

The LORD Jesus gives special revelations of Himself to His people. Even if Scripture did not declare this, there are many children of God who could testify to it from their own experience. They've had manifestations of Jesus Christ in a special way. In the biographies of eminent saints, you'll find many instances recorded in which Jesus has been pleased to speak to their souls and reveal the wonders of His person. At those times, their souls were so steeped in happiness that they thought they were in heaven, and even though they weren't, they were close to its threshold—for when Jesus reveals Himself to His people, it's heaven on earth. Special manifestations of Christ have a holy influence on a believer's heart—one is *humility*. If someone says, "I have had such-and-such spiritual communications with Christ, and so I'm a great Christian," that person has never had any communion with Jesus. "The LORD ... looks upon the lowly, but the proud He knows from afar.[512] He doesn't need to come near them to know them, and will never give them any visits of love. Another effect will be *happiness*, for in God's presence there are eternal pleasures.[513] And still another is *holiness*. A person who has no holiness has never had this manifestation. Some profess a great deal, but we mustn't believe anyone unless we see that their deeds equal what they say. "Do not be deceived: God cannot be mocked."[514] He will not bestow His favors upon the wicked. While He won't cast away a holy person, neither will He respect an evildoer.

Weeping may remain for a night, but rejoicing comes in the morning (Psalm 30:5).

Christian, if you're in a night of trial, think of the future. Cheer your heart with the thought of the coming of your LORD. Be patient, for He will come with a mighty army.[515] Be patient, the farmer waits until He reaps His harvest.[516] Be patient; for you know who has said, "Behold, I am coming soon! My reward is with Me, and I will give to everyone according to what he has done."[517] Your head may be crowned with thorny troubles now, but it will wear a starry crown before long. Your life may be filled with heavy cares now, but one day it'll trade those cares for heaven's glory. Your garments may be soiled with dirt now, but they'll soon be white. Wait a little longer. How trivial our troubles and trials will seem when we look back on them. Looking at them now they seem immense, but when we get to heaven the glory will outshine them all. Our trials will then seem light and momentary afflictions. Let's go on boldly. No matter how dark the night, the morning comes, which is more than they who are shut up in the darkness of hell can say. Do you know what it means to live on the future, to live on expectation, to anticipate heaven? Happy believer, it means to have a certain and comforting hope. It may be all dark now, but it'll soon be light. It may be all trial now, but it'll soon be all happiness. What does it matter though "weeping may remain for a night," when "rejoicing comes in the morning?"

Co-heirs with Christ (Romans 8:17).

Christ is "heir of all things,"[518] and sole proprietor of the vast creation of God. He has enabled us to claim all of it as ours, by reason of that deed of co-heirship that God has enacted with His chosen people. The golden streets of paradise, the pearly gates,[519] the river of life,[520] the transcendent bliss, and the unutterable glory are given to us by our blessed LORD for our everlasting possession. All that He has He shares with His people. He has placed a royal crown upon the head of His Church, appointing her a kingdom and calling her children a royal priesthood[521]— priests and kings to our God.[522] Crown the head and the whole body shares the honor. Behold here the reward of every Christian who overcomes![523] Christ's throne, crown, scepter, treasure, robes, heritage, are yours. Far superior to the jealousy, selfishness, and greed, that allow no participation in their advantages, Christ's happiness is completed by His people sharing it. "I have given them the glory that You gave me."[524] "I have told you this so that My joy may be in you and that your joy may be complete."[525] The smiles of His Father are all the sweeter to Him, because His people share them. The honors of His kingdom are more pleasing because His people appear with Him in glory. More valuable to Him are His conquests, since they've taught His people to overcome. He delights in His throne because on it there is a place for them. He delights all the more in His joy because He calls them to enter into it.

☙ May 15 ☜

Everyone who believes is justified (Acts 13:39).

The believer in Christ is justified here and *now*. Faith does not produce this fruit after awhile, but *now*.[526] Since justification is the result of faith, it's given to the soul at the moment it receives Christ as its all in all. If those who stand before the throne of God are justified *now*, so are we, as truly and as clearly justified as they who walk in white and sing melodious praises[527] to golden harps.[528] The thief upon the cross was justified the moment that he turned the eye of faith to Jesus.[529] After years of service, the Apostle Paul was not more justified than was the thief with no service at all. We are *today* accepted in the Beloved,[530] *today* absolved from sin, *today* acquitted before the judgment seat of God. We are *now*—even *now* pardoned. Even *now* our sins are put away. Even *now* we stand in the sight of God accepted—as though we had *never* been guilty. "Therefore, there is *now* no condemnation for those who are in Christ Jesus."[531] There is not a sin in the books of God, even *now*, against one of His people. All their names are written *now* in the Book of Life.[532] Who dares to lay anything to their charge?[533] There is *now* neither speck, nor spot, nor wrinkle, nor any such thing remaining upon any believer[534] in the matter of justification in the sight of the Judge of all the earth. Let present privilege awaken us to present duty—and *now*, while life lasts, let us spend and be spent for our glorious LORD.

Who richly provides us with everything for our enjoyment (1 Timothy 6:17).

Our LORD Jesus is always giving, and doesn't withdraw His hand for a single instant. As long as there's a vessel of grace not yet full to the brim, the oil will not stop.[536] The rain of His grace is always dropping, the river of His bounty is ever-flowing, and the well-spring of His love is constantly overflowing. As the King can never die, so His grace can never fail. Daily we pluck His fruit, and daily His branches bend down to our hand with a fresh store of mercy. There are seven feast days in His weeks, and there are as many banquets in His years as there are days. Who has ever risen from His table unsatisfied? His mercies are new every morning and fresh every evening. Who can know the number of His benefits,[537] or recount the list of His bounties? The wings of our hours are covered with the silver of His kindness, and with the yellow gold of His affection. The river of time bears the golden sands of His favor from the mountains of eternity. The countless stars are like standard bearers of a more innumerable host of blessings. Who can count the dust of the benefits that He bestowed on Jacob, or tell the number of the fourth part of His mercies toward Israel? How shall my soul extol Him who daily loads us with benefits,[538] and who crowns us with loving kindness?[539] O that my praise could be as ceaseless as His bounty! How can I be silent? "Awake, my soul! Awake, harp and lyre! I will awaken the dawn."[540]

⊰ *May 17* ⊱

Walk as Jesus did (1 John 2:6).

Why should Christians imitate Christ?[541] First, for *their own sakes*. If they desire to be in a healthy state of soul, escape the sickness of sin, and enjoy the vigor of growing grace, let Jesus be their model. If they would enjoy holy and happy communion with Jesus, if they would be lifted up above the cares and troubles of this world, let them walk even as He walked. Nothing can help you to walk toward heaven rapidly as much as wearing the image of Jesus on your heart to rule all its actions. It's when the power of the Holy Spirit enables you to walk with Jesus in His very footsteps, that you are most happy, and most known to be the children of God. Second, strive to be like Jesus for *Christianity's sake*. Christianity has been painfully shot at by cruel enemies, but it hasn't been wounded half as dangerously by its enemies as by its friends. Who made those wounds in the fair hand of Godliness? The professor of religion who used the dagger of hypocrisy. There's no weapon half as deadly as a Judas kiss. Inconsistent Christians injure the gospel more than the sneering critic. Third, imitate Christ's example especially for *His own sake*. Christian, do you love your Savior? Is His name precious to you? Is His cause dear to you? Would you see the kingdoms of the world become His? Is it your desire that He should be glorified? Are you longing that souls be won to Him? If so, *imitate* Jesus—be a "letter from Christ, known and read by everybody."[542]

⊰ *May 18* ⊱

For in Christ all the fullness of the Deity lives in bodily form, and you have been given fullness in Christ (Colossians 2:9-10).

All the attributes of Christ, as God and man, are at our disposal. All the fullness of the Godhead is ours to make us complete. He cannot endow us with the attributes of Deity, but His omnipotence, omniscience, omnipresence, immutability, and infallibility, are all combined for our salvation. The LORD Jesus has yoked the whole of the divine Godhead to the chariot of salvation. How vast His grace, how firm His faithfulness, how unswerving His immutability, how infinite His power, how limitless His knowledge. Jesus made all these pillars of the temple of salvation, and all are covenanted to us as our perpetual inheritance. Every drop of the fathomless love of the Savior's heart is ours. Every muscle in the arm of might, every jewel in the crown of majesty, the immensity of divine knowledge, and the sternness of divine justice, are all ours, and will be used for us. The whole of Christ, in His adorable character as the Son of God, is by Himself made over to us to richly enjoy. His wisdom is our direction, His knowledge our instruction, His power our protection, His love our comfort, His mercy our solace, and His immutability our trust. He holds nothing back, but opens the recesses of the Mount of God and bids us dig in its mines for the hidden treasures. "Everything is yours," He says, "be satisfied with favor and full of the goodness of the LORD."[543] How comforting to call upon Him with the certain confidence that in seeking His love or power, we're only asking for what He has already faithfully promised.

*I have seen slaves on horseback, while princes go
on foot like slaves (Ecclesiastes 10:7).*

Upstarts frequently usurp the highest places, while the
truly great wither away in obscurity. This is a riddle of
providence whose answer will one day gladden the hearts
of the upright, but it's so common a fact that none of
us should murmur if it falls to our own lot. When our
King of kings was upon earth He walked the footpath of
weariness and service as the Servant of servants. So what
wonder is it if His followers should also be looked down
upon as inferior and contemptible persons?[544] The world
is upside down, and therefore, the first are last and the
last first.[545] See how the servile sons of Satan lord it in the
earth! Haman is in the court, while Mordecai sits in the
gate.[546] David wanders on the mountains, while Saul reigns
in state. Elijah is complaining in the cave while Jezebel is
boasting in the palace.[548] Yet who would wish to take the
places of the proud rebels? And who might not envy the
despised saints? Patience, then, believer, eternity will right
the wrongs of time. Let's not fall into the error of letting
our passions and carnal appetites ride in triumph while
our nobler powers walk in the dust. Grace must reign as
a prince, and make the members of the body instruments
of righteousness. The Holy Spirit loves order, and He
therefore gives the highest room to those spiritual faculties
that link us with the great King. So let's ask for grace that
we may keep under our body and bring it into subjection
for the glory of God the Father.

☙ *May 20* ❧

The wonder of Your great love (Psalm 17:7).

When we give our hearts with our offerings, we give well—but we often fail in this respect. Not so our Master and LORD. His favors are always given with the love of His heart. He doesn't send us cold meat and broken pieces of bread from the table of His bounty. He dips our morsel into His own dish, and seasons our provisions with the spices of His fragrant affections. He comes into our houses on His errands of kindness, and He doesn't act as some cheerless visitors do in a poor person's home. Not despising our poverty or blaming our weakness, He sits by our side and encourages us with gracious words, embraces us affectionately, and bestows upon us abundantly. If He gave us only pennies, the way of His giving would turn them into gold. It's impossible to doubt the sincerity of His charity, for there's a bleeding heart stamped upon the face of all that He gave us. He gives generously and without finding fault.[549] There is not one hint that we are burdensome to Him, not one cold look for those who depend upon His bounty. Instead, He rejoices in His mercy, and presses us to His heart while He pours out His life for us. There's a fragrance in His perfume that nothing but His heart could produce. There is a sweetness in His honeycomb that could not be in it unless the very essence of His soul's affection had been mingled with it. O the rare communion that comes from such unique love. May we continually taste and know its blessedness!

◄ *May 21* ►

If so be you have tasted that the LORD *is gracious
(1 Peter 2:3,* KJV*).*

"*If*" said Peter. So there is a possibility and a probability
that some may not have tasted that the LORD is gracious.
That means this is not a general but a special mercy, and
we need to inquire whether we know the graciousness of
God by inward experience. There's no spiritual favor that
doesn't require heart searching. But while this should be
a matter of earnest and prayerful inquiry, no one should
be content while there is any such thing as an "if" about
having tasted that the LORD is gracious. A jealous and holy
distrust of self may give rise to the question even in the
believer's heart, but the *continuance* of such a doubt would
be an evil indeed. We mustn't rest without a desperate
struggle to clasp the Savior in the arms of faith, and say, "I
know whom I have believed, and am convinced that He is
able to guard what I have entrusted to Him."[550] Don't rest
until you have a full assurance of your interest in Jesus. Let
nothing satisfy you until the infallible witness of the Holy
Spirit bears witness with your spirit that you're a child
of God.[551] Don't trifle here—let no "if" or "perhaps" or
"maybe" satisfy your soul. Get the sure mercies of David,
and surely get them.[552] Let your anchor be fixed firmly
within the veil,[553] and see to it that your soul is linked
to the anchor by an unbreakable cable. Advance beyond
these dreary "ifs." Don't live in the wilderness of doubt
anymore—cross the Jordan of distrust and enter the land
of peace.

He led them by a straight way (Psalm 107:7).

Changes often cause the anxious to ask, "Why's this happening to me?" I looked for light, but darkness came—for peace, but found only trouble. I said in my heart, *my mountain stands firm, I will never be shaken.* But when you hid your face, LORD, I was dismayed.[554] Yesterday I could see my name clearly.[555] Today the writing is dim, and my hopes are clouded. Yesterday I could climb to Pisgah's top,[556] and view all the land and rejoice with confidence in my future inheritance. Today, my spirit has no hopes, but many fears—no joys, but many distresses. Is this part of God's plan for me? Can this be the way by which God would bring me to heaven? Yes, it may be. The clouding of your faith, the darkness of your mind, the dimming of your hope, all these things are parts of God's method of making you ready for the great inheritance that you will soon receive. These trials are for the testing and strengthening of your faith, they are waves that wash you further upon the rock, they are winds that move your ship more swiftly toward the desired haven.[557] According to David's words, so it's of you, "He guided them to their desired haven." By plenty and by poverty, by joy and by distress, by persecution and by peace, by all these things the life of your soul is maintained, and by each of these you're helped on your way. "We must go through many hardships to enter the kingdom."[558] So "consider it pure joy … whenever you face trials."[559]

*The LORD will fulfill His purpose for me
(Psalm 138:8).*

The confidence that the Psalmist expressed here was a *divine confidence*. He did not say, "*I* have grace enough to perfect that which concerns me—my faith is so steady that it will not stagger—my love is so warm that it will never grow cold—my resolution is so firm that nothing can move it. No, his dependence was on the LORD alone. If we indulge in any confidence that is not grounded on the Rock of ages, our confidence is worse than a dream—it will fall upon us, and cover us with its ruins, to our sorrow and confusion. The Psalmist was wise, he rested upon nothing short of the LORD's work. It's the LORD who began a good work in us, it is He who will complete it[560]—if He does not, it will never be completed. If there is one stitch in our robe of righteousness[561] that we are to insert ourselves, then we're lost. But we're confident that the LORD who began will perfect. He *has* done it all, *must* do it all, and *will* do it all. Our confidence must not be in what we have done, nor in what we have resolved to do, but entirely in what *the* LORD will do.[562] Unbelief says, "You'll never be able to stand. Look at the evil in your heart. You can never conquer sin." We would indeed perish if left to our own strength. But God will fulfill His purpose in us, and bring us to the desired haven.[563] We can never be too confident when we confide in Him alone.

*Praise be to God, who has not rejected my prayer
(Psalm 66:20).*

If we look back honestly upon the character of our prayers, we'll wonder that God has ever answered them. There may be some who think their prayers worthy of acceptance—as the Pharisee did, but the true Christians weep over their prayers, and if they could retrace their steps they would desire to pray more earnestly. Remember, Christian, how *cold* your prayers have been. When in your closet you should have wrestled as Jacob did.[564] Instead, your petitions have been faint and few—far removed from that humble, believing, persevering faith, that cries, " "I will not let You go unless You bless me." [565] Yet, wonderful to say, God has heard these cold prayers of yours, and not only heard but answered them. Reflect, also, how *infrequently* you have prayed—unless you were in trouble, and then you went often to the mercy seat.[566] But when deliverance came, your praying stopped. In all matters you have stopped praying the way you once did. When you've neglected the mercy seat, God hasn't deserted it—the bright light of the Shekinah[567] has always been visible between the wings of the cherubim.[568] What a God is He to hear the prayers of those who come to Him when they have pressing needs but neglect Him when they have received a mercy, who approach Him when they're forced to come but forget to speak to Him when mercies are plentiful and sorrows are few. Let His gracious kindness in hearing such prayers touch our hearts, so that we henceforth "pray in the Spirit on all occasions with all kinds of prayers and requests."[569]

O Lord, do not forsake me (Psalm 38:21).

Frequently we pray that God will not forsake us in the hour of trial and temptation, but we often forget that we need to use this prayer at *all times*. There is no moment of our life, however holy, in which we can do without His constant upholding. Whether in light or in darkness, in communion or in temptation, we need the prayer, "do not forsake me." "Uphold me, and I will be delivered."[570] While learning to walk, a little child always needs help. We cannot do without continual help from above.[571] So pray this day: "Do not forsake me, Father, lest I fall by the hand of the enemy. Great Shepherd,[572] do not forsake Your lamb, lest I wander from the safety of the fold. Great Husbandman,[573] do not forsake Your branch, lest it wither and die. Do not forsake me in my joys, lest they absorb my heart. Do not forsake me in my sorrows, lest I murmur against You. Do not forsake me in the day of my strongest faith, lest faith degenerate into presumption. Do not forsake me ever, for without You I am weak, but with You I am strong.[574] Do not forsake me for my path is dangerous and full of snares, and I cannot do without Your guidance. The hen does not forsake her brood, so always cover me with your feathers and let me find refuge under Your wings.[575] Do not be far from me, for trouble is near and there is no one to help.[576] Do not reject me or forsake me, O God my Savior."[577]

Cast your cares upon the LORD *and He will sustain you (Psalm 55:22).*

Carried to excess, care[578] has in it the nature of sin. We are told many times by our LORD and the Apostles not to worry[579] or be anxious for anything.[580] Such precepts cannot be neglected without involving transgression, for the very essence of anxiety is imagining that we're wiser than God, and putting ourselves in His place to do what He has undertaken to do for us.[581] We take upon ourselves our weary burden as if He were unable or unwilling to take it for us. This unbelief in His Word, this presumption in intruding upon His province, is sinful. Yet more than this, worry often leads to acts of sin. Those who cannot leave their affairs in God's hand are likely to use wrong means to help themselves. This sin leads to forsaking God as our counselor and resorting instead to human wisdom.[582] This is going to the "broken cistern" instead of to the "fountain of living waters," a sin that was laid against Israel.[583] Anxiety makes us doubt God's loving kindness,[584] and our love for Him grows cold. We feel mistrust and grieve the Spirit of God. So our prayers are hindered, our consistent example marred, and our life one of self-seeking. Through lack of confidence in God we wander far from Him. But if by faith we cast each burden as it comes upon Him, and are "anxious for nothing"[585] because He undertakes to care for us, it will keep us close to Him, and strengthen us against much temptation. "You will keep in perfect peace him whose mind is steadfast, because he trusts in You."[586]

And Mephibosheth lived in Jerusalem, because he always ate at the king's table, and he was crippled in both feet (2 Samuel 9:13).

Mephibosheth was no great ornament to a royal table, yet he had a continual place at David's table because the king could see in Mephibosheth his beloved father, Jonathan.[587] Like Mephibosheth, we may cry unto the King of Glory, "What is your servant, that You should notice a dead dog like me?"[588] But still God has intimate communion with us because He sees in us His dearly-beloved Son, Jesus. God's people are *loved for another's sake*. Such is the love that the Father has for His only begotten Son, that for His sake He raises His lowly brothers and sisters from poverty and banishment to courtly companionship, noble rank, and royal provision. Their *disability will not rob them of their privileges*. Lameness is no bar to sonship.[589] The disabled are as much heirs as if they could run like Asahel.[590] A king's table is a noble resting place for lame legs, and at the gospel feast we learn to glory in infirmities because the grace of Christ rests upon us.[591] Yet grievous *disability may affect the best-loved saints*. Here is one feasted by David—a young man who was injured when he was five when his nurse dropped him as she tried to flee after hearing of the deaths of Saul and Jonathan.[592] Saints whose faith is weak and knowledge is little are great losers and spiritually disabled. Poor nursing in their spiritual infancy often causes converts to fall into sin and despair from which they never recover. LORD, help the lame to leap like a deer,[593] and satisfy Your people with the bread of the King's table!

And those He predestined, He also called; those He called, He also justified; those He justified, He also glorified (Romans 8:30).

Christian, here is a precious truth for you. You may be poor, or suffering, or unknown, but for your encouragement review your *calling* and the consequences that flow from it—especially that blessed result spoken of here. As surely as you are God's child today, so surely will all your trials soon be at an end, and you'll be rich to all the fullness of God's blessings. Wait awhile, and that weary head will wear the crown of glory, and that hand of labor will grasp the palm branch of victory. Don't grieve over your troubles, but rejoice that before long you'll be where "there will be no more mourning or crying or pain."[594] The chariots of fire are at your door, and a moment will be enough to carry you to the glorified.[595] The portals of heaven stand open for you. Don't think that you can fail to enter into rest. If He's called you, nothing can separate you from His love.[596] Distress cannot sever the bond, the fire of persecution cannot burn the link, the hammers of Satan cannot break the chain. You are secure! The voice that called you at first will call you again from earth to heaven, from death's gloomy voice to immortality's unuttered splendors. Rest assured, the heart of Him who justified you beats with infinite love towards you. You'll soon be with the glorified, where your portion is. You're only waiting here to be made ready for the inheritance. When that's done, you'll be carried far away to the mount of peace, joy, and blessedness, where you'll rest forever and ever.

≤ *May 29* ≥

You ... hate wickedness (Psalm 45:7).

"In your anger do not sin."[597] There can hardly be goodness in us if we aren't angry at sin. Those who love truth must hate every false way. How our LORD Jesus hated it when the temptation came! Three times it assailed Him in different forms, but each time He rebuked it with, "Get behind Me, Satan." He hated it in others more often in tears of pity than in words of rebuke. Yet what could be sterner, more Elijah-like, than the words, "Woe to you, scribes and Pharisees, hypocrites![598] For you devour widows' houses, and for a pretense make long prayers." He hated wickedness so much that He bled on the Cross to destroy it.[599] He died that it might die. He was buried that He might bury it in His tomb. He rose that He might forever trample it under His feet.[600] Christ is in the Gospel, and that Gospel is opposed to wickedness in every shape. Wickedness clothes itself in pleasant clothes, and imitates the language of holiness, but the precepts of Jesus will not tolerate it in the Church. So, too, there is war between Christ and Belial in the heart where Christ reigns![601] And when our Redeemer comes to be our Judge, those thundering words, "Depart, you who are cursed,"[602] will manifest His loathing of sin. As perfect as is His righteousness, so perfect will be the destruction of every form of wickedness. O you glorious champion of right and destroyer of wrong, for this cause "God, your God, has set you above your companions by anointing you with the oil of joy."[603]

✝ *May 30* ✝

Catch for us the foxes, the little foxes that ruin the vineyards (Song of Songs 2:15).

A little thorn may cause much suffering. A little cloud may hide the sun. Little foxes ruin the vineyards—and little sins do mischief to the tender heart. These little sins burrow into the soul and make it so full of what is hateful to Christ that He will have no close fellowship and communion with us. A great sin cannot destroy Christians, but a little sin can make them miserable. Christ will not walk with His people unless they drive out every known sin. He said, "If you obey My commands, you will remain in My love, just as I have obeyed My Father's commands and remain in His love."[604] Some Christians very seldom enjoy their Savior's presence. Why is this? Surely it is sad for tender children to be separated from their loving father—and how much sadder for Christians to be separated from their loving LORD. What has driven Christ from you? He hides His face behind the wall of your sins. That wall may be built up of pebbles, as easily as of great stones. The sea is made of drops of water, and the sea that divides you from Christ may be filled with the drops of your little sins. If you would live with Christ, and walk with Christ, and see Christ, and have companionship with Christ, take heed of "the little foxes that spoil the vineyards, our vineyards that are in bloom."[605] Christ invites you to go with Him and take the grapes. Like Samson, He will surely catch the foxes at once and easily.[606] Go with Him to the hunting.

⚞ May 31 ⚟

The king also crossed the Kidron Valley
(2 Samuel 15:23).

David passed that gloomy brook when fleeing from his traitor son. The man after God's own heart was not exempt from trouble—his life was full of it. He was both the LORD's anointed and the LORD's afflicted. Why then should we expect to escape? The noblest saints have sat with ashes on them,[607] so why should we complain as though some strange thing had happened to us? The King of kings[608] himself was not favored with a more cheerful or royal road. He passed over the filthy ditch of Kidron, through which the filth of Jerusalem flowed. God had one Son without sin, but not a single child without the rod. It's a great joy to know that Jesus was tempted in all points like as we are.[609] What is our Kidron this morning? Is it a faithless friend, a tragic loss, or a slanderous accusation? The King has passed over all these. Is it bodily pain, poverty, persecution, or contempt? Through each of these the King has gone before us. "In all our distress He too was distressed."[610] The idea of strangeness in our trials must be banished at once and forever. Christ Jesus knows by experience the grief that we think is so peculiar, and was victorious over it. Let us then be of good courage, for we will be victorious also. We will yet with joy "draw water from the wells of salvation,"[611] though now we have to pass over the sickening streams of sin and sorrow. Be courageous, Christian, the King Himself triumphed after going over the Kidron Valley,[612] and so will you.

June

⇥ June 1 ⇤

*And there was evening, and there was morning—
the first day (Genesis 1:5).*

Did light and darkness divide the realm of time in the first day? Then it's little wonder if I also have changes in my circumstances from the sunshine of prosperity to the midnight of adversity. It won't always be the blaze of noon even in the concerns my soul. At times, I must expect to mourn the absence of my former joys, and seek my Beloved in the night. I'm not alone in this, for all the LORD's saints have had to sing the mingled song of trial and deliverance, mourning and delight. It's the way of Divine providence that day and night won't cease[613] either in the spiritual or natural creation till we reach the land where "there will be no more night."[614] What our heavenly Father ordains is wise and good. What, then, is it best for you to do? Learn first to be content with this divine order, and be willing, like Job, to accept trouble from God as well as good.[615] Then study ways to make the morning sunrises and the evening sunsets reasons to rejoice. Praise the LORD for the sun of joy when it rises, and for the dark of evening when it falls. There's beauty both in sunrise and sunset—sing of it and glorify the LORD. Like the nightingale, pour forth your notes at all hours. Believe that the night is as useful as the day. The dews of grace fall heavily in the night of sorrow, and the stars of promise shine forth gloriously amid the darkness of grief. So thank Him for both the day *and* the night.

☙ June 2 ☚

For the sinful nature desires what is contrary to the Spirit, and the Spirit what is contrary to the sinful nature (Galatians 5:17).

In every believer's heart there's a constant struggle between the old nature and the new. The old nature is very active, and loses no opportunity of using all the weapons in its deadly armory against newborn grace. At the same time, the new nature is always on the watch to resist and destroy its enemy. Grace within us will employ prayer, faith, hope, and love to cast out the evil. It puts on the "full armor of God," and fights earnestly.[616] These two opposing natures will never cease to struggle so long as we are in this world. The battle of "Christian" with "Apollyon" lasted three hours, but the battle of Christian with himself lasted all the way from the Wicket Gate to the river Jordan.[617] The enemy is so securely entrenched within us that he can never be driven completely out while we're in this body. But although we are attacked from all sides, and often in painful conflict, we have an almighty helper—Jesus Christ, the captain of our salvation, [618]who is always with us. He assures us that we'll eventually come off more than conquerors through Him.[619] With such help the newborn nature is more than a match for its enemies. Are you fighting with the adversary today? Are Satan, the world, and the flesh, all against you? Don't be discouraged or dismayed. Fight on! God Himself is with you. Don't be afraid—you'll overcome, for who can defeat Omnipotence? Fight on, "looking unto Jesus."[620] And though the conflict is long and hard, the victory will be sweet, and the promised reward will be glorious.

⚝ June 3 ⚝

They were the potters who lived at Netaim and Gederah;[621] *they stayed there and worked for the king (1 Chronicles 4:23).*

Potters were the highest grade of workers. But since the king needed potters, they were in royal service, even though the material they worked with was nothing but clay. We, too, may be engaged in the most menial part of the LORD's work, but it's a great privilege to do anything for the King, so we will do whatever He gives us to do. In Netaim and Gederah there were also those who had rough, rustic, hedging and ditching work to do. They may have desired to live in the city and enjoy its society and refinement, but they kept their appointed places, for they also were doing the king's work. The place of our habitation is fixed, and we are not to leave it out of whim and impulse, but seek to serve the LORD in it by being a blessing to those among whom we reside.[622] These potters and gardeners had *royal company*, for they stayed *with the king*. No menial occupation can keep us from communion with our divine LORD. In visiting crowded tenements, poverty-stricken area, or jails, we may go *with the King*. We can count on the LORD's fellowship in all works of faith. It's when we're in His work that we can depend on His approval. You unknown workers who are occupied for your LORD among the lowest of the low, be of good cheer, for jewels have been found upon dunghills, clay pots have been filled with heavenly treasure, and unhealthy weeds have been transformed into precious flowers. Work for the King and your name will be recorded in His chronicles.

The kindness and love of God our Savior
(Titus 3:4).

How delightful it is to behold the Savior communing with His own beloved people! There is nothing greater than to be led by the Holy Spirit into this wondrous field of delight. When we meditate upon Christ's amazing love, and behold the all-glorious Kinsman of the Church endowing her with all His ancient wealth, our souls may well be overwhelmed with joy. Who is the Christian who can endure such a weight of love? That partial sense of it that the Holy Spirit is sometimes pleased to manifest to us, is more than the soul can hold. How glorious must be a complete view of it! When the soul has understanding to discern all the Savior's gifts, wisdom by which to evaluate them, and time in which to meditate upon them, we will then commune with Jesus more closely than ever. But who can imagine the delight of such a relationship? It must be one of the things that "no mind has conceived," but which "God has prepared for those who love him."[623] Oh, to burst open the door of our Joseph's granaries,[624] and see the abundance[625] that He has stored up for us! This would overwhelm us with love. By faith we see, as in a glass darkly,[626] the reflected image of His unbounded treasures. But when we actually see the heavenly things themselves, with our own eyes, how deep will be the stream of fellowship in which our soul will bathe itself! Till then our grandest songs will be reserved for our loving benefactor, Jesus Christ our LORD, whose love for us surpasses all other loves.

✒ *June 5* ✒

Then the LORD *shut him in (Genesis 7:16).*

Noah was shut in away *from all the world* by the hand of divine love. The door of electing purpose interposes between us and the world that is under the control of the evil one.[627] We are not of the world even as Jesus was not of the world.[628] We cannot play with the children of darkness, for our Father has shut us in. Noah was shut in *with his God*. *"Come into the ark,"*[629] was the LORD's invitation, by which He clearly showed that He Himself intended to dwell in the ark with them. All the chosen dwell in God and God in them.[630] What joy to be enclosed in the same circle that contains God in the Trinity of His persons: Father, Son, and Spirit. Noah was so shut in that *no evil could reach him*. Floods only lifted him heavenward, and the winds only hurried him on his way. Outside the ark all was chaos, but inside all was peace. Without Christ we perish, but in Christ Jesus there is perfect safety. Noah was so shut in that *he could not even desire to come out*, and those who are in Christ Jesus are in Him forever. They will go out no more, for eternal faithfulness has shut them in. In the last days the LORD will rise and shut the door. It will then be useless for those who only profess to be Christians to knock and cry "LORD, LORD open for us."[631] The same door that shuts in the wise will shut out the foolish forever.[632] LORD, shut me in by Your grace.

✠ *June 6* ✠

I am unworthy (Job 40:4).

Poor lost sinner, I have an encouraging word for you! You think you mustn't come to God because YOU are unworthy. Now, there isn't a saint living on earth who hasn't been made to feel that he or she is unworthy. If Job, and Isaiah, and Paul were all obliged to say "I am not worthy,"[633] are you ashamed to join in the same confession? If divine grace doesn't eradicate all sin from the believer, how do you hope to do it yourself? And if God loves His people while they are yet unworthy, do you think your unworthiness will prevent His loving you?[634] Believe on Jesus who calls *you* just as you are.[635] Even now say, "You died for sinners.[636] I am a sinner. LORD Jesus, sprinkle Your blood on me."[637] If you will confess your sins you will find pardon.[638] If now, with all your heart, you will say, "I am unworthy, wash me," you will be washed now. If the Holy Spirit enables you to cry from your heart for forgiveness of your sins,[639] you will rise from reading this morning's portion with all your sins pardoned. And though you woke this morning with every sin that you've ever committed on your head, you will rest tonight accepted in the Beloved.[640] Although once clothed with the filth of sin, you will be adorned with a robe of righteousness.[641] For *"now* is the time of God's favor."[642] If you "trust God who justifies the wicked, [your] faith is credited as righteousness."[643] May the Holy Spirit give you saving faith in Him who receives the unworthy.

Let those who love the LORD *hate evil
(Psalm 97:10).*

You have good reason to hate evil. Think of what harm it has already done to you. Sin blinded you so that you could not see the beauty of the Savior.[644] It made you deaf so you could not hear the Redeemer's tender invitations. Sin turned your feet into the way of death, and poured poison into the very fountain of your being. It soiled your heart and made it "deceitful above all things, and desperately wicked."[645] Before grace intervened, you were a lost creature because of what evil had done to you. You were an heir of wrath even as others. You followed "the crowd in doing wrong."[646] We were all like that. But Paul reminds us, "You were washed, you were sanctified, you were justified in the name of the LORD Jesus Christ and by the Spirit of our God."[647] We have good reason, indeed, for hating evil when we look back and trace its deadly workings. Our souls would have been lost if omnipotent love hadn't intervened to redeem us. Even now sin is an active enemy, always watching for ways to harm us. Therefore hate evil, Christian, unless you desire trouble. If you would live a happy life, and die a peaceful death, then walk in all the ways of holiness, hating evil until the end. If you truly love your Savior, and would honor Him, then hate evil. There's no better cure for the love of evil in a Christian than communing with the LORD in prayer. If you spend much time with Him, you'll find it impossible to be friends with sin.

☀ *June 8* ☞

*Many others fell slain, because the battle was God's
(1 Chronicles 5:22).*

When you are fighting under the banner of the LORD Jesus,
observe this verse with holy joy, for as it was then so is it
now. If the battle is God's, the victory is certain. The sons
of Reuben, the Gadites, and the half tribe of Manasseh
could barely muster 44,760 fighting men,[648] and yet in
their war with the Hagarites, they captured a hundred-
thousand prisoners and slew many others: "because they
cried out to God during the battle. He answered their
prayers, because they trusted in Him."[649] The LORD saves
neither by many nor by few. If we go forth in Jehovah's
name with but a handful, the LORD of Hosts is with us as
our Captain. They did not neglect buckler, sword, and bow,
but neither did they put their trust in these weapons. We
must use all proper means, but our confidence must be in
the LORD alone, for He is the sword and the shield of His
people.[650] The great reason of their extraordinary success
lay in the fact that "the battle was God's." Beloved, in
fighting with sin externally and internally, with doctrinal
or practical error, with spiritual wickedness in high places
or low places,[651] with demon's and the devil's allies, you
are fighting Jehovah's war, and unless He Himself can be
beaten, you need not fear defeat. The battle is the LORD's,[652]
and He will deliver His enemies into our hands. Rush to
the conflict with steadfast foot, strong hand, dauntless
heart, and flaming zeal. Do not be afraid, the hosts of evil
will fly before you like dust before the wind.

⚜ *June 9* ⚜

The LORD has done great things for us, and we are filled with joy (Psalm 126:3).

Some Christians are sadly prone to look on the dark side of everything, and to dwell more upon what they've gone through than upon what God has done for them. Ask for their impression of the Christian life, and they'll describe their continual conflicts, their deep afflictions, their sad adversities, and the sinfulness of their hearts, yet with scarcely any mention of the mercy and help that God has given them. But a Christian whose soul is in a healthy state, will say joyously: "I won't speak about myself, but to the honor of my God. 'He lifted me out of the slimy pit, out of the mud and mire; He set my feet on a rock and gave me a firm place to stand. He put a new song in my mouth, a hymn of praise to our God.[653] The LORD has done great things for me, and I am filled with joy.'"[654] Abstract experiences like these are the best that any child of God can give. It's true that we endure trials, but it's just as true that we're delivered out of them. It's mournfully true that we have our corruptions, but it's quite as true that we have an all-sufficient Savior who overcomes these corruptions and delivers us from their dominion. In looking back, it would be wicked to forget that we have been brought through them safely and profitably. The deeper our troubles, the louder our thanks to God. Our griefs cannot mar the melody of our praise, "The LORD has done great things for us, and we are filled with joy."

✎ June 10 ✎

We live to the LORD (Romans 14:8).

If God had willed it, each of us might have entered heaven at the moment of our conversion. It wasn't necessary for our preparation for immortality that we stay here. It's possible for a person to be taken to heaven, and to be found qualified to be a partaker of the inheritance of the saints in light,[655] though just having believed in Jesus. It's true that our sanctification is a long and continued process, and we will not be perfected until we lay aside our bodies and enter within the veil. Nevertheless, had the LORD so willed it, He could have changed us from imperfection to perfection and taken us to heaven at once. Why then are we still here? Would God keep His children out of paradise a single moment longer than was necessary? Why is the army of the living God still on the battlefield when one charge might give them the victory? Why are His children still wandering through the maze of this world when a solitary word from His lips would bring them into the center of their hope in heaven? The answer is: they are here that they may *"live to the LORD,"* and bring others to know His love. We remain on earth as sowers to scatter good seed,[656] as plowers to break up the fallow ground,[657] as heralds of the glorious Gospel.[658] We are here to glorify Christ in our daily life. We are here as workers for Him, and as "workers together with Him."[659] So let us live earnest, useful, holy, lives, to "the praise of His glorious grace."[660]

⊰ June 11 ⊱

We love Him because He first loved us
(1 John 4:19).

There is no light in the planet except that which comes from the sun, and there is no true love to Jesus in the heart except that which comes from the LORD Jesus Himself. From this overflowing fountain of the infinite love of God, all our love to God must spring. This is a great and certain truth—we love Him for no other reason than because He first loved us. Anyone may have cold admiration when studying the works of God, but the warmth of love can only be kindled in the heart by God's Spirit. How wonderful that people like us should ever have been brought to love Jesus at all. How marvelous that when we had rebelled against Him, He sought to draw us back by a display of such amazing love. We would never have had a grain of love toward God unless it had been sown in us by the sweet seed of His love to us. The parent of love is the love of God poured out into the heart.[661] But after it is divinely born, it must be divinely nourished. Love for Jesus is a flower of a delicate nature, and if it received no nourishment but that which could be drawn from the rock of our hearts it would soon wither. Since love comes from heaven, it must feed on heavenly bread. It cannot exist in the wilderness unless it is fed by manna from on high. Love must feed on love. The very soul and life of our love for God is His love for us.

☆ *June 12* ☆

You have been weighed on the scales and found
wanting (Daniel 5:27).

It's well to frequently weigh ourselves on the scale of God's Word. You'll find it a holy exercise to read some psalm of David, and, as you meditate upon each verse, to ask yourself, "Can I say this? Have I felt as David felt? Has my heart ever been broken on account of sin, as his was when he wrote his penitential psalms?[662] Has my soul been full of true confidence in the hour of difficulty as his was when he sang of God's mercies?[663] Do I take the cup of salvation and call upon the name of the LORD?"[664] Then turn to the life of Christ, and as you read, ask yourselves how far you are conformed to His likeness.[665] Endeavor to discover whether you have the meekness, the humility, the lovely spirit that He constantly displayed. Then read the epistles, and see whether you can go with Paul in what he said of his experience. Have you ever cried out as he did, "What a wretched man I am! Who will rescue me from this body of death?"[666] Have you considered yourself the chief of sinners,[667] and less than the least of all saints?[668] Could you join with him and say, "For to me, to live is Christ and to die is gain?"[669] If we read God's Word as a test of our spiritual condition, we'll have good reason to often stop and say, "LORD, I've never been here. Bring me here! Let me no longer be found wanting when weighed in the scales of Your word, lest I be found wanting in the scales of judgment."

✥ June 13 ✥

*Whoever wishes, let him take the free gift of the
water of life (Revelation 22:17).*

Jesus says, "take the free gift." He wants no payment
or preparation. He seeks no recommendation from our
virtuous emotions. If you have no good feelings but you
are willing, you are invited—therefore come! You have no
belief and no repentance? Come to Him, and He will give
them to you. Come just as you are, and take the free gift
without money and without price. He gives Himself to
needy ones. Who would be so foolish as to stand before a
drinking fountain and cry, "I cannot drink because I haven't
any money"? However poor the person is, there is the
fountain, free for all to drink from. Whether expensively
dressed or poorly dressed, no one looks for permission to
drink—the fountain being there is permission enough to
drink freely from it. Perhaps the only persons who would
go thirsty where there is a drinking fountain, are the proud
ones who are very thirsty but cannot think of being so lowly
as to drink from a public fountain. They think it would
demean them to drink from a fountain that everyone may
drink from, and so they pass it by with dry and parched
throats—looking for a place to drink in keeping with their
station. "I won't be saved," they say, "in the same way as
immoral people. What! go to heaven in the same way as
a thief. There must be other ways. I won't be saved that
way." Such proud boasters must remain without the living
water, but, "Whoever wishes, let him take the free gift of
the water of life."

❦ *June 14* ❧

Delight yourself in the LORD *(Psalm 37:4).*

The teaching of these words must be surprising to those who are strangers to vital godliness, but to the sincere believer it's only the repetition of a recognized truth. The life of the believer is described here as a delight in God, and so we learn the great fact that true Christianity overflows with happiness and joy. Ungodly persons and those who merely profess Christianity never see it as a joyful thing. To them it's service, duty, or necessity, but never pleasure or delight. If they pay attention to it at all, it's either that they may profit from it, or because they don't dare do otherwise. The thought of delight in Christianity is so strange to most people, that no two words in their language stand further apart than "holiness" and "delight." But believers who know Christ understand that delight and faith are so blessedly united that the gates of Hades cannot prevail[670] to separate them. They who love God with all their hearts find that His ways are ways of pleasantness, and all His paths are peace. True saints find such joys, such brimful delights, such overflowing blessings, that they would follow Him though all the world cast out His name as evil. We don't fear God because of any compulsion. Our faith is no chain, our profession is no bondage. We're not dragged to holiness or driven to duty. Our piety is our pleasure, our hope is our happiness, our duty is our delight. Delight and true Christianity are as allied as root and flower, as indivisible as truth and certainty.

Sarah said, "God has brought me laughter, and everyone who hears about this will laugh with me"
(Genesis 21:6).

It was far above the power of nature, and even contrary to its laws, that the aged Sarah should be honored with a son. And it's beyond all ordinary rules that I, a helpless, sinner, should be given grace to bear in my soul the indwelling Spirit of Christ.[671] Even I who once despaired—for my nature was as dry and withered and barren and accursed as a howling wilderness—have been made to bring forth fruit unto holiness. My mouth is filled with joyous laughter because of the surprising grace I received, for I have found Jesus, the promised seed,[672] and He is mine forever. This day I will lift up psalms of triumph to the LORD, for "My heart rejoices in the LORD; in the LORD my horn is lifted high. My mouth boasts over my enemies, for I delight in your deliverance."[673] I would have all those that hear of my great deliverance from hell, and my most blessed visitation from on high, laugh for joy with me. I would surprise my family with my abundant peace, delight my friends with my ever-increasing happiness, edify the Church with my grateful confessions, and even impress the world with the cheerfulness of my daily conversation. The LORD Jesus is a deep sea of joy that my soul will dive into and be swallowed up in the delights of His presence. Sarah looked on her Isaac and laughed with excess of rapture, and all her friends laughed with her. And you, my soul, look on your Jesus, and bid heaven and earth join you in your unspeakable joy.

⚘ *June 16* ⚘

I give them eternal life, and they shall never perish
(John 10:28).

The Christian should never think or speak lightly of unbelief. For a child of God to mistrust His love, truth, and faithfulness, must be greatly displeasing to Him. How can we grieve Him by doubting His sustaining grace? Christian, it's contrary to every promise of God's precious Word that you would ever be forgotten or left to perish. If it could be so, how could He be true who has said: ""Can a mother forget the baby at her breast and have no compassion on the child she has borne? Though she may forget, I will not forget you!"[674] What would be the value of that promise, "Though the mountains be shaken and the hills be removed, yet My unfailing love for you will not be shaken nor my covenant of peace be removed," says the LORD, who has compassion on you."[675] Where would be the truth of Christ's words: I give them (my sheep) eternal life, and they shall never perish; no one can snatch them out of My hand. My Father, who has given them to Me, is greater than all; no one can snatch them out of My Father's hand."[676] Where would be the doctrines of grace? They would be all disproved if one child of God should perish. Where would be God's truthfulness, honor, power, grace, covenant, oath, if any of those who have put their trust in Christ should nevertheless be cast away? Banish those unbelieving fears that so dishonor God. It's sinful to doubt His promise that you will never perish. Let the eternal life within you express itself in confident rejoicing.

⚜ June 17 ⚜

Help, Lord (Psalm 12:1).

The prayer itself is remarkable: short, timely, precise, and suggestive. David mourned the fewness of faithful men, and therefore lifted up his heart in supplication—when the creature failed, he flew to the Creator. He evidently felt his own weakness or he would not have cried for help. At the same time he intended to exert himself for the cause of truth, for the word "help" is inappropriate when we ourselves do nothing. There's directness, clearness of perception, and distinctness of utterance in this petition of two words. The Psalmist runs to his God with a well-considered prayer—he knows what he is seeking and where to seek it. Lord, teach us to pray in the same blessed manner. We often have occasions to use this prayer.[677] How suitable it is for tested believers in providential afflictions who find all helpers failing them. Students in doctrinal difficulties may often obtain aid by lifting up this cry of "Help, Lord." Spiritual warriors in inward conflicts may send to the throne for reinforcements, and this is a model for their request. Workers in heavenly labor may obtain grace in time of need. "Help, Lord," will suit us whether living or dying, suffering or laboring, rejoicing or sorrowing. Our help is found in Him.[678] Let's not be slack to cry to Him. The answer to the prayer is certain, if it is sincerely offered through Christ.[679] The Lord's character assures us that He won't leave His people. His gift of Jesus is a pledge of every good thing,[680] and His sure promise stands, "Do not fear; I will help you."[681]

⇗ *June 18* ⇖

Your Redeemer (Isaiah 54:5).

Jesus the Redeemer is ours forever. All His offices are held on our behalf. He is king, priest, and prophet for us. Whenever we read a new title of the Redeemer, let us appropriate Him as ours under that name as much as under any other. The shepherd's staff,[682] the captain's sword,[683] the prophet's mantle,[684] all are ours. Jesus has no dignity that He will not employ for our exaltation, and no prerogative that He will not exercise for our defense. His fullness of Godhead is our unfailing, inexhaustible treasure house. To us our gracious LORD communicates the spotless virtue of a stainless character, to us He gives the meritorious power of a devoted life, to us He gives the reward obtained by obedient submission and incessant service. He makes the unsullied garment of His life our covering beauty; the glittering virtues of His character our ornaments and jewels, and the superhuman meekness of His death our boast and glory. He bequeaths us His manger, from which to learn how God came down to us, and His Cross to teach us how we may go up to God. All His thoughts, emotions, actions, words, miracles, and prayers, were for us. He trod the road of sorrow on our behalf, and has given us as His heavenly legacy the full results of all the labors of His life. Though He is the blessed and only Potentate, the King of kings, and LORD of lords, He is not ashamed to acknowledge Himself *"our* LORD Jesus Christ."[685] O my soul, by the power of the Holy Spirit,[686] call Him, "your Redeemer."

All of them were filled with the Holy Spirit
(Acts 2:4).

The blessings of this day would be rich if we were all filled with the Holy Spirit. The results of this sacred filling of the soul would be impossible to overestimate. Life, comfort, light, purity, power, peace, and many other precious blessings are inseparable from the Spirit's presence. As sacred oil, He anoints the head of the believers,[687] sets them apart to the priesthood of saints,[688] and gives them grace to do His work properly. As the only truly purifying water,[689] He cleanses us from the power of sin and sanctifies us to holiness,[690] working in us to will and to do of the LORD's good pleasure.[691] As the light, He first revealed to us our lost condition, and now He reveals the LORD Jesus to us and in us,[692] and guides us in the way of righteousness. Enlightened by His pure celestial ray, we are no more darkness but light in the LORD.[693] As fire, He both purges us from dross, and sets our consecrated nature on fire.[694] He is the sacrificial flame by which we are enabled to offer our whole souls as a living sacrifice unto God.[695] As the dove, with wings of peaceful love He hovers over His Church and over the souls of believers, and as a Comforter,[696] He dispels the cares and doubts that mar the peace of His beloved. As the wind, He brings the breath of life,[697] blowing wherever He pleases[698] He performs the life-giving operations by which the spiritual creation is animated and sustained. Would to God, that we might feel His presence this day and every day.

◄ *June 20* ►

"For I will give the command, and I will shake the house of Israel among all the nations as grain is shaken in a sieve, and not a pebble will reach the ground" (Amos 9:9).

Every sifting comes by divine command and permission. Satan had to ask for permission before he could lay a finger upon Job.[699] Even more, in some sense our siftings are directly the work of heaven, for the text says, "I will shake the house of Israel." Satan may hold the sieve, hoping to destroy the wheat, but the overruling hand of the Master is accomplishing the purity of the grain by the very process that the enemy intends to be destructive. If you are much-sifted wheat, be comforted by the blessed fact that the LORD directs the sieve to His own glory and to your eternal profit. The LORD Jesus will surely use the fan that is in His hand, and will divide the precious wheat from the unworthy chaff.[700] In the sieve true weight alone has power. Chaff has no substance and flies before the wind—only solid wheat remains. Observe the complete safety of the LORD's wheat, even the least grain has a promise of preservation. God Himself sifts, and therefore it is stern and terrible work. He sifts them in all places, "among all the nations." He sifts them in the most effective manner, "as grain is shaken in a sieve." Yet for all this, not the smallest, lightest, or most shriveled grain, is permitted to fall to the ground. Every individual believer is precious in the sight of the LORD. A shepherd would not lose one sheep, nor a mother one child, and the LORD will not lose one of His redeemed people. We may rejoice that we are each preserved in Christ Jesus.

You are the most excellent of men (Psalm 45:2).

Jesus is altogether complete, not only in His several parts, but as a gracious all-glorious whole. His character is not a mass of fair colors mixed confusedly, nor a heap of precious stones laid carelessly one upon another. He's a picture of beauty and a breastplate of glory. In Him, all good things are in their proper places, and assist in adorning each other. Not one feature in His glorious person attracts attention at the expense of others—but He is perfectly and altogether lovely. Oh, Jesus! Your power, Your grace, Your justice, Your tenderness, Your truth, Your majesty, and Your immutability make up a person that neither heaven nor earth has seen elsewhere. Your infancy, Your eternity, Your sufferings, Your triumphs, Your death, and Your immortality, are all woven into one gorgeous tapestry without seam or tear. You are music without discord. You are many, and yet not divided. You are all things, and yet not diverse. As all the colors blend into one resplendent rainbow, so all the glories of heaven and earth meet in You, and unite so wondrously that there is none like You in all things. Indeed, if all the most excellent virtues were bound in one bundle, they could not rival You. You are a mirror of all perfection. You have been anointed with the holy oil of myrrh and cassia,[701] which Your God has reserved for You alone. As for Your fragrance, it's as the holy perfume,[702] the like of which none can ever mingle, even with the art of the apothecary. Each spice is fragrant, but the compound is divine.

☀ *June 22* ☀

He ... will build the temple of the LORD, *and He will be clothed with majesty (Zechariah 6:13).*

Christ Himself is the builder of His spiritual temple, and He has built it on the mountains of His unchangeable affection, His omnipotent grace, and His infallible truthfulness. But as it was in Solomon's temple, so in this—the materials need to be made ready. There are the cedars of Lebanon that are not yet framed for the building—they are not cut down[703] and shaped and made into those planks of cedar whose beautiful fragrance will make glad the courts of the LORD's house in Paradise. There are also the rough stones still in the quarry that must be cut and squared.[704] All this is Christ's own work. Each individual believer is being prepared, polished, and made ready for their place in the temple. But Christ's own hand performs the preparation work. Afflictions cannot sanctify, except as they are used by Him to that end. Our prayers and efforts cannot make us ready for heaven, apart from the hand of Christ, who fashions our hearts.[705] As in the building of Solomon's temple, "no hammer, chisel or any other iron tool was heard at the temple site,"[706] because all was brought perfectly ready for the exact spot it was to occupy. So it is with the temple that Jesus Christ builds—the making ready is all done on earth. When we reach heaven, there will be no sanctifying us there, no squaring us with affliction, no perfecting us with suffering.[707] No, we must be made ready here. Then we will be carried to the heavenly Jerusalem. There to abide as eternal pillars in the temple of our LORD.

Ephraim is a flat cake not turned over (Hosea 7:8).

A pancake that is not turned over is *uncooked on one side.* In many respects, Ephraim was untouched by divine grace, although there was some partial obedience, there was very much rebellion left. Christian, see whether this is how you are. Are you thorough in the things of God? Has grace gone into the very center of your being so that you feel its divine operations in all your powers, actions, words, and thoughts? To be sanctified, spirit, soul, and body, should be your aim and prayer.[708] And although sanctification may not be completely perfect in you anywhere, it must be universal in its action. There must not be the appearance of holiness in one place and reigning sin in another, or you, too, will be a pancake not turned over. A cake not turned over is soon burned on the side nearest the fire, and there are some who seem burnt black with bigoted zeal for that part of truth they've received. The assumed appearance of superior sanctity frequently accompanies a total absence of all vital godliness. The saint in public is a devil in private. The cake that is burned on one side, is dough on the other. If it is so with me, O Lord, turn me over! Turn my unsanctified nature to the fire of Your love and let it feel the sacred glow, and let my burnt side cool a little while I learn my own weakness and lack of heat when I am removed from Your heavenly flame. Let me not be double-minded,[709] but one entirely under the powerful influence of sovereign grace.

↗ *June 24* ↘

A woman in the crowd called out, "Blessed is the mother who gave You birth and nursed You." He replied, "Blessed rather are those who hear the word of God and obey it" (Luke 11:27-28).

It's fondly thought by some that it must have involved very special privileges to have been Jesus' mother, because they imagine she had the benefit of looking into His heart in a way in that we cannot hope to do. We don't know, however, that Mary knew more than others. From what we read in the gospels, she doesn't appear to have been better instructed than any other of Jesus' disciples. All that she knew we also may learn. Do you wonder that we should say so? Here is a text to prove it: "The LORD confides in those who fear Him; He makes His covenant known to them."[710] Remember the Master's words: "I no longer call you servants, because a servant does not know his master's business. Instead, I have called you friends, for everything that I learned from My Father I have made known to you."[711] So blessedly does this divine revealer of secrets tell us His heart, that He keeps back nothing that is profitable to us. His own assurance is, "if it were not so, I would have told you."[712] Doesn't He manifest Himself to us this day in ways He doesn't to the world? He does, and so we won't ignorantly cry out, "Blessed is the mother who gave You birth and nursed You." We will instead intelligently bless God that, having heard the Word and kept it, we have as true a communion with the Savior as Mary had, and as true an acquaintance with the secrets of His heart as she's imagined to have obtained. We're blessed to be so privileged!

⇜ *June 25* ⇝

Go up on a high mountain (Isaiah 40:9).

Our knowledge of Christ is like climbing a mountain. When you're at the base you see very little, and the mountain itself appears half as high as it really is. In the valley, you see hardly anything but the brooks descending into the stream at the foot of the mountain. Climb the first knoll, and the valley opens beneath your feet. Go higher, and you see the country for four or five miles around, and you're delighted with the widening prospect. Climb higher, and the scene enlarges. When you reach the summit, the view in all directions seems unlimited. There's a forest perhaps two hundred miles away, far to the other side is a lake, and over there are the towering buildings of a city. All these things delight you, and you say, "I never imagined so much could be seen at this height." The Christian life is the same. When we first believe in Christ we see very little of Him. The higher we climb the more we discover of His beauties. But who's ever reached the summit? Who's known all the heights and depths of the love of Christ that surpasses knowledge?[713] When sitting in a dungeon in Rome, Paul could say with greater emphasis than we can, "I know whom I have believed."[714] For each of his experiences had been like climbing another summit, and his death was like reaching the top of the mountain. From there he could see the whole of the faithfulness and the love of Him to whom he had committed his soul. Go up, dear friend, on a high mountain.

You have become like us (Isaiah 14:10).

What must be the apostate professing Christians' doom when their naked souls appear before God? How will they bear that voice, "Depart, you cursed. You have rejected Me, and I reject you. You have played the harlot, and departed from Me.[715] I also have banished you forever from My presence,[716] and will not have mercy upon you."[717] What will be their shame at the last great day when the apostates will be unmasked before assembled multitudes?[718] No greater eagerness will ever be seen among hell's tormentors, than in that day when the souls of hypocrites are cast down into perdition.[719] John Bunyan pictures this with massive but awful grandeur of poetry when he speaks of the back way to hell. Seven devils bound the wretch with nine cords, and dragged him from the road to heaven in which he had professed to walk, and thrust him through the back door into hell. Mind that back way to hell, you who profess to be Christians! "Examine yourselves to see whether you are in the faith."[720] Look well to your condition and see whether Christ is in you or not. It's the easiest thing in the world to give a lenient verdict when you are judging yourself. O friend, for the sake of your immortal soul, be just and true and rigorous to yourself. Remember, if it isn't a rock on which you build, the house will fall with a great crash.[721] May the LORD give you sincerity, faithfulness, and firmness—and no matter how evil the day, may you never be led to turn aside.

◁ June 27 ◁▷

"But you must not go very far" (Exodus 8:28).

This is a crafty word from Pharaoh. If the enslaved Israelites must go out of Egypt, then he bargains with them that it won't be very far away—at least not far enough for them to escape the terror of his arms and the observation of his spies. In the same way, the world would have us be more tolerant and not be too severe about spiritual matters. Death to the world and burial with Christ are experiences that carnal minds treat with ridicule. Thus the Scriptures that set them forth are almost universally neglected and condemned. Worldly wisdom recommends compromise and moderation. According to this carnal policy, purity is admitted to be desirable, but we're warned against being too strict. Truth is to be followed, of course, but error isn't to be severely denounced. "Yes," says the world, "be spiritually minded by all means, but don't deny yourself a little frivolous socializing, an occasional dance, and a visit to a theatre. What's the good of denouncing a thing when everybody does it?" Multitudes of professing Christians yield to this cunning advice to their own eternal ruin. If we would follow the LORD wholly, we must go right away into the wilderness of separation, and leave the Egypt of the carnal world behind us. We must leave its maxims, pleasures, and carnal religion, and go far away to the place where the LORD calls His sanctified ones. When the town is on fire, our house cannot be too far from the flames. To all true believers let the trumpet-call be sounded, "come out from them and be separate."[722]

☙ *June 28* ☙

Fix our eyes on Jesus (Hebrews 12:2).

It's the Holy Spirit's work to turn our eyes away from self to Jesus. but Satan's work is just the opposite of this. He is constantly trying to make us look at ourselves instead of Christ. He insinuates, "Your sins are too great for pardon and you have no faith." All these are thoughts about self, and we'll never find comfort or assurance by looking within. But the Holy Spirit turns our eyes entirely away from self. He tells us that we're nothing but that "Christ is all, and is in all."[723] Remember, therefore, it's not your hold on Christ that saves you, it's Christ. It's not your joy in Christ that saves you, it's Christ. It's not even faith in Christ—though that's the instrument—it's Christ's blood and merits. So don't look so much at your hand with which you're grasping Christ, as at Christ. Don't look to your hope, but to Jesus, the source of your hope. Don't look to your faith, but to Jesus, the author and perfecter of your faith.[724] We'll never find happiness by looking at our prayers, works, or feelings. It's what *Jesus* is, not what *we* are, that gives rest to the soul.[725] If we would at once overcome Satan and have peace with God, it must be by "fixing our eyes on Jesus." Keep your eye simply on Him. Let His death, sufferings, merits, glories, intercession, be fresh upon your mind. When you wake in the morning look to Him. When you lie down at night look to Him. Follow hard after Him and He will never fail you.

☄ June 29 ☄

God will bring with Jesus those who have fallen
asleep in Him (1 Thessalonians 4:14).

Let's not imagine that the soul sleeps in insensibility.
"Today you will be with Me in paradise,"[726] is the whisper
of Christ to every dying saint. They fall "asleep in Jesus,"
but their souls are before the throne of God, praising Him
day and night in His temple, and singing hallelujahs to
Him who washed them from their sins in His blood.[727] The
body sleeps beneath the cover of grass—but what is this
sleep? The idea connected with sleep is *rest*, and that's the
thought the Spirit of God would convey to us. Sleep shuts
fast the door of the soul, and bids all intruders wait for
a while that the life within may enter its summer garden
of ease. The toil-worn believer quietly sleeps like a weary
child slumbering on its mother's breast. Oh, happy those
who die in the LORD! They rest from their labors, and
their works follow them.[728] Their quiet repose will never
be broken until God awakes them to give them their full
reward. Guarded by angel watchers, curtained by eternal
mysteries, they sleep on—the inheritors of glory—until the
fullness of time brings the fullness of redemption. What
an awaking will be theirs! They were laid in their last
resting place weary and worn, but they won't rise that way.
They went to their rest with furrowed brows and wasted
features, but they'll wake in beauty and glory. Blessed is
death, because through God's power it disrobes us of this
workday garment and clothes us with the wedding garment
of incorruption. Blessed are those who "have fallen asleep
in Him."

∗ *June 30* ∗

I have given them the glory that You gave Me
(John 17:22).

Behold the unsurpassed generosity of the Lord Jesus—He
has given us His all. Although a tithe of His possessions
would make a universe of angels rich beyond all thought,
He wasn't content until He gave us all that He had. It would
have been surprising grace if He had allowed us to eat the
crumbs of His bounty, but He'll do nothing by halves. He
makes us sit with Him and share the feast. Had He given
us some small pension from His royal treasures, we would
have cause to love Him eternally. But no, He will have His
bride as rich as Himself, and He will not have a glory or a
grace in which she won't share. He wasn't content with less
than making us co-heirs with Himself,[729] so that we might
have equal possessions. He emptied all His estate into the
treasures of the Church, and has all things common with
His redeemed. There's not one room in His house that He
withholds the key from His people. He gives them full
liberty to take all that He has to be their own. He loves
them to be free with His treasure, and take as much as
they can possibly carry. The boundless fullness of His all-
sufficiency is as free to the believers as the air they breathe.
Christ has put the cup of His love and grace to our lips,
and bids us to drink on forever. If we could drain it, we're
welcome to do so. But since we cannot exhaust it, we're
bid to drink abundantly, for it belongs to us.

July

≍ July 1 ≍

*Living water will flow ... in summer and in winter
(Zechariah 14:8).*

The streams of living water that flow from Jerusalem are
not dried up by the parching heats of sultry midsummer any
more than they were frozen by the cold winds of blustering
winter. Rejoice, O my soul, that you are spared to testify of
the faithfulness of the LORD. The seasons change and you
change, but your LORD remains the same forever,[730] and
the streams of His love are as deep, broad, and full as ever.
The heats of daily cares and scorching trials make me need
the cooling influences of the river of His grace. I may go at
once and drink to the full from the inexhaustible fountain,
for in summer and in winter it pours forth its flood. Job
said his brethren were as a deceitful brook,[731] but he found
his God an overflowing river of consolation. The Nile is
the great confidence of Egypt, but its floods are variable.
Our LORD is always the same. By turning the course of the
Euphrates, Cyrus took the city of Babylon, but no power,
human or infernal, can divert the current of divine grace.
The tracks of ancient rivers have been found all dry and
desolate, but the streams that are fed by the mountains of
divine sovereignty and infinite love will always be full to
the brim. Generations melt away, but the course of grace
is unaltered. How happy are you, my soul, to be led beside
such still waters![732] Never wander to other streams, lest you
hear the LORD's rebuke, "Now why go to Egypt to drink
water from the Shihor?"[733]

≈ July 2 ≈

In Him our hearts rejoice (Psalm 33:21).

The fact that Christians can sing even when surrounded by troubles is a blessing. Waves may roll over them, but their souls soon rise to the surface and see the light of God's countenance. They have a buoyancy about them that keeps their head always above water, and helps them to sing in the middle of the storm. Trouble doesn't necessarily bring consolation with it to the believer, but the presence of the Son of God in the fiery furnace[734] with us fills our heart with joy. When we're sick and suffering, Jesus visits us and makes our bed for us. When a believer is dying and sinking deep into the cold waters of the Jordan, Jesus puts His arms around the dying one and cries, "Fear not, beloved. To die is to be blessed. The waters of death have their fountainhead in heaven. They are not bitter, they are sweet as nectar, for they flow from the throne of God."[735] As the departing saint wades through the stream and heart and flesh begin to fail, the same voice speaks, "Fear not, I am with you.[736] Do not be dismayed, for I am your God."[737] As the believer nears the borders of the infinite unknown and fear begins to rise, Jesus says, "Do not be afraid, for your Father has been pleased to give you the kingdom."[738] Thus strengthened and consoled, the believer is not afraid to die, for having seen Jesus as the morning star, there's a longing to look upon Him in all His glory. Truly, the presence of Jesus is all the heaven we desire.

And the cows that were ugly and gaunt ate up the seven sleek, fat cows (Genesis 41:4).

Pharaoh's dream has too often been my waking experience. My days of laziness have ruinously destroyed all that I had achieved in times of zealous industry. My seasons of coldness have frozen all the pleasant glow of my periods of fervency and enthusiasm. My fits of worldliness have thrown me back from my advances in the divine life. I need to beware of lean prayers, lean praises, lean duties, and lean experiences, for these will eat up the fat of my comfort and peace. If I neglect prayer for a short time, I lose all the spirituality that I had attained. If I draw no fresh supplies from heaven, the old grain in my granary is soon consumed by the famine that rages in my soul. How anxious I should be to have no lean-fleshed days, no ill-favored hours. If every day I journeyed towards the goal of my desires I would soon reach it. But backsliding[739] leaves me still far from the prize of my high calling,[740] and robs me of the advances that I had so laboriously made. The only way in which all my days can be as the "fat cows," is to feed them in the right meadow—in the company of the LORD, in His service, in His company, in His fear, and in His way. Why shouldn't every year be richer in love, usefulness, and joy? I've had more experience of my LORD and should be more like Him. LORD, keep the curse of leanness of soul far from me. May I be well-fed and nourished that I may praise Your name.

Sanctify them by the truth; Your word is truth
(John 17:17).

Sanctification begins in regeneration. The Spirit of God infuses into us that new living principle by which we become a new creation in Christ.[741] This work, which begins in the new birth, is carried on in two ways—mortification, whereby the lusts of the flesh are subdued and kept under; and vivification,[742] by which the life that God has put within us is made to be a well of water springing up to eternal life.[743] This is carried on every day in what is called *perseverance*, by which the Christian is preserved and continued in a gracious state, and is made to abound in good works to the praise and glory of God. It culminates, or comes to perfection, in glory, when the soul is caught up to dwell with the Majesty on high. But while the Spirit of God is the author of sanctification, there is a visible agency employed that must not be forgotten. "Sanctify them," said Jesus, "by the truth; Your word is truth." There are many passages of Scripture that prove that the instrument of our sanctification is the Word of God. The Spirit of God brings to our minds the precepts and doctrines of truth, and applies them with power. The truth is the sanctifier, and if we do not hear or read the truth, we will not grow in sanctification. We only progress in sound living as we progress in sound understanding. "Your word is a lamp to my feet and a light for my path."[744] Hold fast the truth, for by it you'll be sanctified by the Spirit of God.

Called to be saints (Romans 1:7).

We're tend to think that the apostolic saints were saints in a more special way than we are. All whom God called by His grace are saints and sanctified by His Spirit. But we tend to look upon the *apostles* as extraordinary beings, scarcely subject to the same weaknesses and temptations as us. Yet in so doing, we're forgetting this truth: the nearer we live to God the more intensely we have to mourn over our own evil heart; and the more our Master honors us in His service, the more the evil of our flesh annoys and teases us every day. The fact is, if we had seen the apostle Paul we would have thought he was remarkably like the rest of us. If we had talked with him, we would have said, "His experience and ours are much the same. He's more faithful, more holy, and more deeply taught than we are, but he has the same trials to endure." Don't look on the ancient saints as being exempt either from infirmities or sins. Don't regard them with that mystic reverence that will almost make us idolaters. Their holiness is attainable even by us. It's our Christian duty to force our way into the inner circle of saintship. We have the same light they had, the same grace is accessible to us, so why should we rest satisfied until we've equaled them in heavenly character? They lived *with* Jesus, they lived *for* Jesus, therefore they grew *like* Jesus. Let's live by the same Spirit they did, "looking unto Jesus,"[745] and our saintship will soon be apparent.

Whoever listens to Me will live in safety and be at ease, without fear of harm (Proverbs 1:33).

Divine love is most conspicuous when it shines in the midst of judgments. When the Israelites provoked God by their continued idolatry, He punished them by withholding both dew and rain, so that their land was visited by a severe famine.[746] But while He did this, He took care that His chosen ones would be secure. Though all other brooks are dry, one will be reserved for Elijah.[747] And when that fails, God will still preserve a place of sustenance for him.[748] But the LORD had not just one Elijah," He had a remnant according to the election of grace[749] who were hidden by fifty in two caves. And though the whole land was subject to famine, these in the caves were fed from Ahab's table by his God-fearing steward, Obadiah.[750] From this we can draw the inference that no matter what comes, God's people are safe. Though the world be shaken and the sky torn in two, the believer will be as secure as in the calmest hour of rest. If God cannot save His people *under* heaven, He will save them *in* heaven. If the world becomes too hot to hold them, then heaven will be the place of their reception and safety. Be confident when you hear of wars and rumors of wars.[751] Let no agitation distress you, and don't fear evil. Secure yourself upon His promise, rest in His faithfulness, and bid defiance to the blackest future, for there's nothing in it dreadful for you. Your sole concern should be to show to the world the blessedness of listening to the voice of wisdom.

⊰ July 7 ⊱

Brothers, pray for us (1 Thessalonians 5:25).

This one morning in the year we reserved to refresh the reader's memory upon the subject of prayer for ministers, and we earnestly implore every Christian to answer the fervent request of the words first written by the apostle and now repeated by us. A very heavy responsibility rests upon every minister of the Gospel, and it will be no small mercy if at the last they are found clean of the blood of all people.[752] As officers in Christ's army, they are the special mark of the enmity of people and demons. Their sacred calling involves them in temptations from which other Christians are exempt. Above all, it often draws them away from personal enjoyment of truth into a ministerial and official consideration of it. They meet with many difficult cases, and their wits are baffled. They observe sad backslidings, and their hearts are wounded. They see millions perishing, and their spirits sink. They wish to profit you by their preaching, be a blessing to your children, and long to be useful both to saints and sinners. Therefore, dear friends, intercede for them with our God. They are miserable men and women if they don't have the help of your prayers, but happy if they live in your supplications. You don't look to them but to our LORD for spiritual blessings, and yet how many times has He given those blessings through His ministers. Pray again and again that they may be the earthen vessels into which the LORD may put the treasure of the gospel. Every day pray for all the pastors, teachers, evangelists, and missionaries!

☆ *July 8* ☆

"Tell me the secret of your great strength"
(Judges 16:6).

What's the secret strength of faith? It's the food it feeds on. Faith studies what the promise is—a sending forth of divine grace, an overflowing of the great heart of God—and then says, "God gave this promise from love and grace; therefore, I'm certain He will do what He promised."[753] Then faith thinks, "*Who* gave this promise?" It doesn't consider so much the greatness of the promise as it does, "Who is the author of it?" It remembers that it's God who cannot lie, and who is omnipotent and immutable. It therefore concludes that the promise *must* be fulfilled. It remembers why the promise was given— namely, for God's glory, and feels perfectly sure that God's glory is secure. Therefore the promise must and will stand. Faith also considers the work of Christ as being clear proof of the Father's intention to fulfill His word. "He who did not spare his own Son, but gave Him up for us all—how will He not also, along with him, graciously give us all things?"[754] Faith also looks back upon the past and remembers that God never has failed it. No, He never once failed any of His children. It recollects times of great peril, when deliverance came, hours of awful need when strength was received, and cries, "Always before the LORD has helped me, and He will help me now." Thus faith views each promise in its relation with the giver of the promise, and because it does, it can say with assurance, "Surely goodness and love will follow me all the days of my life."[755]

☙ July 9 ☚

Forget not all His benefits (Psalm 103:2).

It's a profitable occupation to note the hand of God in the lives of ancient saints, and to observe His goodness in delivering them, His mercy in pardoning them, and His faithfulness in keeping His covenant with them. But it would be even more profitable to note the hand of God in our own lives. We should look upon our own history as being at least as full of His goodness and truth, as much a proof of His faithfulness, as the lives of any of the saints who have gone before. We do God an injustice when we suppose that He performed all His mighty acts for those in the early time, but doesn't perform wonders for the saints now. Surely in our own lives we may discover some happy incidents, refreshing to ourselves and glorifying to our God. Have you had any deliverances? Have you passed through any rivers, supported by the divine presence? Have you walked through any fires unharmed? Have you had any manifestations? Has God ever listened to you and answered your requests? Have you ever been made to lie down in green pastures? Have you ever been led by the still waters?[756] Surely the goodness of God has been the same to us as to the saints of old. So then let us take the pure gold of thankfulness, and the jewels of praise and make them into another crown for the head of Christ. Let our souls give forth music as sweet and as exhilarating as came from David's harp, while we praise the LORD whose mercy endures for ever.[757]

Fellow citizens with God's people (Ephesians 2:19).

What's meant by our being citizens in heaven? It means that we're under heaven's government. Christ the King of heaven reigns in our hearts, and our daily prayer is, "Your kingdom come, Your will be done on earth as it is in heaven."[758] We freely receive the proclamations issued from the throne of glory, and we cheerfully obey the decrees of the Great King. Then, as citizens of the New Jerusalem, we share heaven's honors. The glory that belongs to beatified saints belongs to us, for we are already children of God. We wear the spotless robe of Jesus' righteousness, angels to serve us,[759] saints for our companions, Christ for our Brother, God for our Father, and a crown of immortality for our reward. We share the honors of citizenship, for we have come to the general assembly and Church of the first-born whose names are written in heaven.[760] As citizens, we have common rights to all the property of heaven. There's nothing in heaven that doesn't belong to us. "Things present or things to come," all are ours.[761] Also as citizens of heaven we enjoy its delights. Do they there rejoice over sinners that repent, prodigals that have returned? So do we. Do they chant the glories of triumphant grace? We do the same. Do they cast their crowns at Jesus' feet?[762] Whatever honors we have we cast there too. Do they look forward and long for His second advent? We also look and long for His appearing.[763] If, then, we are truly citizens of heaven, let our walk and actions be consistent with our high dignity.

After you have suffered a little while, will Himself restore you and make you strong, firm and steadfast (1 Peter 5:10).

You've seen the rainbow as it spans the plain. Its colors are glorious but it passes away. The beautiful colors give way to the fleecy clouds and the sky is no longer brilliant with the tints of heaven. It's not *established*. How can it be? It's only a glorious show made up of transitory sunbeams and passing raindrops, so how can it abide? The graces of the Christian character must not resemble the rainbow in its short-lived beauty. They must be established. May every good thing you have, believer, be established. May your character not be writing upon the sand, but upon the rock. May your faith be built of material able to endure that awful fire that will consume the wood, hay, and stubble of the hypocrite.[764] May you be rooted and grounded in love.[765] May your convictions be deep, your love real, your desires earnest. May your whole life be so settled and established, that all the blasts of Satan and all the storms of earth will never be able to remove you. But notice how this blessing of being "established in the faith"[766] is gained. The apostle's words point us to *suffering* as the means employed: *"After you have suffered a little while."* It's no use hoping we'll be well rooted if no rough winds pass over us. Those old knots on the root of the oak tree tell of the many storms that have swept over it and how deep the roots have forced their way into the earth. Thus the Christian is made strong and firmly rooted by the trials and storms of life.

Sanctified by God the Father (Jude 1, KJV).
Sanctified in Christ Jesus (1 Corinthians 1:2).
Through the sanctifying work of the Spirit
(1 Peter 1:2).

Note the union of the Three Divine Persons in all their gracious acts. How unwise are the believers who talk of preferences in the Persons of the Trinity. They think of Jesus as if He were the embodiment of everything lovely and gracious, while the Father they regard as severely just, but destitute of kindness. Equally wrong are those who magnify the decree of the Father and the atonement of the Son in a way that diminishes the work of the Spirit. In deeds of grace, none of the Persons of the Trinity act apart from the rest. They are as united in their deeds as in their essence. In their love towards the chosen they are one, and in the actions that flow from that great central source they are still undivided. Especially note this in the matter of sanctification. While we may without mistake speak of sanctification as the work of the Spirit, yet we must be careful that we don't view it as if the Father and the Son had no part in it. It's correct to speak of sanctification as the work of the Father, of the Son, and of the Spirit. See the value that God sets upon real holiness, since the Three Persons in the Trinity are represented as working together to produce a Church without "without stain or wrinkle or any other blemish."[767] As a follower of Christ, you must also set a high value on holiness—upon purity of life and godliness of conversation. This day let's so live as to manifest the work of the Triune God in us.

God said to Jonah, "Do you have a right to be angry?" (Jonah 4:9)

Anger isn't always or necessarily sinful, but it has such a tendency to run wild that whenever it displays itself we should quickly question its character with this inquiry, "Do you have a right to be angry?" It may be that we can answer, "Yes." Most often anger is a mad person's firebrand, but sometimes it's Elijah's fire from heaven.[768] We do well when we're angry with sin, because of the wrong that it commits against our good and gracious God, or with ourselves because we remain so foolish after so much divine instruction, or with others because of the evil they do. Anyone who isn't angry at transgression becomes a partaker in it. Sin is a loathsome and hateful thing, and no renewed heart can patiently endure it. God Himself is angry with the wicked every day, and it's written in His Word, "Let those who love the Lord hate evil."[769] Far more frequently, however, our anger is not commendable or even justifiable, and then we must answer, "No." Why should we be angry with children, irritable with spouses, and irate with co-workers? Is such anger honorable to our Christian profession or glorifying to God? Many Christians give way to temper as though it were useless to attempt resistance, but we must be overcomers in every point, or else we cannot be crowned.[770] If we cannot control our tempers, what has grace done for us? Whenever anger rears its ugly head, we must fly to the Cross and pray the Lord to crucify our tempers, and renew us in gentleness and meekness after His own image.[771]

You will defile it if you use a tool on it
(Exodus 20:25).

God's altar was to be built of unhewn stones so no trace of human skill or labor would be seen upon it. Human wisdom delights to trim and arrange the doctrines of the Cross into a system more congenial with the depraved tastes of fallen nature. But instead off improving the gospel, carnal wisdom pollutes it until it becomes another gospel and not the truth of God at all. All alterations and amendments of the LORD's Word are defilements and pollutions. Proud hearts are anxious to have a hand in the justification of the soul before God. Preparations for Christ are dreamed of, humblings and repentings are trusted in, good works are proclaimed, and natural ability is boasted about. The carnal confidences of sinners pollute the Savior's work. The LORD alone must be exalted in the work of atonement, and not a single mark of a human chisel or hammer will be endured. There's an inherent blasphemy in seeking to add to what Christ Jesus in His dying moments declared to be finished,[772] or to improve that in which the LORD Jehovah finds perfect satisfaction. Sinner, put away your tools, fall upon your knees in humble supplication, accept the LORD Jesus to be the altar of your atonement, and rest in Him alone. There's far too much inclination among Christians to square and reconcile the truths of revelation. This is a form of irreverence and unbelief. Strive against it and receive truth as you find it, rejoicing that the doctrines of the Word are unhewn stones, and all the more fit to build an altar for the LORD.

The fire must be kept burning on the altar continuously; it must not go out (Leviticus 6:13).

Keep the altar of private prayer burning. This is the very life of all piety. Burn here the fat of your sacrifices.[773] The sanctuary and family altars borrow their fires here, therefore let this burn well. Secret devotion is the very essence, evidence, and barometer, of vital and experimental religion. Let your closet seasons be regular, frequent, and undisturbed. "The prayer of a righteous person is powerful and effective."[774] Pray for the Church, the ministry, your own soul, your children, your relations, your neighbors, your country, and the cause of God and truth throughout the world. Let's examine ourselves on this important matter. Do we engage in private devotion with lukewarmness?[775] Is the fire of devotion burning dimly in our hearts? If so, we should be alarmed at this sign of decay. Let us go with weeping, and ask for the Spirit of grace and of supplication.[776] Let us set apart special seasons for extraordinary prayer. For if this fire should be smothered beneath the ashes of a worldly conformity, it will dim the fire on the family altar, and lessen our influence both in the Church and in the world. Our text also applies to the altar of the heart. This is a golden altar indeed.[777] Let us give to God our hearts all blazing with love, and seek His grace that the fire may never be quenched. For it won't burn if the LORD doesn't keep it burning. Let us use texts of Scripture as fuel for our heart's fire, they are live coals. But above all, let us be much alone with Jesus.

☙ *July 16* ☙

Each morning everyone gathered as much as he needed (Exodus 16:21).

Labor to maintain a sense of your entire dependence upon the LORD's good will and pleasure for the continuance of your richest enjoyments. Never try to live on the old manna, nor seek to find help in Egypt. All must come from Jesus. Old anointings won't impart unction to your spirit—your head must have fresh oil poured upon it from the golden horn of the sanctuary[778] or its glory will cease. Today you may be upon the summit of the mount of God, but He who has put you there must keep you there, or you will sink faster than you can imagine. Your mountain only stands firm when He settles it in its place. If He hide His face, you'll soon be troubled. If the Savior should see fit, there's not a window through which you see the light of heaven that He couldn't darken in an instant. He can withdraw the joy of your heart, the light of your eyes, and the strength of your life. In His hand your comforts lie, and at His will they can depart from you. Our LORD is determined that we will feel and recognize this continual dependence, for He only permits us to pray for daily bread,[779] and only promises that "your strength will equal your days."[780] It's best for us that it should be so, that we may often go to His throne and constantly be reminded of His love. LORD Jesus, we bow at Your feet, conscious that we can do nothing without You,[781] and in every favor that we receive, we acknowledge Your inexhaustible love.

For we know ... that He has chosen you
(1 Thessalonians 1:4).

Many persons want to know their election before they look to Christ, but they cannot, for it is only to be discovered by "looking unto Jesus."[782] Do you feel that your a lost, guilty, sinner? If you do, go immediately to the Cross of Christ and tell Him so. Tell Him also that you've read in the Bible, "whoever comes to Me I will never drive away."[783] Tell Him that it's also written, "Christ Jesus came into the world to save sinners."[784] Look to Jesus and believe on Him, and you will prove your election instantly, for as surely as you believe, you are elect. If you will give yourself wholly to Christ and trust Him, then you are one of God's chosen ones. But if you stop and say, "I want to know first whether I am elect," you don't know what you asked.[785] No matter how guilty, go to Jesus just as you are. Leave all curiosity about election alone. Go straight to Christ and you will know your election. The assurance of the Holy Spirit will be given to you,[786] so that you will be able to say, "I know whom I have believed, and am convinced that He is able to guard what I have entrusted to Him."[787] Christ can tell you whether you were chosen or not, but you cannot learn it any other way. Put your trust in Him, and His answer will be, "I have loved you with an everlasting love; I have drawn you with loving-kindness."[788] When you've chosen *Him*, there will be no doubt about His having chosen *you*.

⊰ July 18 ⊱

*They will set out last, under their standards
(Numbers 2:31).*

The camp of Dan brought up the rear when the armies of Israel were on the march. The Danites occupied *the last place*, but they were as much part of the host as were the foremost tribes. They followed the same fiery pillar,[789] ate the same manna,[790] drank from the same spiritual rock,[791] and journeyed to the same inheritance. Cheer up my heart, though last and least it's your privilege to be in the army, and to fare as those fare who lead. Some one must be last in honor and esteem, some one must do menial work for Jesus, and why not me? Danites occupy a very useful place. Stragglers have to be picked up during the march, and lost property has to be gathered from the field. Fiery spirits may dash forward over untrodden paths to learn fresh truth, and may win more souls to Jesus, but those of a more conservative spirit are often used to remind the Church of her ancient faith and restore her fainting sons and daughters.[792] Every position has its duties, and the slower moving children of God will find their peculiar state one in which they may eminently bless the whole host. The rear guard is a place of danger. There are foes behind us as well as before us. Attacks come from all directions. Amalek fell upon Israel[793] and slew all those who were lagging behind. Weary Christians must not be left unaided, and therefore it's the duty of experienced saints to bear their standards among the last. My soul, tenderly watch to help today those who are last.

✦ July 19 ✦

"The LORD our God has shown us His glory"
(Deuteronomy 5:24).

How will God's glory be manifested to fallen creatures like us? Our eye is not single, We always have a side glance towards our own honor, have too high an opinion of our own powers, and so are not qualified to behold the LORD's glory. It's clear, then, that self must stand out of the way so there is room for God to be exalted. This is why He often bring His people into needs and difficulties. Being made conscious of their own foolishness and weakness, they will be able to see the majesty of God when He comes to work their deliverance. Those whose lives are an even and smooth path will see little of the glory of the LORD, for they have few occasions of self-emptying, and so little fitness for being filled with the revelation of God. Among the trials of bereavement, poverty, temptation, and reproach, we learn the power of Jehovah, because we feel the littleness of ourselves. Thank God, then, if you have been led by a rough road—it's this that has given you your experience of God's greatness and loving-kindness. Your troubles have enriched you with a wealth of knowledge that is gained by no other means. Your trials have been the cleft of the rock in which Jehovah has set you, that you might behold His glory as it passed by.[794] Praise God that you've not been left to the darkness and ignorance that continued prosperity might have involved. In the great fight of affliction you've been qualified for the manifestations of His glory in His wonderful dealings with you.

A deposit guaranteeing our inheritance
(Ephesians 1:14).

Oh, what enlightenment, what joys, what consolation, what delight of heart is experienced by that person who has learned to feed on Jesus, and on Jesus alone. Yet the realization that we've tasted in this life of Christ's preciousness is imperfect at the best. As an old writer says, "'Tis but a taste!" We have tasted "that the LORD is gracious,"[795] but we don't yet know *how* good and gracious He is, although what we know of His sweetness makes us long for more. We've enjoyed the firstfruits of the Spirit,[796] and they've made us hungry and thirsty for the fullness of the heavenly vintage. We groan within ourselves, waiting for the adoption.[797] *Here* we are like Israel in the wilderness, who had but one cluster from Eshcol,[798] *there* we shall be in the vineyard. We are but beginners now in spiritual education. We have learned the first letters of the alphabet but cannot read words yet, much less put sentences together. As one says, "The person who has been in heaven but five minutes, knows more than the entire assembly of saints on earth." We have many ungratified desires at present, but soon every wish will be satisfied, and all our abilities will find the sweetest expression in that eternal world of joy. O Christian, in a little while you'll be rid of all your trials and troubles. Your tear-filled eyes will weep no longer. You'll look in unutterable rapture upon the splendor of Christ. You'll sit upon His throne and share in His triumph. You'll be co-heir with Him who is the heir of all things.

*The Daughter of Jerusalem tosses her head as you
flee (Isaiah 37:22).*

Reassured by the Word of the LORD, the poor trembling
citizens of Zion grew bold, and shook their heads at
Sennacherib's boastful threats. Strong faith enables
the servants of God to look with calm contempt upon
their most haughty foes. We know that our enemies are
attempting impossibilities. They seek to destroy the eternal
life that cannot die while Jesus lives—to overthrow the
citadel that the gates of Hades will not overcome.[799] They
kick against the goads[800] and wound themselves, and rush
upon the raised ornament of Jehovah's shield and hurt
themselves. We know their weakness. What are they but
people? And what is mankind but a worm?[801] They roar
and swell like waves of the sea, foaming out their own
shame. When the LORD arises,[802] they will fly as chaff before
the wind, and be consumed as crackling thorns. Their utter
powerlessness to do damage to the cause of God and His
truth, should cause the weakest soldiers in Zion's ranks to
laugh scornfully at them. Above all, we know that the Most
High is with us, and when He dresses Himself for battle,
where are His enemies? If He comes forth from His place,
the broken vessels of the earth will not long contend with
their Maker. His rod of iron will dash them to pieces like a
potter's vessel,[803] and the memory of them will perish from
the earth.[804] Away, then, all fears, the kingdom is safe in
the King's hands. Let us shout for joy, for the LORD reigns,
and His foes will be as straw for the manure pile.[805]

☙ *July 22* ❧

I am your husband (Jeremiah 3:14).

Christ Jesus is joined to His people in marriage. In love He took His Church in marriage as a chaste virgin, long before she fell under the yoke of bondage. Full of burning affection He toiled, like Jacob for Rachel,[806] until the whole of her purchase money had been paid. Having sought her by His Spirit, and brought her to know and love Him, He now awaits the glorious hour when their mutual bliss will be consummated at the marriage-supper of the Lamb.[807] The glorious Bridegroom hasn't yet presented His betrothed, perfected and complete, before the Majesty of heaven. She hasn't yet actually entered upon the enjoyment of her dignities as His wife and queen. She is still a wanderer in a world of misery, a dweller in the tents of Kedar.[808] But she is even now the bride, the spouse of Christ, dear to His heart, precious in His sight, written on His hands, and united with His person. On earth He exercises toward her all the affectionate offices of Husband. He makes rich provision for her wants, pays all her debts, and allows her to assume His name and share in all His wealth. He will never act otherwise to her. He will never mention the word divorce, for "He hates divorce."[809] Death severs the marriage tie between the most loving mortals, but it cannot divide the links of this immortal marriage. In heaven they do not marry, but are as the angels.[810] There is, however, this one marvelous exception to the rule—in heaven Christ and His Church will celebrate their joyous nuptials.

You were like one of them (Obadiah 1:11).

Special stress in our text is laid upon the word *you*, as when Caesar cried to Brutus, "*You* too, Brutus."[811] A bad action may be all the worse because of the person who has committed it. When *we* who are the chosen favorites of heaven sin, we sin with an emphasis. If an angel laid his hand upon us while we're sinning, he need not use any other rebuke than the question, "What are *you* doing?" Much forgiven, delivered, instructed, enriched, and blessed, will we dare to put our hand to evil? God forbid! A few minutes of confession may be beneficial to you, gentle reader, this morning. Have you ever acted like the wicked? If at a gathering people laughed at an unclean joke, and the joke wasn't completely offensive to your ear, *you were like one of the*m. When hard things were said about the ways of God and you were silent; *you were like one of the*m. When worldlings were doing business and driving hard bargains, weren't you like one of them? Weren't you not as greedy for gain as they were? Could any difference be discerned between you and them? Is there any difference? Here we come to close quarters. Be honest with your own soul, and make sure that you're a new creation in Christ Jesus.[812] When this is sure, walk jealously lest any should again be able to say, "You were like one of them." If you don't desire to share their eternal doom, then why be like them here? Side with the afflicted people of God, and not with the world.

⊠ *July 24* ⊠

Stand firm and you will see the deliverance the
LORD will bring you today (Exodus 14:13).

These words contain God's command to the believer who is
brought into extraordinary difficulties. The person cannot
retreat or go forward or to either side—what is there to do?
The Master's word is, "Stand firm."[813] At such times it's
well to listen only to the Master's word, for evil advisers
will soon come with their suggestions. *Despair* whispers,
"Give up and die."[814] But God would have us put on a
cheerful courage and rejoice in His love and faithfulness
even in our worst times. *Cowardice* says, "Retreat and
go back to the world's way of acting. You can't play the
Christian's part, it's too difficult." However much Satan
may urge this course upon you, you can't follow it if you're
a child of God. His divine decree has directed you to go
from strength to strength.[815] If for a while you're called
to stand firm, it's to renew your strength for some greater
advance in due time. *Hastiness* cries: "Do something. Stir
yourself. To just stand still and wait is sheer idleness." We
must be doing something at once—instead of confidently
looking to the LORD. *Presumption* boasts, "If the sea is
before you, march into it and expect a miracle." But Faith
doesn't listen to Presumption, Despair, Cowardice, or
Hastiness. It hears God say, "Stand firm," and it stands
immovable as a rock. Keep the posture of an alert person—
ready for action, expecting further orders, and cheerfully
and patiently awaiting the directing voice. It won't be long
before God will say to you, as distinctly as to Moses and
the people of Israel, "Go forward."[816]

He left his cloak in her hand and ran out of the house (Genesis 39:12).

In contending with certain sins there remains no way of winning but by running. Those who would be safe from acts of evil must run away from opportunities for it. A covenant must be made with our eyes to not even look upon the cause of temptation,[817] for such sins only need a spark to begin with and a blaze follows in an instant. Who would wantonly enter Sodom and live amid its horrible corruption? Only those who desire to be as its inhabitant would so court contagion. If a ship's captain knows how to avoid a storm, he does anything rather than run the risk of weathering it. Today I may be exposed to great peril—let me have the wisdom to keep out of it and avoid it.[818] The wings of a dove may be of more use to me today than the jaws of a lion. It's true I may be an apparent loser by declining evil company, but I had would rather leave my cloak than lose my character. It's isn't necessary that I be rich, but it's essential to me to be pure. No ties of friendship, no chains of beauty, no flashings of talent, no shafts of ridicule must turn me from the wise resolve to flee from sin. I only need to resist the devil and he will flee from me,[819] but the lusts of the flesh, I must flee. God of holiness, preserve your Josephs, that Potiphar's wife doesn't bewitch them with her vile suggestions.[820] May the horrible trinity of the world, the flesh, and the devil, never overcome us!

*Make every effort to add to your faith goodness; and to
goodness, knowledge; and to knowledge, self-control;
and to self-control, perseverance; and to perseverance,
godliness; and to godliness, brotherly kindness; and to
brotherly kindness, love (2 Peter 1:5-7).*

If you would enjoy the eminent grace of the full assurance
of faith, under the blessed Spirit's influence and assistance,
do what the Scripture tells you, *"Make very effort."* Take
care that your faith is of the right kind—that it's not a
mere belief of doctrine, but a simple faith that depends on
Christ and on Christ alone. Give diligent attention to your
courage. Plead with God that He would give you the face
of a lion, so that with a consciousness of right, you may
go on boldly. Study well the Scriptures and get *knowledge*,
for a knowledge of doctrine will tend to confirm *faith*. Try
to understand God's Word and let it dwell richly in your
heart. When you have done this, "Add to your knowledge
self-control." Pay attention to your body—have eternal
self-control. Pay attention to your soul—have internal
self-control. Control your tongue,[821] life, heart, and
thoughts. Add to this *perseverance*. Ask God to give you
the perseverance that endures affliction, which, when tried,
comes forth as gold.[822] Array yourself with perseverance so
you don't murmur or get depressed when afflicted. When
that grace is won look to *godliness*. Godliness is something
more than religion. Make God's glory your object in life.
Live in His sight, dwell close to Him, seek fellowship with
Him, and you have "godliness." To that add *brotherly
kindness*. Be kind to all the saints.[823] And then add a *love*
that opens its arms to everyone and loves their souls.[824]
When you're adorned with these jewels you will come to
know by clearest evidence your calling and election.

Very great and precious promises (2 Peter 1:4).

If you would know experimentally the preciousness of the promises, and enjoy them in your own heart, meditate much upon them. Thinking over God's words will often be the prelude to their fulfillment. Many Christians who have thirsted for the fulfillment of a promise have received the blessing they sought even while still meditating on the Word. Besides meditating on the promises, receive them in your soul as the very words of God. Speak to your soul this way: "If I were dealing with a person's promise, I would carefully consider the ability and the character of the person who had made the promise to me. So with the promise of God, I mustn't so much look upon the greatness of the promise, which may stagger me,[825] but upon the greatness of He who promised.[826] That will cheer me. My soul, it's God, even your God, who cannot lie, who speaks to you. This word of His that you are now considering is as true as His own existence. He is an unchangeable God.[827] He has not altered the thing that has gone out of His mouth,[828] nor called back one single comforting sentence. Nor does He lack power, for He who has spoken is the God who made the heavens and the earth. Nor can He fail in wisdom as to the time when He will give the favors, for He knows when it is best to give and when it's better to withhold." If we meditate upon the promises in this way, and consider the Promiser, we will experience their sweetness and obtain their fulfillment.

✥ *July 28* ✥

*So foolish was I, and ignorant; I was as a beast
before Thee (Psalm 73:22, KJV).*

Remember this is the confession of the man after God's
own heart,[830] and in telling us his inner life, he writes,
"So foolish was I, and ignorant." The word *foolish* here,
means more than it signifies in ordinary language. David,
in a former verse of the Psalm, writes, "I was envious at
the foolish when I saw the prosperity of the wicked,"[831]
which shows that the folly he intended had sin in it. He
puts himself down as being "foolish," and adds a word
that gives intensity to it: "*so* foolish was I." How foolish he
could not tell. It was a sinful foolishness, a foolishness that
was not to be excused, but to be condemned because of its
perverseness and willful ignorance. He had been envious
of the present prosperity of the ungodly, forgetting the
dreadful end awaiting them. Are we better than David that
we should call ourselves wise! Do we profess that we've
attained perfection,[832] or have been so chastened that the
rod has taken all our sinfulness out of us?[833] This would
be pride indeed! Look back, believer, and think of your
doubting God when He has been so faithful to you. Think
of the many times you've misunderstood His providences,
misinterpreted His dispensations, and complained, "All
these things are against me," when they're all working
together for your good.[834] Think how often you've chosen
sin because of its pleasure, when that pleasure was a root
of bitterness to you.[835] If we know our own heart we must
plead guilty to sinful foolishness and resolve that God will
be our counsel and guide.[836]

Yet I am always with you (Psalm 73:23).

"Yet,"—As if, notwithstanding all the foolishness and ignorance that David had just been confessing to God, it was still true and certain that David was saved, accepted, and blessed by being constantly in God's presence. Fully conscious of his own lost estate, and of the deceitfulness and vileness of his nature, yet, by a glorious outburst of faith, he sings "yet I am always with You." Believer, in like spirit endeavor to say "yet, since I belong to Christ I am always with God!" By this is meant always upon His mind—He's always thinking of me for my good. Always before His eye—the eye of the LORD never shuts, but is always watching over my welfare.[837] Always in His hand—none will be able to pluck me out. Always on His heart—worn there as a memorial, even as the high priest bore the names of the twelve tribes upon his heart forever.[838] You always think of me, O God. The depths of Your love continually yearn towards me. You're always making providence work for my good. Your love for me is strong as death, many waters cannot quench it, and no floods drown it.[839] Surprising grace! You see me in Christ, and though in myself sinful, You see me as wearing Christ's garments and washed in His blood, and so I stand accepted in Your presence. Thus I am always in Your favor: "always with You." Here is comfort for the tried and afflicted soul: "*Yet.*" O say it in your heart and take the peace it gives. "Yet I am always with You."

And he broke down and wept (Mark 14:72).

Some believe that as long as Peter lived, he wept whenever he remembered denying his LORD. It's not unlikely that it was so, for his sin was great and afterward grace had done a perfect work in him. This same experience is common to all the redeemed family according to the degree in which the Spirit of God has removed the natural heart of stone. Like Peter we remember our boastful promise: "Even if all fall away on account of you, I never will."[840] We eat our own words with the bitter herbs of repentance. When we think of what we vowed we would be, and of what we've been, we may weep showers of grief. Peter thought about how he denied knowing his LORD.[841] Can we, when we're reminded of our sins and their exceeding sinfulness, remain unemotional and stubborn? May we never take a dry-eyed look at sin, lest our tongue be parched in the flames of hell. Peter also thought about his Master's look of love.[842] The LORD followed the cock's warning voice with an admonitory look of sorrow, pity, and love. Without doubt, that glance was never out of Peter's mind so long as he lived. It was far more effectual than ten thousand sermons would have been without the Spirit. The penitent apostle would be sure to weep when he recollected the Savior's full forgiveness, which restored him to his former place. To think that we have offended so kind and good a LORD is more than sufficient reason for being constant weepers. LORD, strike our rocky hearts and make the waters flow.

I in them (John 17:23).

If such is the union that exists between our souls and our LORD, how deep and broad is the channel of our communion. This is no narrow pipe through which a thread-like stream may wind its way. It's a channel of amazing depth and breadth, along whose glorious length an abundant volume of living water may roll. This city of communion has many pearly gates.Lo43 Each gate is made of one pearl, and is thrown completely open so we may enter assured of welcome. If there were but one small loophole through which to talk with Christ, it would be a high privilege, but how much we are blessed in having so large an entrance. Had the LORD Jesus been far away from us, we would have longed to send a messenger to Him to carry our love to Him and bring us word from His Father's house. But see His kindness, He's built His house next door to ours. More than that, He dwells with us, and tabernacles in poor humble hearts, so He may have perpetual communion with us. How foolish we are if we don't live in habitual communion with Him. When her husband's on a journey, a loving wife may go days without having conversation with him, but she could never endure to be separated from him if she knew he was in one of the rooms of their house. Seek your LORD, for He is near. Embrace Him, for He is your Brother. Hold Him fast, for He is your Husband. Press Him to your heart, for He is of your own flesh.

August

✄ *August 1* ✄

"Let me go to the fields and pick up the leftover grain" (Ruth 2:2).

Downcast and troubled Christian, come and take what you need today in the broad field of promise. Here are abundant promises that exactly meet your needs. Take this one: "A bruised reed He will not break, and a smoldering wick He will not snuff out."[844] Does that suit your case? A reed, helpless and weak, a bruised reed—yet, He won't break you, but will restore and strengthen you. You're like the smoking wick, no light or warmth, can come from you, but He won't quench you. He'll breathe on you[845] with His sweet breath of mercy until He fans you to a flame. Do you need more grain? "Come to me, all you who are weary and burdened, and I will give you rest."[846] What soft words! Your heart is tender, and the Master knows it, and so He speaks gently to you. Won't you obey Him and come to Him now? Take more grain: "'Do not be afraid, O worm Jacob, O little Israel, for I myself will help you,' declares the LORD, your Redeemer, the Holy One of Israel."[847] How can you fear with such wonderful assurances? You may pick up tons of golden grain like this! "I have swept away your offenses like a cloud, your sins like the morning mist."[848] Or this: "Though your sins are like scarlet, they shall be as white as snow."[849] Our Master's field is rich. Pick the promises and make them your own, for Jesus bids you take them. Don't be afraid, only believe! Grasp these sweet promises, thresh them out by meditation and feed on them with joy.

⊲ *August 2* ⊳

Who works out everything in conformity with the
purpose of His will (Ephesians 1:11).

Our belief in God's wisdom necessitates that He has a settled purpose and plan in the work of salvation. What would creation have been without His design? Is there a fish in the sea or a fowl in the air that was left to chance for its formation? No, in every tissue and bone you see the presence of God working everything according to His infinite wisdom. And will God rule over everything in creation and not in grace? Since divine counsel rules the old creation, will the new creation be allowed the fickle genius of free will to preside over it? Look at Providence! Not a sparrow falls to the ground without your Father.[850] Even the hairs of your head are all numbered.[851] God weighs the mountains of our grief in scales, and the hills of our tribulation in balances.[852] And will there be a God in providence and not in grace? No! He knows the end from the beginning.[853] He sees in its appointed place not only the cornerstone that He has laid in pleasing colors, in the blood of His dear Son, but He beholds in their ordained position each of the chosen stones taken out of the quarry of nature and polished by His grace. He has a clear knowledge of every stone that will be laid in its prepared space. At the last it will be clearly seen that in every chosen vessel of mercy, Jehovah did as He willed with His own, and that in every part of the work of grace He accomplished His purpose[854] and glorified His own name.[855]

❧ *August 3* ❧

The Lamb is its lamp (Revelation 21:23).

Quietly contemplate the Lamb as the light of heaven. Light in Scripture is the emblem of joy. The joy of the saints in heaven is comprised in this: Jesus chose us,[856] loved us,[857] bought us,[858] cleansed us,[859] robed us,[860] kept us,[861] glorified us[862]—we are here entirely through the LORD Jesus. Light is also the cause of beauty. Nothing of beauty is left when light is gone. No radiance flashes from the sapphire without light, and the saints above have no beauty except what comes from Jesus. Like planets they reflect the light of the Sun of Righteousness. If He withdrew, they must die. If His glory were veiled, their glory must expire. Light is also the emblem of knowledge. In heaven our knowledge will be perfect, but the LORD Jesus Himself will be the source of it. Dark providences that were never understood before will then be clearly seen, and all that puzzles us now will become plain to us in the light of the Lamb. Oh, what unfolding there will be and what glorifying of the God of love. Light also means manifestation. Light manifests. In this world it does not yet appear what we will be.[863] When Christ receives His people into heaven, He will change them into the image of His manifested glory. What a transformation! They were stained with sin, but with one touch of His hand they're bright as the sun. Oh, what a manifestation! All this proceeds from the exalted Lamb. Oh, to be present and to see Him in His own light, the King of kings, and LORD of lords![864]

☙ *August 4* ☙

The people who know their God shall be strong
(Daniel 11:32, NKJV).

Every believer understands that to know God is the highest and best form of knowledge, and this spiritual knowledge is a source of strength to Christians.[865] It strengthens their faith. Believers are constantly spoken of in the Scriptures as being persons who are enlightened and taught of the LORD[866]—they are said to have "an anointing from the Holy One."[867] It's the Spirit's special office to lead them into all truth,[868] and all for the increase and the fostering of their faith. Knowledge strengthens love, as well as faith. Knowledge opens the door, and through that door we see our Savior. Or, to use another similitude, knowledge paints the portrait of Jesus, and when we see that portrait then we love Him. We cannot love a Christ we know only a little about. If we know but little of the excellencies of Christ, what He has done for us, and what He is doing now, we cannot love Him much. But the more we know Him, the more we'll love Him. Knowledge also strengthens hope. How can we hope for a thing if we do not know of its existence? Knowledge gives us reasons for patience. How can we have patience unless we know something of the sympathy of Christ, and understand the good that comes out of the correction that our heavenly Father sends us?[869] There's not a single grace of the Christian that isn't fostered and brought to perfection by holy knowledge. How important it is then that we grow not only in grace, but in the knowledge of our LORD and Savior Jesus Christ.[870]

⚜ August 5 ⚜

We know that in all things God works for the good of those who love Him (Romans 8:28).

Upon some points believers are absolutely sure. They know that God sits in the stern of the vessel when it rocks most. They believes that an invisible hand is always on the world's tiller, and that wherever providence may drift, Jehovah steers it. That reassuring knowledge prepares them for everything. They looks over the raging waters and see the spirit of Jesus treading the waves, and hear a voice saying, "It is I. Don't be afraid."[872] They know, too, that God is always wise. Knowing this, they're confident that there can be no accidents and no mistakes in their lives, and that that nothing happens that should not. They can say, "If I should lose all I have, it's better to lose than have, if God so wills." If God ordains it, the worst calamity is the wisest and the kindest thing that could befall me." "We know that in all things God works for the good of those who love him." Christians don't merely hold this as a theory, they *know it* as a matter of fact. Everything *has* worked for good thus far. Every event so far has worked out the most divinely blessed results. And so, believing that God rules all, that He governs wisely, that He brings good out of evil, believers' hearts are assured, and they are able to calmly meet each trial as it comes. Believers can in the spirit of true submission pray, "Send me what you will, my God, so long as it comes from You. Nothing truly harmful has ever come from Your table to any of Your children."

Watchman, what is left of the night? (Isaiah 21:11)

What enemies are abroad? Errors are a numerous horde, and new ones appear every hour. What heresy must I guard against? Sins creep from their lurking places when the darkness reigns. I must myself mount the watchtower, and watch in prayer.[873] Our heavenly Protector foresees all the attacks that are about to be made upon us. When Satan desires to sift us as wheat, He prays for us that our faith may not fail.[874] Continue O gracious Watchman, to forewarn us of our foes, and for Zion's sake do not hold your peace. "Watchman, what is left of the night?" What weather is coming for the Church? Are the clouds darkening, or is it all clear and fair overhead? We must care for the Church of God with anxious love. Now that heresy and infidelity are threatening from every side, let us observe the signs of the times[875] and prepare for conflict. "Watchman, what is left of the night?" What stars are visible? What precious promises fit our present condition? You sound the alarm—give us the consolation, also. Christ, the polestar,[876] is ever fixed in His place, and all the stars are secure in the right hand of their Lord. But watchman, when does the morning come? The Bridegroom tarries.[877] Aren't there any signs of His coming forth as the Sun of Righteousness?[878] Hasn't the morning star[879] arisen as the pledge of day? When will the day dawn and the shadows flee away?[880] O Jesus, if You don't come today to Your waiting Church, come in Spirit to my sighing heart and make it sing for joy.

How right they are to adore you! (Song of Songs 1:4)

Believers love Jesus with a deeper affection then they dare to give to any other being. They would sooner lose father and mother then part with Christ. They hold all earthly comforts with a loose hand, but they carry Him tightly locked in their hearts. They voluntarily deny themselves for His sake, but they won't be driven to deny *Him*. It's meager love that persecution fire can dry up—the true believer's love is a deeper stream than that. Many have labored to divide the faithful from their Master, but their attempts have been fruitless in every age. This's no day by day attachment that the world's power eventually dissolve. Neither human nor demon have found a key that opens this lock. Never has Satan's craft been more defective than when he's exercised it in trying to tear apart this union of two divinely welded hearts. It is written, and nothing can blot out the sentence: "How right they are to adore you!" The intensity of the love of the believers, however, is not so much to be judged by what it appears as by what the believers long for. It's our daily lament that we cannot love enough. If only our hearts were capable of holding more and reaching further. Alas, our love is only as a drop of water in an ocean compared to what He deserves. Yet measure our love by our intentions, and it's high indeed. Oh, if only we could give all the love in all hearts in one great mass, a gathering together of all loves to Him who is altogether lovely!

≈ *August 8* ≈

They spin ... a spider's web (Isaiah 59:5).

See the spider's web, and behold in it a most suggestive picture of the hypocrite's religion. It's meant to catch his prey. Foolish persons are easily entrapped by the loud professions of pretenders, and even the careful can't always escape. Custom, reputation, praise, advancement, and other flies are the small game that hypocrites take in their nets. A spider's web is a marvel of skill. Look at it and admire the cunning hunter's wiles. Isn't a deceiver's religion equally wonderful? How does he make so barefaced a lie appear to be a truth? How can he make his tinsel look so much like gold? A spider's web comes from the creature's own stomach. The bee gathers her wax from flowers, the spider sucks no flowers, and yet he spins out his material to any length. Even so hypocrites find their trust and hope within themselves. They lay their own foundation, and hew out the pillars of their own house, scorning to be debtors to the sovereign grace of God. But a spider's web is very frail. It's no match for the servant's broom. It takes no battery of Christians to blow the hypocrite's hope to pieces, a mere puff of wind will do it. Hypocritical cobwebs will soon come down when the broom of destruction begins its purifying work. This reminds us of another thought: cobwebs aren't to be endured in the LORD's house. He will see to it that they and those who spin them are destroyed forever. O my soul, rest on something better than a spider's web. Let the LORD Jesus your eternal hiding place.

↘ August 9 ↙

*The city has no need of the sun, neither of the
moon, to shine in it (Revelation 21:23).*

Over there in the better world, the inhabitants are
independent of all creature comforts. They've no need
of clothing. Their white robes never wear out, neither
will they ever be defiled. They need no medicine to heal
diseases, for "no one living in Zion will say, 'I am ill.'"
They need no sleep to refresh themselves—they do not rest
day or night, but untiringly praise Him in His temple.[881]
They need no social relationship to minister comfort, and
whatever happiness they may derive from association with
their companions is not necessary to their bliss, for their
LORD's company is enough for their largest desires. They
need no teachers there. They undoubtedly talk with one
another about the things of God, but they do not require
this to teach them, they will all be taught of the LORD.[883]
Here we lean on the friendly arm, but there they lean on
their Beloved and on Him alone. Here we must have the
help of our companions, but there they find all their help
in Christ Jesus. Here we labor for the food that perishes,
but there they find everything in God. Here the angels
bring us blessings, but we will need no messengers from
heaven then. We will not need Gabriels there to bring us
love notes from God,[884] for there we will see Him face
to face.[885] Oh, what a blessed time that will be. What a
glorious hour when God and not His creatures, the LORD
and not His works, will be our daily joy! Our souls will
then have attained the perfection of bliss.

Christ, who is your life (Colossians 3:4).

Paul's marvelously rich expression indicates that *Christ is the source of our life.* "You He made alive, who were dead in trespasses and sins."[886] The same voice that brought Lazarus out of the tomb raised us to newness of life. He's now the substance of our spiritual life.[887] It's by His life that we live.[888] He is in us, the hope of glory.[889] *Christ is the sustenance of our life.* What can Christians feed upon but Jesus' flesh and blood? "This is the bread which comes down from heaven, that one may eat of it and not die."[890] *Christ is the solace of our life.* All our true joys come from Him, and in times of trouble His presence is our consolation. There is nothing worth living for but Him, and His loving kindness is better than life.[891] *Christ is the object of our life.* As the arrow to its target, so flies the Christian towards the perfection of fellowship with Christ Jesus. As the soldiers fight for their commander, and are crowned in their commander's victory, so believers contend for Christ, and get triumphs out of the triumphs of their Master. "For to them to live is Christ."[892] *Christ is the example of our life.* Where there is the same life internally, there will be, to a great extent, the same developments externally. If we live in near fellowship with the LORD Jesus we'll grow like Him. We'll seek to walk in His footsteps, until He becomes *the crown of our life in glory.* Oh, how safe and happy is the Christian, because Christ is our life!

⊰ *August 11* ⊱

"How I long for the months gone by" (Job 29:2).

Many Christians view the past with pleasure, but regard the present with dissatisfaction. Once they lived near to Jesus, but now they feel that they've wandered from Him, and they say, "How I long for the months gone by!" They complain that they've lost their peace of mind, or that they have don't have much zeal for God's glory. The causes of this mournful state of things are manifold. It may arise through a *neglect of prayer*, for a neglected prayer is the beginning of all spiritual decline. Or it may be the result of *idolatry*. The heart has been occupied with something else, more than with God. The affections have been set on the things of earth, instead of the things of heaven.[893] A jealous God won't be content with a divided heart. He must be loved first and best. He'll withdraw the sunshine of His presence from a cold, wandering, heart. Or the cause may be found in *self-confidence* and *self-righteousness*. Pride is busy in the heart, and self is exalted instead of lying low at the foot of the Cross.[894] Christian, if you're not now as you were in "the months gone by," don't rest satisfied with wishing for a return of former happiness, but go at once to seek your Master and tell Him your sad state. Ask His grace and strength to help you to walk more closely with Him. Humble yourself before Him, and He will lift you up,[895] and give you again the enjoyment you once had. While the beloved Physician lives there is hope and certain recovery for the worst cases.

The LORD *reigns, let the earth be glad (Psalm 97:1).*

There's no reason for anxiety so long as this blessed Scripture is true. On earth the LORD's power as readily controls the rage of the wicked as the rage of the sea. His love as easily refreshes the poor with mercy as the earth with showers. Majesty gleams in flashes of fire in the center of the storms fury, and the glory of the LORD is seen in its grandeur in the rise and fall of empires. In all our conflicts and tribulations, we may behold the hand of the divine King. God is God, and He sees and hears all our troubles and sorrows. We must not forget in the midst of our afflictions that He forever reigns. Evil spirits acknowledge with misery His undoubted supremacy.[896] When permitted to roam abroad, it is with a chain at their heel—the bit is in the mouth of behemoth,[897] and the hook in the jaws of leviathan.[898] Death's darts are under the LORD's lock, and the grave's prisons have divine power as their overseer. The terrible vengeance of the Judge of all the earth makes demons cower down and tremble.[899] Don't fear death or Satan's attacks. God defends those who trust in Him. *In heaven* none doubt the sovereignty of the King Eternal, but all fall on their faces to do Him homage.[900] Angels are His royal attendants, the redeemed His favorites, and all delight to serve Him day and night. May we soon reach the city of the great King! Until that glorious day, however, let us remember that God, and God alone, reigns in all His universe.

The cedars of Lebanon that He planted
(Psalm 104:16).

Lebanon's cedars are symbolic of the Christian, in that *they owe their planting entirely to the* LORD. This is quite true of every child of God. We're not planted by people, or by ourselves, but by God. The mysterious hand of the divine Spirit dropped the living seed into a heart that He had Himself prepared for its reception. All true heirs of heaven recognizes the great Farmer as their planter. Moreover, the cedars of Lebanon *are not dependent upon human beings for their watering*. They stand on the lofty rock, unmoistened by human irrigation, and yet our heavenly Father waters them. So it is with Christians who have learned to live by faith. They're independent of humankind, even in temporal things. For their continued maintenance they look to the LORD their God alone. Again, the cedars of Lebanon *are not protected by any mortal power*. They owe nothing to humankind for their preservation from stormy winds and rain. They're God's trees, kept and preserved by Him alone. It's the same with Christians. They're not hothouse plant, sheltered from temptation. They stand in the most exposed positions, with no protection except the wings of the eternal God. Like cedars, believers are *full of sap* having vitality enough to always be green, even in winter. Lastly, the majestic condition of the cedar *is to the praise of God only*. Thus David says, "Praise the LORD … fruit trees and all cedars."[901] In believers there's nothing that can magnify humankind. They're planted, nourished, and protected by the LORD's own hand. To Him let all the glory be given.

⊰ *August 14* ⊱

You make me glad by your deeds, O LORD
(Psalm 92:4).

Do you believe that your sins are forgiven, and that Christ has made a full atonement for them? Then what a joyful Christian you should be! You should live above the common trials and troubles of the world! Since sin is forgiven, can it matter what happens to you now? Luther said, "Strike, LORD, strike, for my sin is forgiven. If You have but forgiven me, strike as hard as You will." Christian, if you're saved, be grateful and loving. Cling to the Cross that took your sin away—serve Him who served you. "Therefore, I urge you, in view of God's mercy, to offer your bodies as living sacrifices, holy and pleasing to God—this is your spiritual act of worship."[902] Don't let your zeal evaporate. Show your love in expressive tokens. Love the brothers and sisters of Him who loved you. If there's a Mephibosheth anywhere who is lame or halt, help him for Jonathan's sake.[903] If there's a poor tried believer, weep with her, and bear her cross for the sake of Him who wept for you and carried your sins.[904] Since you're forgiven freely for Christ's sake, go and tell to others the joyful news of pardoning mercy. Don't be contented with this unspeakable blessing for yourself alone, but publish abroad the story of the Cross. Holy gladness and holy boldness will make you a good preacher. Cheerful holiness is the most forcible of sermons, but the LORD must give it to you. Seek it this morning. When it's the LORD's work in which we rejoice, we needn't be afraid of being too glad.

*He went out to the field one evening to meditate
(Genesis 24:63).*

His activity was admirable. Those who spend many hours in idle company, light reading, and useless pastimes, would find more profit in meditation than in the vanities they now enjoy so much.[905] We would all know more, live nearer to God, and grow in grace, if we were alone more. Meditation chews slowly and extracts the real nourishment from the mental food gathered elsewhere. When Jesus is the theme, meditation is sweet indeed. *His choice of place was also admirable.* In a field we have a study surrounded with texts for thought. From the cedar to the oak, from the soaring eagle to the chirping grasshopper, from the blue expanse of heaven to a drop of dew, all things are full of teaching, and when the eye is divinely opened, that teaching flashes upon the mind far more vividly than from written books. Our little rooms are not as healthy, suggestive, agreeable, or inspiring as the fields. If we count nothing common or unclean,[906] but feel that all created things point to their Maker, the field will at once be hallowed. *The time of day was equally admirable.* As the sunset draws a veil over the day, it harmonizes well with the soul that is yielding earthborn cares to the joys of heavenly communion. If your time and place allow it, it would be well, dear reader, if you could make nature your prayer closet this evening. But if not, the LORD is everywhere, and will meet with you in your room or in the crowded street. Let your heart go forth to meet Him.

Ascribe to the LORD *the glory due His name
(Psalm 29:2).*

God's glory is the result of His nature and acts. He's glorious in His character, for there's such a abundance of everything that's holy and good in God that He must be glorious. The actions that flow from His character are also glorious. But while He intends that they manifest to His creatures His goodness, mercy, and justice, He equally intends that the glory associated with them be given only to Him. There's nothing in us to glory about. What do we have that we didn't receive from God?[907] Then how careful we should be to walk humbly before Him.[908] Since there's room for only one glory in the universe, the moment we glorify ourselves we set ourselves up as rivals of God. Will a piece of broken pottery exalt itself above the one who fashioned it upon the wheel? "Ascribe to the LORD . . . ascribe to the LORD glory and strength. Ascribe to the LORD the glory due His name."[909] Yet it's perhaps one of the hardest struggles of the Christian life to learn, "Not to us, O LORD, not to us but to Your name be the glory."[910] It's a lesson God is always teaching us, and teaching us sometimes by very painful discipline. Just begin to boast, "I can do all things," without adding "through Christ who strengthens me,"[911] and before long you'll be groaning, "I can do nothing." When we do anything for the LORD, and He's pleased to accept it, let us lay our crown at His feet, and exclaim, "Not I, but the grace of God which was with me!"[912]

☙ *August 17* ☙

God's unfailing love (Psalm 52:8).

Meditate a little on God's unfailing love. *It's tender love.* With a gentle loving touch He heals the brokenhearted and binds up their wounds.[914] He's as gracious in the manner of His unfailing as in the matter of it. *It's great love.* There's nothing little in God. His unfailing love is so great that it forgives great sins to great sinners, after great lengths of time, and then gives great favors and great privileges, and raises us up to great enjoyments in the great heaven of the great God. *It's undeserved love,* as indeed all true love must be. There was no right on the sinner's part to the kind consideration of God. If rebels were doomed at once to eternal fire they would have merited the doom, and if delivered from wrath, sovereign love alone has found a cause, for there's nothing in sinners themselves that deserves eternal life. *It's rich love.* Some things are great, but have little power in them. But this is a garden of love for your trembling heart. *It's manifold love and mercy.* John Bunyan says, "All the flowers in God's garden are double."[915] There's no single mercy. You may think you receive but one mercy, but you'll find that it's a whole cluster of mercies. *It's abounding love.* Millions have received it, yet it's far from being exhausted. *It's unfailing love.* It will never leave you nor forsake you.[916] It will be with you in every temptation and trouble, will be the light and life of your days, and will be the comfort and joy of your soul when you're dying.

⊲ *August 18* ⊳

"Foreigners have entered the holy places of the
Lord's house" (Jeremiah 51:51).

Because of this, the faces of the Lord's people were covered with shame, for it was a terrible thing that laypeople intruded into the Holy Place reserved for the priests alone. Everywhere about us we see similar reason for sorrow. Many ungodly people are now studying for the ministry! How dreadful that the unconverted are being ordained, and that there's such laxity of discipline among the more enlightened churches. If the thousands who read these words will take this matter before the Lord Jesus, He'll intervene and avert the evil that will otherwise come upon His Church. To adulterate the Church is to pollute a well, to pour water upon fire, to sow a fertile field with stones. May we all have grace to maintain the purity of the Church as an assembly of believers and not an unsaved community of unrepentant people. Our zeal must, however, begin at home. Let's examine ourselves as to our right to eat at the Lord's table. Let's see to it that we have on our wedding clothes, lest we ourselves be intruders in the Lord's sanctuaries. Many are called, but few are chosen[918]—the gate is small and the way is narrow[919] O for grace to come to Jesus properly, with the faith of God's elect. Uzzah was struck for touching the ark.[920] As a believer I may come freely to God's sacraments, but as a foreigner I mustn't touch them lest I die. Heart searching is essential for all who are baptized or come to the Lord's table.[921] "Search me, O God, and know my heart."[922]

*He will stand and shepherd His flock in the strength
of the LORD (Micah 5:4).*

Christ's reign in His Church is that of a *shepherd-king*.[923]
He has supremacy, but it's the supremacy of a wise and
tender shepherd over His needy and loving flock. He
commands and receives obedience, but it's the willing
obedience of the well-cared-for sheep, rendered joyfully to
their beloved Shepherd whose voice they know so well.[924]
He rules by the force of love and the energy of goodness.
His reign is *practical in its character*. It's written, "He will
stand and shepherd." The great Head of the Church is
actively engaged in providing for His people. He doesn't
sit upon a throne without authority,[925] or hold a scepter
without wielding it in government. No, He stands and
shepherds. The expression *shepherd* in Greek means to
shepherdize—to do everything expected of a shepherd:
guide, watch, preserve, restore, tend, and feed. His reign
is *continual in its duration*. It's written, *"He will stand
and shepherd."* Not, "He will shepherd now and then,
and leave His position." Not, "He will one day grant a
revival, and then leave His Church to barrenness." His eyes
never slumber, and His hands never rest. His heart never
ceases to beat with love, and His shoulders are never weary
of carrying His people's burdens. His reign is *effectually
powerful in its action*; "He will shepherd in the strength
of Jehovah." Wherever Christ is, there is God—and
whatever Christ does is the act of God. He who stands
today representing the interests of His people is very God
of very God to whom every knee will bow.[926] Blessed are
those who belong to such a shepherd.

Israel's singer of songs (2 Samuel 23:1).

Among all the saints whose lives are recorded in Scripture, David possesses the most striking, varied, and instructive character. In his history we find trials and temptations not to be discovered, as a whole, in other saints of ancient times, and therefore he's all the more suggestive a type of our LORD. David knew the trials of all ranks and conditions. Kings have their troubles, and David wore a crown. Peasants have cares, and David was a shepherd. Wanderers have many hardships, and David lived in the caves of En Gedi.[927] He was also tried in his friends—his counselor Ahithophel abandoned him:[928] "He who shared my bread, has lifted up his heel against me."[929] His worst foes were of his own household[930]—his children were his greatest affliction. The temptations of poverty and wealth, honor and reproach, health and weakness, all tried their power upon him. He had temptations externally to disturb his peace, and internally to mar his joy. He no sooner escaped from one trial than he fell into another, and no sooner emerged from one season of despondency and alarm than he was again in the lowest depths. It's probably from this cause that David's psalms are so universally the delight of experienced Christians. Whatever our frame of mind, whether ecstasy or depression, David has exactly described our emotions. He was an able master of the human heart, because he had been tutored in the school of heart-felt, personal, experience. As we are instructed in the same school, we increasingly appreciate David's psalms. My soul, let David's experience cheer and counsel you this day.

Those who refresh others will themselves be refreshed (Proverbs 11:25).

Here we are taught a great lesson—to get we must give, to accumulate we must scatter, to make ourselves happy we must make others happy, and to become spiritually vigorous we must seek the spiritual good of others. In helping others we are helped. How? Our efforts to be useful bring out our powers for usefulness. We have latent talents and abilities that are brought to light by exercise. Our strength for labor is often unknown until we begin to climb difficult mountains. We don't know what tender sympathies we possess until we try to dry someone's tears. We often find in attempting to teach others we ourselves learn. What gracious lessons we've learned at sick beds! We went to teach the Scriptures and came away blushing that we knew so little. In talking with poor saints we're taught the way of God more accurately.[931] Helping others makes us humble. We discover how much grace there is where we hadn't looked for it, and how much a poor saint may outstrip us in knowledge. Our own comfort is also increased by helping others. We endeavor to cheer them, and the consolation gladdens our own heart. Like the two men in the snow—one rubbed the other's limbs to keep him from dying, and in so doing kept his own blood circulating and saved his own life. The poor widow in Zarephath supplied the prophet's from her scanty store, and from that day she never again knew what need was.[932] "Give, and it will be given to you. A good measure, pressed down, shaken together and running over."[933]

⚜ *August 22* ⚜

O daughters of Jerusalem, I charge you— if you find my lover, what will you tell him? Tell him I am faint with love (Song of Songs 5:8).

Gracious souls are never perfectly at rest except when they are near Christ, for when they are away from Him they lose their peace. The nearer to Him, the nearer to the perfect calm of heaven. The nearer to Him, the fuller the heart is—not only of peace, but of life, vigor, and joy, for these all depend on constant communion with Christ. What the sun is to the day, what the moon is to the night, what the dew is to the flower, is what Jesus Christ is to us. What bread is to the hungry, clothing to the naked, shade to the traveler in a sun-baked land, is what Jesus Christ is to us. Therefore, if we are not consciously one with Him, our spirit cries in the words of the Song, "I charge you—if you find my lover, tell him I am faint with love." This deep longing after Christ has a blessing attending it: "Blessed are those who hunger and thirst for righteousness."[934] Supremely blessed are those who thirst after the Righteous One. That hunger is blessed because it comes from God. If I may not feed on Christ, it will be next door to heaven to hunger and thirst after Him. There's a sacredness about that hunger, since it sparkles among the beatitudes of our LORD. But the blessing involves a promise. Hungry ones "will be filled" with what they're seeking. So if Christ causes us to long after Himself, He will certainly satisfy those longings. When He does come to us, as come He will, how glorious it will be!

The sound of weeping and of crying will be heard
... no more (Isaiah 65:19).

The glorified weep no more, for *all outward causes of grief are gone.* There are no broken friendship or ruined prospects in heaven. Poverty, famine, peril, persecution, and slander are unknown there. No pain distresses, no thought of death or bereavement saddens. They weep no more, for *they are perfectly sanctified.*[935] No "sinful, unbelieving heart" prompts them to depart from the living God.[936] They're without fault before His throne,[937] and are fully conformed to His image.[938] Those who have ceased to sin, cease to mourn. They weep no more, because *all fear of change is past.* They know they're eternally secure. Sin is shut out, and they're shut in. Countless cycles may revolve, but eternity will not be exhausted, and while eternity endures their immortality and blessedness co-exist with it. They're forever with the LORD.[939] They weep no more, because *every desire is fulfille*d. They cannot wish for anything that they don't already possess. No matter what is wanted, all the faculties are completely satisfied. Imperfect as our present ideas are of the things that "God has prepared for those who love Him,"[940] the Spirit has revealed enough for us to know that the saints above are supremely blessed. The joy of Christ, which is an infinite fullness of delight, is in them. That same joyful rest remains for us. It may not be far distant. Before long the weeping willow will be exchanged for the palm branch of victory, and sorrow's tears will be transformed into pearls of everlasting bliss. "Therefore encourage each other with these words."[941]

*One who breaks open the way will go up
before them (Micah 2:13).*

Because Jesus has gone before us, things are not as they would have been if had He never passed that way. He has conquered every foe that obstructed the way. Cheer up now. Not only has Christ traveled the road, but He's slain your enemies. Do you dread sin? He's nailed it to His cross. Do you fear death? He's been the death of death. Are you afraid of hell? He's barred it against the entrance of any of His children—they will never see the abyss of perdition. Whatever foes may be before the Christian, they're all overcome. There are lions, but their teeth are broken. There are serpents, but their fangs are pulled. There are rivers, but there are bridges across. There are flames, but we wear that matchless garment that renders us invulnerable to fire.[942] The sword that has been forged against us is already blunted. The instruments of war the enemy is preparing have already lost their point. God has taken away in the person of Christ all the power that anything can have to hurt us. Well then, the army may safely march on, and you may go joyously along your journey, for all your enemies are conquered beforehand. They are beaten, they are vanquished, and all you have to do is to divide the spoil. It is true, you will often be engaged in combat; but your fight is with a vanquished foe. He may attempt to injure you, but his strength is not sufficient for his malicious attacks. Your victory will be easy, and your treasure will be beyond all measure.

His fruit is sweet to my taste (Song of Songs 2:3).

In the Scriptures, faith is spoken of as belonging to all the senses. It is *sight*: "Look to Me, and be saved."[943] It is *hearing*: "Hear, and your soul shall live."[944] Faith is spiritual *touch*. By this faith the woman came behind and touched the hem of Jesus' garment,[945] and by this we handle the things of the good Word of life.[946] One of the first performances of faith is hearing. We hear the voice of God, not with the outward ear alone, but with the inward ear. We hear it as God's Word, and we believe it to be so—that is the *hearing* of faith. Then our mind looks on the truth as it is presented to us. That is to say, we understand it, we perceive its meaning—that is the *seeing* of faith. Next we discover its preciousness; we begin to admire it, and find how fragrant it is—that is faith in its *smell*. Then we appropriate the mercies that are prepared for us in Christ—that is faith in its *touch*. Then follow the enjoyments: peace, delight, communion, which are faith in its *taste* Any one of these acts of faith is saving. To hear Christ's voice as the sure voice of God in the soul will save us. But that which gives true enjoyment is the aspect of faith wherein Christ, by holy taste, is received into us, and made by inward and spiritual understanding, to be the food of our souls. It is then we sit "under His shadow with great delight,"[947] and find His fruit sweet to our taste.

⊰ August 26 ⊱

He ordained His covenant forever (Psalms 111:9).

The LORD's people delight in the covenant. It's an unfailing source of consolation to them whenever the Holy Spirit leads them into its banqueting house and waves its banner of love. They delight to contemplate *the antiquity* of that covenant, remembering that before the daystar knew its place, or planets circled in their rotations, the interests of the saints were made secure in Christ Jesus.[948] It's peculiarly pleasing to them to remember *the sureness* of the covenant, while meditating upon "the sure mercies of David."[949] They delight to celebrate it as signed, sealed, and ratified in all things. It often brings them joy to think of its *immutability*, as a covenant that neither time nor eternity, life nor death, will ever be able to violate—a covenant as old as eternity and as everlasting as the Rock of Ages. They rejoice also in *the fullness* of this covenant, for they see in it all things provided for them. God is their portion, Christ their companion, the Spirit their Comforter, earth their lodge, and heaven their home. They see in it an inheritance reserved for every soul possessing salvation. More especially it's the pleasure of God's people to contemplate *the graciousness* of this covenant. They see that the law was made void because it was a covenant of meritorious works. But this they perceive as enduring because grace is the basis, grace the condition, grace the foundation, grace the capstone. The covenant is a treasury of wealth, a granary of food, a fountain of life, a storehouse of salvation, a charter of peace, and a haven of joy.

How long will they refuse to believe in Me?
(Numbers 14:11)

Strive with all diligence to keep out unbelief. It so dishonors Christ that He will withdraw His manifested presence if we insult Him by indulging it. Among hateful things it's the most to be loathed. In your case, believer, it's most wicked, for the mercies of your LORD in the past increase your guilt in doubting Him now. When you do distrust the LORD Jesus, He may well cry out, "Behold, I am weighed down by you, As a cart full of sheaves is weighed down."[950] The sin is needless, foolish, and unwarranted. Jesus has never given the slightest ground for suspicion, and it's bitter to be doubted by those to whom our conduct is uniformly affectionate and true. Jesus is the Son of the Highest, and has unbounded wealth. It's shameful to doubt Omnipotence and distrust all-sufficiency. The cattle on a thousand hills will suffice for our most hungry feeding,[951] and the granaries of heaven are not likely to be emptied by our eating. If Christ were only a cistern, we might soon exhaust His fullness, but who can drain a fountain? Multitudes of spirits have drawn their supplies from Him, and not one of them has murmured at the scantiness of His resources. Do away with this lying traitor unbelief, for its only errand is to cut the bonds of communion and make us mourn an absent Savior. John Bunyan tells us that unbelief has "as many lives as a cat." If so, let's kill one life now, and continue the work until the whole nine are gone. Down with you, traitor, my heart loathes you.

Olive oil for the light (Exodus 25:6).

My soul, how much you need this, for your lamp will not burn long without it. Your charred wick will smoke and become an offense if light is gone, and gone it will be if there's no oil. Even the consecrated lamps[952] could not give light without oil. Though they shone in the tabernacle they needed to be fed. Though no rough winds blew upon them, they needed to be trimmed. And your need is equally as great. Under the most happy circumstances you can not give light for another hour unless fresh oil of grace is given you. Not every oil was to be used in the LORD's service. Neither the petroleum that exudes so plentifully from the earth, nor the produce of fishes, nor that extracted from nuts would be accepted. Only the best olive oil was selected. Pretended grace from natural goodness, fancied grace from priestly hands, or imaginary grace from outward ceremonies will never serve the true saints of God. They know that the LORD would not be pleased with rivers of such oil. They go to the olive press of Gethsemane, and draw their supplies from Him who was crushed there. Our churches are the Savior's golden candle sticks, and if they are to be lights in this dark world, they must have a large supply of holy oil. Let's pray for our ministers and churches, that they may never lack oil for the light. Truth, holiness, joy, knowledge, love, are all beams of the sacred light, but they will not shine unless in private we receive oil from the Holy Spirit.

Have mercy upon me, O God (Psalm 51, KJV).

When Dr. Carey[953] was suffering from a dangerous illness, the question was asked, "If this sickness should prove fatal, what passage would you select as the text for your funeral sermon?" He replied, "Oh, I feel that such a poor sinful creature is unworthy to have anything said about him. But if a funeral sermon must be preached, let it be from the words, 'Have mercy upon me, O God, according to Thy loving kindness; according unto the multitude of Thy tender mercies blot out my transgressions.'" In the same spirit of humility, he directed in his will that the following inscription and nothing more should be cut on his gravestone:

WILLIAM CAREY, BORN August 17th, 1761: DIED ...
A wretched, poor, and helpless worm
On Thy kind arms I fall.

Only on the footing of free grace can the most experienced and most honored of the saints approach their God. The best of saints are conscious above all others that they are mere mortals at the best. Merely professing Christians can boast, but true children of God cry for mercy on their unprofitableness. We need the LORD's mercy upon our good works, our prayers, our preachings, our alms-givings,[954] and our holiest things. The blood wasn't sprinkled only upon the doorposts of Israel's houses,[955] but upon the tabernacle,[956] the mercy seat,[957] and the altar,[958] because as sin intrudes into our holiest things, the blood of Jesus is needed to purify them from defilement.

Wait for the LORD *(Psalm 27:14).*

It may seem an easy thing to wait, but it takes years of teaching before we learn. We are anxious to serve the LORD, and it's much easier to forge ahead than to wait. But don't—simply wait. *Wait in prayer,* however. Call upon God, and spread the case before Him. Tell Him your difficulty, and plead His promise of aid. When uncertain about which way to move, be humble as a child and *wait with simplicity of soul* upon the LORD. It's sure to be well with us when we feel and know our own foolishness, and are highly willing to be guided by the will of God. But *wait in faith.* Express your unstaggering confidence in Him. Unfaithful, untrusting, waiting, is an insult to the LORD. Believe that if He keeps you tarrying even many days, He'll come at the right time. The vision will come and will not linger.[959] *Wait in quiet patience,* not rebelling because you're under an affliction, but blessing your God for it. Never murmur against the second cause, as the children of Israel did against Moses.[960] Never wish you could go back to the world again,[961] but accept the situation as it is, and with your whole heart and without any self-will, put it into the hand of your God. Say, "Now, LORD, not my will, but Yours be done.[962] I don't know what to do, but I'll wait, for my heart is fixed upon You alone, O God, and my spirit waits in full conviction that You'll yet be my joy and my salvation,[963] my refuge[964] and my strong tower."[965]

My arm they will trust (Isaiah 51:5, NKJV).

In seasons of severe trial, Christians have nothing on earth that they can trust in, and are therefore compelled to cast themselves on their God alone. There is no human deliverance, and they must trust themselves entirely to the providence and care of God. There is no getting to our God sometimes because of the multitude of our friends who want to help, but when we're so poor, so friendless, so helpless that we have nowhere else to turn, we fly into our Father's arms, and are blessedly held close! When we're burdened with troubles so pressing and so peculiar that we can't tell them to anyone but God, we may be thankful for them, for we will learn more of our Father then than at any other time. Oh, storm-tossed believer, it's a happy trouble that drives you to your Father! Now that you have only your God to trust in, see that you put your full confidence in Him. Don't dishonor your God by unworthy doubts and fears, but be strong in faith, giving glory to God.[966] Show the world that your God is worth ten thousand worlds to you. Show wealthy people how rich you are in your poverty when the LORD is your helper.[967] Show the strong person how strong you are in your weakness when underneath you are the everlasting arms.[968] Now's the time for feats of faith and valiant exploits. Be strong and very courageous,[969] and the LORD your God will surely glorify Himself in your weakness. May the Holy Spirit give you rest in Christ this closing day of the month.

September

﹏ *September 1* ﹏

You will guide me with your counsel, and afterward
you will take me into glory (Psalm 73:24).

The Psalmist felt his need for divine guidance. He had just been discovering the foolishness of his own heart, and resolved that God's counsel would hereafter guide him. A sense of our own foolishness is a great step toward being wise, when it leads us to rely on the wisdom of the LORD. We should give ourselves up implicitly to divine guidance, nothing doubting,[970] assured that though we're blind and cannot see, it's always safe to trust the All-seeing God. *"You will,"* is a blessed expression of confidence. He was certain the LORD would not decline the task. Be assured that God will be your counselor and friend. He will guide you and direct all your ways. This assurance is partly fulfilled in His Word, for Scripture is His counsel to you. We're blessed to have God's Word always to guide us! Without a compass the mariner would be lost. So would Christians without the Bible. This is the unerring chart in which is described all the channels from the quicksands of destruction to the haven of salvation, mapped by one who knows all the way.[971] Bless You, O God, that we can trust You to guide us now, and guide us to the end! After this guidance through life, the psalmist anticipates a divine reception at last — *"and afterward you will take me into glory."* What a thought for you, believer! God Himself will receive *you* to glory—*you!* Wandering, erring, straying, yet He will bring you safe at last to glory. This is your inheritance, go straight to the throne in the strength of this text.

Simon's mother-in-law was in bed with a fever, and they told Jesus about her (Mark 1:30).

This glimpse into the house of the apostolic fisherman is very interesting. We see at once that household joys and cares are no hindrance to the full exercise of ministry. Often they furnish an opportunity for personally witnessing the LORD's gracious work upon one's own flesh and blood. They may even instruct the teacher better than any other earthly discipline. Some of the Church may decry marriage, but true Christianity and household life go well together. Peter's house was probably a poor fisherman's hut, but the LORD of Glory[972] entered it, lodged in it, and worked a miracle in it. If this is being read in some humble house this morning, let this fact encourage the inhabitants to seek the company of King Jesus. God is more often in humble houses than in rich palaces. Jesus is looking around your room now, and is waiting to be gracious to you. Sickness had entered Simon's house sickness, and a deadly fever had prostrated his mother-in-law. As soon as Jesus came they told Him of the sad affliction, and He hurried to the patient's bed. Have you any sickness in the house this morning? You'll find Jesus to be an excellent physician.[973] Go to Him at once and tell Him all about the matter. Immediately lay the case before Him. It concerns one of His people, and therefore won't be trivial to Him. The LORD may not immediately remove all disease from those we love, but believing prayer for the sick is often followed by restoration.[974] The tender heart of Jesus waits to hear your griefs, so tell Him now.[975]

⚹ *September 3* ⚹

You whom I love (Song of Songs 1:7).

It's good to be able to say of the LORD Jesus, without any "ifs," "ands," or "buts," *"You whom I love."* Many can only say of Jesus that they *hope* they love Him, or that they *trust* they love Him. But only a poor and shallow experience will be content to stay there. We shouldn't allow our spirit to rest until we're certain about a matter of such vital importance. We shouldn't be satisfied with a superficial *hope* that Jesus loves us, and with a mere trust that we love Him. The old saints did not moderate what they said, but they spoke positively and plainly. "I know whom I have believed," said Paul.[976] "I know that my Redeemer lives," said Job.[977] Get positive knowledge of your love for Christ, and don't be satisfied until you can speak of your interest in Him as a reality, which you have made sure by having received the witness of the Holy Spirit.[978] True love for Christ is the Holy Spirit's work. He is the *efficient cause* of it, but the logical reason lies in Jesus *Himself. Why* do we love Jesus? Because He first loved us.[979] *Why* do we love Jesus? Because He "gave Himself for us."[980] We have life through His death[981] and peace through His blood.[982] Though He was rich, yet for our sakes He became poor.[983] *Why* do we love Jesus? Because of the excellency of His person. We're filled with a sense of His beauty, an admiration of His charms, a consciousness of His infinite perfection! "Yes, He is altogether lovely."[984] This is blessed love, indeed!

"I am willing," he said. "Be clean!" (Mark 1:41)

Primeval darkness heard the Almighty decree, "light be,"[985] and immediately light was, and the word of the LORD Jesus is equal in majesty to that ancient word of power. Redemption, like creation, has its word of might. Jesus speaks and it's done. Leprosy yielded to no human remedies, but it fled at once at the LORD's "Be clean!" The disease exhibited no hopeful signs of recovery, nature contributed nothing to its own healing, but the unaided word brought about the entire work immediately and forever. Sinners are in conditions more miserable than the leper. Let them imitate his example and go to Jesus, "imploring Him, and kneeling down to Him."[986] Let them exercise what little faith they have, even if it goes no further than, "If you are willing, you can make me clean." The result need not be doubted. Jesus heals all who come to Him, and casts out none.[987] In reading this morning's Scripture, note that Jesus *touched* the leper. This unclean person had broken the ceremonial law[988] by coming among the multitude.[989] But instead of rebuking him, Jesus broke through the Levitical law and became unclean Himself in order to heal him.[990] In the same way, Jesus, who had no sin, was made "to be sin for us, so that in Him we might become the righteousness of God."[991] If only poor sinners would go to Jesus, believing in the power of His blessed substitutionary work, they would soon learn the power of His gracious touch. The love of Jesus is the source of salvation. He loves, He looks, He touches us, WE LIVE!

⊲ *September 5* ⊳

*Woe to me that I dwell in Meshech, that I live
among the tents of Kedar! (Psalm 120:5)*

As a Christian you have to live in the midst of an ungodly world, and it's of little use for you to cry "Woe to me." Jesus did not pray that you should be taken out of the world, and what He didn't pray for you need not desire. Far better to meet the difficulty in the LORD's strength, and glorify Him in it. The enemy is always watching to detect inconsistency in your conduct,[992] so be holy. Remember that everyone's watching you, and that more is expected from you than from others. Strive to give no opportunity for blame. Like Daniel, let your goodness be the only fault they can find in you.[993] Seek to be useful as well as consistent. Perhaps you think, "If I were in a more favorable position I might serve the LORD's cause, but I can't do any good where I am." But the worse the people are around you, the more they need your efforts. If they're crooked, the more need there is that you set them straight. If they're perverse, the more they need you to turn their proud hearts to the truth. If you grow weary of the strife and sin that meets you on every hand, consider that all the saints have endured the same trial. You mustn't expect to travel more easily than they. Some had to risk their lives to the death in the high places of the field, and you'll not be crowned until you've endured hardness as a good soldier of Jesus Christ. So "stand firm in the faith ... be strong."[994]

In a crooked and depraved generation, in which you shine like stars in the universe (Philippians 2:15).

We use lights to *reveal*. As Christians, we should so shine in our lives that a person could not live with us a week without knowing the gospel. Our conversation should be such that all those around us clearly understand whom we belong to and serve. They should see the image of Jesus reflected in our daily actions. Lights are intended for *guidance*. We're to help those around us who are in the dark. We're to hold forth the Word of life to them. We're to point sinners to the Savior, and the weary to a divine resting place. People sometimes read their Bibles, and fail to understand them. Like Philip,[995] we should be ready to instruct the inquirer in the meaning of God's Word, the way of salvation, and the life of godliness. Lights are also used for *warning*. Lighthouses are erected to warn ships of dangerous reefs. Christians should know that there are many false lights shown everywhere in the world, and therefore the right light is needed. The wreckers of Satan are always abroad, tempting the ungodly to sin under the name of pleasure, and shining a false light. We must shine the true light upon every dangerous rock and point out every sin and tell what it leads to, so we may be clean of the blood of all people[996] and shine as lights in the world. Lights also have a *cheering* influence, and so have Christians. Christians should be comforters,[997] with kind words on their lips, and sympathy in their hearts. They should carry sunshine wherever they go, and diffuse happiness around them.

✍ *September 7* ✍

Since they could not get him to Jesus because of the crowd, they made an opening in the roof above Jesus and, after digging through it, lowered the mat the paralyzed man was lying on (Mark 2:4).

Faith is full of inventions. The house was full, a crowd blocked the door, but faith found a way of getting at the LORD and placing the paralyzed man before Him. If we cannot get sinners where Jesus is by ordinary methods, we must use extraordinary ones. Luke 5:19 seems to indicate that roof tiles had to be removed, which create dust and some hazard to those below, but where the case is very urgent we mustn't mind running some risks and shocking some proprieties. Jesus was there to heal, and, therefore, fall what might, faith risked all so that the poor paralyzed person might have his sins forgiven. O that we had more daring faith among us! We should seek it this morning for ourselves and for others, and try to perform some gallant act today for the love of souls and the glory of the LORD. The world is constantly inventing. Cannot faith invent too, and by some new means reach the outcasts who are perishing around us? It was the presence of Jesus that created victorious courage in the four bearers of the paralyzed man.[998] Isn't the LORD among us now? Have we seen His face for ourselves this morning? Have we felt His healing power in our own souls? If so, then through doors or through roofs, let's break through all obstructions and labor to bring poor souls to Jesus. Many means are acceptable when love is set on winning souls. O LORD, make us quick to suggest methods of reaching Your poor sin-sick ones, and bold to carry them out despite the hazards.

⊰ *September 8* ⊱

"Your fruitfulness comes from me" (Hosea 14:8).

Our fruitfulness comes from God by union. The fruit of the branch is directly traceable to the root. Sever the connection, the branch dies, and no fruit is produced. By virtue of our union with Christ we bring forth fruit. Every cluster of grapes was first in the root, passed through the vine, flowed through the sap vessels, and fashioned itself externally into fruit—but it was first in the vine. So also every good work was first in Christ, and then is brought forth in us.[999] Christian, prize this precious union with Christ, for it must be the source of all the fruitfulness that you can hope to know. If you were not joined to Jesus Christ, you would be a barren branch indeed.[1000] Our fruit comes from God by spiritual providence. The fruit owes much to the root—it's essential for fruitfulness—but it owes much also to external influences. We owe much to God's grace of providence in which He provides us constantly with stimulation, teaching, consolation, strength, or whatever else we need. To this we owe all our usefulness. The gardener's sharp-edged knife promotes the fruitfulness of the vine by thinning the clusters, and by cutting off superfluous shoots. So is it, Christian, with that pruning that God gives to you. "My Father is the gardener. He cuts off every branch in me that bears no fruit, while every branch that does bear fruit he prunes so that it will be even more fruitful."[1001] Since God is the source of our spiritual graces, let us give to Him all the glory of our salvation.

≤ *September 9* ≥

*"I will answer you and tell you great and
unsearchable things you do not know"
(Jeremiah 33:3).*

There are different translations of these words. One version
says, "I will show you great and fortified things." Another,
"Great and reserved things." There are reserved and special
things in Christian experience—not all the developments
of spiritual life are attained with the same ease. There
are the common conditions and feelings of repentance,
faith, joy, and hope that are enjoyed by the entire family.
But there is an upper realm of rapture, communion, and
conscious union with Christ that is far from being the
common dwelling place of believers. We haven't all the
high privilege of leaning on Jesus' chest like John,[1002] or
being caught up into the third heaven like Paul.[1003] There
are heights in experimental knowledge of the things of
God that philosophic thought has never seen. God alone
can take us there. The chariot in which He takes us up,
and the fiery steeds with which that chariot is pulled, are
prevailing prayers. Prevailing prayer takes the Christian
to Carmel, and enables him to cover heaven with clouds
of blessing, and earth with floods of mercy.[1004] Prevailing
prayer bears the Christian aloft to Pisgah,[1005] and shows
him the inheritance reserved. It elevates us to the Mount
of Transfiguration[1006] and changes us into the likeness of
our LORD, so that as He is, so are we in this world. If you
would reach to something higher than ordinary experience,
look to the Rock that is higher than you,[1007] and look with
eyes of faith through the window of persistent prayer.[1008]
When you open the window on your side, it won't be
bolted on the other.

Jesus went up on a mountainside and called to Him those he wanted, and they came to Him (Mark 3:13).

Here was sovereignty. Impatient spirits may fret and fume, because they're not called to the highest places in the ministry, but rejoice that Jesus calls whom He wills. If He makes me a doorkeeper in His house, I'll cheerfully bless Him for His grace in permitting me to do anything in His service. The call of Christ's servants comes from above. Jesus stands on the mountain, forever above the world in holiness, earnestness, love, and power. Those whom He calls must go up the mountain to Him, and must seek to rise to His level by living in constant communion with Him. They may not be able to mount to classic honors, but like Moses they must go up into the mount of God[1009] and have intimate communion with Him. Jesus went up to speak with His Father, and we must do the same if we would bless others. This morning we must endeavor to climb the mount of communion, and there be ordained to the lifework for which we are set apart. Let's not see the face of anyone today until we have seen Christ. We too will cast out demons[1010] and work wonders if we go down into the world filled with that divine energy that Christ alone can give. It's no use going to the LORD's battle until we are armed with heavenly weapons. We *must* see Jesus.[1011] We will stay at the mercy seat[1012] until He manifests Himself to us in a way He does not to the world—until we can truthfully say, "We were with Him in the holy mount."[1013]

September 11

Be separate (2 Corinthians 6:17).

Christians are in the world but not of the world.[1014] For us, "to live," should be "Christ."[1015] Whether we eat, or drink, or whatever we do, we should do all to God's glory.[1016] You may lay up treasure, but lay it up in heaven, "where moth and rust do not destroy, and where thieves do not break in and steal."[1017] You may strive to be rich, but make it your ambition to be rich in faith[1018] and good works.[1019] You may have pleasure, but when you're merry, sing psalms and make melody in your hearts to the LORD.[1020] In your spirit, as well as in your aim, you should differ from the world. Waiting humbly before God,[1021] always conscious of His presence,[1022] delighting in communion with Him, and seeking to know His will, you'll prove that you're of the heavenly race. You should also be separate from the world in your actions. If a thing is right, though you lose by it, it must be done. If it's wrong, though you would gain by it, you must scorn the sin for your Master's sake. You must have no fellowship with the unfruitful works of darkness, but rather expose them.[1023] Walk worthy of your high calling and dignity.[1024] Remember that Christians are sons and daughters of the King of kings.[1025] Therefore, keep yourself unspotted from the world. Don't let your eyes that are soon to see the King in His beauty become windows of lust. Don't let your heart that is soon to be filled with heaven and ecstatic joy become filled with pride and bitterness. "Be separate!"

The LORD is a jealous ... God. (Nahum 1:2)

Your LORD is jealous of your love. He chose you, and He cannot bear that you should choose another. He bought you with His own blood, and He cannot endure that you should think you are your own, or that you belong to this world. He loved you with such a love that He would sooner die than have you perish,[1026] and He cannot endure that anything stand between your heart's love and Him. *He is very jealous of your trust.* He will not permit you to trust in an arm of flesh.[1027] When we lean upon Him,[1028] He is glad, but when we transfer our dependence to another, when we rely upon our own wisdom, or trust in any works of our own, He is displeased and will chasten us that He may bring us to Himself. *He is also very jealous of our company.* There should be no one with whom we converse so much as with Christ. To abide in Him only, this is true love. He would have us enjoy constant fellowship with Him, and many of the trials that come our way are for the purpose of weaning our hearts from others, and fixing them more closely on Him. This jealousy that would keep us near to Christ should be a comfort to us, for if He loves us so much as to care this much about *our* love, we may be sure that He will allow nothing to harm us, and will protect us from all our enemies. Oh, Christian, let us keep our hearts pure and for our Beloved alone!

As they pass through the Valley of Baca, they make it a place of springs; the autumn rains also cover it with pools (Psalm 84:6).

This teaches us that the comfort obtained by one may often prove useful to another,[1029] just as wells would be used by those who came after. We read a book full of consolation, which is like Jonathan's rod, dropping with honey.[1030] Many of them written mainly for the benefit of the authors but which proved quite as useful to others. We especially notice this in the Psalms, such as that beginning, "Why are you downcast, O my soul?"[1031] Travelers have been delighted to see the footprint of a person on a barren shore, and we love to see the evidence of pilgrims while passing through the vale of tears. Pilgrims dig the well, but, strangely enough, it fills from the top instead of the bottom. The well is dug with human hands, but heaven fills it with rain. "The horse is made ready for the day of battle, but victory rests with the LORD."[1032] The means are connected with the end, but they do not of themselves produce it. The rain fills the pools so that the wells become useful as reservoirs for the water. Labor isn't lost, but yet it doesn't supersede divine help. Grace may well be compared to rain for its purity, for its refreshing and vivifying influence, for it's coming alone from above, and for the sovereignty with which it's given or withheld. May you have showers of blessing, and may the wells you've dug be filled with water! Ways and means without the smile of heaven are as clouds without rain. May God open the windows of heaven and pour us out a blessing![1033]

There were also other boats with Him (Mark 4:36).

Jesus was the High Admiral of the sea that night, and His presence preserved the whole convoy. It's well to sail with Jesus, even though it's in a little boat. When we sail in Christ's company, we may not be sure of fair weather, for great storms may toss the vessel that carries the LORD Himself, and we mustn't expect to find the sea less rough around our little boat. If we go with Jesus we must be content to fare as He fares, and when the waves are rough to Him, they'll be rough to us. When the storm swept over Galilee all faces darkened and all hearts filled with dread. When all creature help was useless, the sleeping Savior arose, and with a word transformed the fury of the storm into a deep calm.[1034] Jesus is master of the sea; and though there's sorrow on the sea, when Jesus is on it there is joy, too. His Church is the Admiral's flagship, and He's the great attraction. Let's always follow in His wake, note His signals, steer by His chart, and never fear while He's within hailing distance. Not one ship in the convoy will be wrecked—the great Commodore will safely steer every ship to the desired haven.[1035] By faith we'll host our anchor for another day's cruise, and sail forth with Jesus into a sea of tribulation. Winds and waves won't spare us, but they'll obey Him. Therefore, whatever squalls may occur outside, faith will feel a blessed calm inside. Let's rejoice in Him. His vessel has reached the haven, and so will ours.

He will have no fear of bad news (Psalm 112:7).

Christian, you shouldn't dread the arrival of bad news, because if you're distressed by them, *how are you different from other people?* Others haven't your God to fly to. They've never proved His faithfulness as you have. It's no wonder if they're bowed down with alarm and cower in fear. But you profess to be of another spirit. You've been begotten again unto a lively hope,[1036] and your heart lives in heaven and not on earthly things. Now, if you're seen to be distracted as others, what's the value of that grace that you profess to have received? Where is the dignity of that new nature that you claim to possess? Again, if you're filled with alarm as others are, you will undoubtedly be led into the sins so common to others under trying circumstances. When the ungodly are overtaken by evil, they rebel against God. They murmur and complain and think that God deals harshly with them. Will you fall into that same sin?[1037] Will you provoke the LORD as they do?[1038] Moreover, unconverted people often run to wrong means in order to escape from difficulties, and you'll be sure to do the same if your mind yields to the same pressures. Trust in the LORD, and wait patiently for Him.[1039] Your wisest course is to do as Moses told the Israelites at the Red Sea, "stand still, and see the salvation of the LORD."[1040] If you doubt, will it glorify God? Take courage, and relying in sure confidence upon the faithfulness of your covenant God, "Let not your heart be troubled, neither let it be afraid."[1041]

☙ *September 16* ☜

Participate in the divine nature (2 Peter 1:4).

To be a participant of the divine nature is not, of course, to become God. That cannot be. The essence of Deity is not to be participated in by the creature. Between the creature and the Creator there's fixed a gulf that cannot be crossed. But as the first man Adam was made in the image of God, so in a yet diviner sense the renewal by the Holy Spirit made us in the image of Christ[1043] and participants of the divine nature. In Christ we're made like God. "God is love,"[1044] and we become love. "Everyone who loves has been born of God."[1045] God is truth, and we become true and love what is true. God is good,[1046] and He makes us good by His grace, so that we become the pure in heart who will see God.[1047] Further, we become members of the body of the divine person of Christ. The same blood that flows in the head flows in the hand, and the same life that makes Christ alive makes His people alive: "For you died, and your life is now hidden with Christ in God."[1048] One with Christ—so one with Him that the branch isn't more one with the vine than we're a part of our Savior! While we rejoice in this, let's remember that those who are made participants of the divine nature will manifest their holy relationship in their dealings with others, and make it evident by their daily walk and conversation that they've escaped the corruption that's in the world through evil desires.[1049] O for more holiness of life!

⊰ September 17 ⊱

Bring the boy to Me (Mark 9:19).

The disappointed father turned from the disciples to their Master. His son was in the worst possible condition, and all means had failed. But the possessed child was soon delivered from the evil spirit when the parent in faith obeyed the LORD Jesus' word, "Bring the boy to Me." Children are a precious gift from God, but a great deal of anxiety comes with them. They may be a great joy or a great bitterness to their parents. They may be filled with God's Spirit or possessed by an evil spirit. In all cases, the Word of God gives us one receipt for curing their ills, "Bring the boy to Me." We need more agonizing prayer on their behalf while they're still babes! Sin is there, so let our prayers attack it. Our cries for our children should precede those cries that result from their entrance into a world of sin. When they're young, we will see sad signs of that dumb and deaf spirit that will neither pray properly nor hear God's voice in the soul—but Jesus still commands, "Bring the boy to Me." When they're grown up they may wallow in sin and rage with hatred against God. Yet when our hearts are breaking we should remember the great Physician's words, "Bring the boy to Me." We must not stop praying until they stop breathing. No case is hopeless with Christ.[1050] Whatever our need may be, let it carry us like a strong current to the ocean of divine love. Christ can soon remove our sorrow, so let's hurry to Him—He waits for us.

Since we live by the Spirit, let us keep in step with the Spirit (Galatians 5:25).

The two most important things in our holy religion are the *life of faith* and the *walk of faith*. True faith is always by true godliness, and there is never a truly holy life that isn't rooted in a living faith in the righteousness of Christ. There are some who cultivate faith and forget holiness. They are high in orthodoxy, but will be very deep in condemnation, for they "suppress the truth in unrighteousness."[1051] There are others who have strained after holiness of life, but have denied the faith, like the Pharisees of old whom Jesus said were "whitewashed tombs."[1052] We must have faith, for this is the foundation. We must have holiness of life, for this is the superstructure. Of what service is the mere foundation of a building to people on a day that storms come? Can they hide themselves in it? They need a house to cover them, as well as a foundation for that house. Even so we need the superstructure of spiritual life if we would have comfort in the day of doubt. But don't seek a holy life without faith, for that would be to erect a house that can give no permanent shelter, because its foundation isn't built on a rock.[1053] Let the life of faith and the walk of faith be put together, and like the two abutments of an arch they'll make our godliness enduring. Like the two pillars of the temple, they're for glory and for beauty. They're two streams from the fountain of grace, two lamps lit with holy fire, two olive trees watered by heavenly care.

≈ *September 19* ≈

It is for freedom that Christ has set us free
(Galatians 5:1).

This freedom makes us free to have everything in the Bible. Here's a choice passage, believer, "When you pass through the waters, I will be with you."[1054] You're free to have that. Here's another: "Though the mountains be shaken and the hills be removed, yet my unfailing love for you will not be shaken."[1055] You're free to have that. You're a welcome guest at the table of the promises. Scripture is a never-failing treasury filled with boundless stores of grace. It's the bank of heaven, and you may draw from it as much as you please. Come in faith and you're welcome to all covenant blessings. There's not a promise in the Word that will be withheld. In the depths of tribulations let this freedom comfort you. In the middle of distress let it cheer you. When sorrows surround you let it be your consolation. You're also free to go to the throne of grace. It's the believer's privilege to have access at all times to His heavenly Father.[1056] Whatever our desires, difficulties, or needs, we are free to spread all before Him. It doesn't matter how much we may have sinned, we may ask and expect pardon. How poor we are signifies nothing, we may plead His promise that He will provide all our needs.[1057] Exercise your right, believer, and live up to your privilege. You are free to all of God's glorious riches in Christ— wisdom, righteousness, sanctification, redemption—every need spiritual and material. It matters not what you need, for there is a fullness of supply in Christ, and it is there for you.

"A sword for the LORD and for Gideon!"
(Judges 7:20)

Gideon ordered his men to do two things. First, cover up a torch in an earthen pitcher,[1058] and at an appointed signal break the pitcher and let the light shine. Second, blow their trumpets and cry out, "A sword for the LORD and for Gideon!, "A sword for the LORD and for Gideon!" This is precisely what all Christians must do. First, break the pitcher that conceals your light—throw aside the basket that's been hiding your candle—and shine.[1059] Let your light shine before people.[1060] Let your good works be such, that when people look at you, they'll know you've been with Jesus.[1061] Second, blow the trumpet, sound the gospel call. There must be active exertions for the ingathering of sinners by proclaiming Christ crucified. Take the gospel to sinners—carry it to their door, put it in their way, don't allow them to escape it. Remember that the Church's true call for action is Gideon's watchword, *"A sword for the LORD and for Gideon!"* God must do it, it's His work. But we mustn't be idle. We're God's instruments: "A sword for the LORD and for Gideon!" If we only cry, "A sword for the LORD!" we'll be guilty of idle presumption, and if we shout, "A sword for Gideon!" alone, we'll manifest idolatrous reliance on an arm of flesh. We must blend the two in practical harmony, "A sword for the LORD and for Gideon!" We can do nothing by ourselves, but we can do everything with the help of our God. Let us go, therefore, in Christ's name, and God will be with us.

I will rejoice in doing them good (Jeremiah 32:41).

The delight that God has in His saints should cheer our hearts. We can't see any reason in ourselves why the LORD should take pleasure in us. We can't take delight in ourselves, for we're often burdened with consciousness of our sinfulness and unfaithfulness. We are afraid also that God's people can't take much delight in us, for they must see so much of our imperfections and foolishness that they grieve over our failings rather than admire our graces. So we love to dwell upon this transcendent truth—this glorious mystery—that as the bridegroom rejoices over the bride, so does the LORD rejoice over us.[1062] We don't read anywhere that God delights in the cloud-capped mountains or the sparkling stars, but we do read that He rejoices in His whole world and delights in people.[1063] In what strong language He expresses His delight in His people! Who could have conceived of the eternal One as bursting forth into a song? Yet it is written, "He will take great delight in you, He will quiet you with his love, He will rejoice over you with singing."[1064] As He looked upon the world He had made, He said, "It is very good."[1065] But when He beheld those who were purchased by Jesus' blood,[1066] His own chosen ones,[1067] it seemed as if the great heart of the Infinite could restrain itself no longer, but overflowed in divine exclamations of joy. Shouldn't we proclaim our grateful response to such a marvelous declaration of His love, and sing, "I will rejoice in the LORD, I will be joyful in God my Savior!"[1068]

Let Israel rejoice in their Maker (Psalm 149:2).

Be glad of heart, believer, but be certain your gladness has its source in the LORD. You have many reasons for being glad in your God, for you can sing with David, "God, my joy and my delight."[1069] Rejoice that He sits upon the throne, and rules everything. Every attribute of God should become a fresh ray in the sunlight of our gladness. Knowing He is wise should make us glad, considering our own foolishness. Knowing He is *mighty* should make us rejoice when we tremble at our weakness. Knowing He is everlasting should always be a theme of joy when we know that we wither as the grass.[1070] Knowing He is *unchanging* should always make us sing, since we change every hour. Knowing He is full of grace, that He overflows with it, and that He has given it to us in the New Covenant should make us glad in Him. This gladness in God is as a deep river. So far we've only touched its surface. We know a little of its clear, sweet, heavenly streams. But forward the depth is greater, and the current swift with sudden joy. The Psalms show us that in ancient times God's people were in the habit of thinking about God's actions and having a song for each of them. So let God's people today rehearse the deeds of the LORD! Let them tell of His mighty acts, and "sing to the LORD, For He has triumphed gloriously!"[1071] They should never stop singing, for as new mercies come to them each day their gladness should show itself in continued thanksgiving.

⇗ *September 23* ⇖

He chose us in Him before the foundation of the world,
that we should be holy and without blame before Him
in love, having predestined us to adoption as sons by
Jesus Christ to Himself, according to the good pleasure
of His will, to the praise of the glory of His grace,
by which He has made us accepted in the Beloved
(Ephesians 1:4-6).

This includes our *justification* before God, but the term
"accepted" in the Greek means more than that. It means
we're highly favored, endued with special honor. How
marvelous that we sinners should be highly favored! But
it's only *"in the Beloved."* Some Christians seem to think
they're accepted by their own experiences. When their
souls are cheerful, they think God accepts them, for they
feel so heavenly-minded! But when their souls cleave to
the dust, they fear they're no longer accepted. All their
cheerfulness doesn't exalt them, however, and all their
despondency doesn't lower them in God's sight. They're
accepted in One who never changes,[1072] in One who is
always the Beloved of God, and always without spot or
wrinkle.[1073] How much happier they would be if they would
understand this. Rejoice then, believer, you're accepted "in
the Beloved." You look within yourself and say, "There is
nothing acceptable *here*!" But look at Christ, and see that
everything is acceptable *there*. Your sins trouble you, but
God has cast your sins behind His back.[1074] You do have
to fight corruption and wrestle with temptation, but you're
already accepted in Him who has overcome the devil. Even
glorified souls in heaven aren't more accepted than you
are. They're only accepted in heaven "in the Beloved," and
you're even now accepted in Christ in the same way.

◁ *September 24* ▷

*"I was ashamed to ask the king for soldiers and
horsemen to protect us from enemies on the road,
because we had told the king, "The gracious hand of
our God is on everyone who looks to Him, but His great
anger is against all who forsake Him" (Ezra 8:22).*

There were many reasons why an armed escort for the
pilgrims would have been desirable, but Ezra would not
ask for one. He was afraid that the heathen king would
think his professions of faith in God were mere hypocrisy,
or that the God of Israel wasn't able to preserve His own
worshippers. He couldn't bring his mind to lean on an arm
of flesh[1075] in a matter so evidently of the Lord. Therefore
the caravan set out guarded only by Him who is the sword
and shield of His people.[1076] Few believers seem to feel
this holy jealousy for God. Even those who in a measure
walk by faith, occasionally mar the luster of their life
by craving help from people. It's a most blessed thing to
have no support but the Lord alone. Would any believers
seek state or federal endowments for their church if they
remembered that the Lord is dishonored by their asking
Caesar's aid? By so doing, they imply that the Lord can't
supply the needs of His own cause! Would we run so hastily
to others for assistance if we remembered that the Lord is
magnified by our implicit reliance upon His solitary arm?
"But," says one, "aren't human resources to be used?"
Certainly, but our fault seldom lies in their neglect. Far
more frequently it springs out of foolishly believing in them
instead of believing in God. Few neglect human resources,
but many sin greatly in making too much of them.

❧ *September 25* ❧

To be just and the One who justifies those who have faith (Romans 3:26).

Being justified by faith, we have peace with God. Conscience no longer accuses.[1078] Judgment now decides for us instead of against us. Memory looks back upon past sins with deep sorrow for the sin, but with no dread of any penalty to come. Christ has paid the debt of His people to the smallest sin, and received the divine receipt. Unless God can be so unjust as to demand double payment for one debt, no soul for whom Jesus died as a substitute can ever be cast into hell. It seems to be one of the very principles of our enlightened nature to believe that God is just. We feel that it must be so, and this causes us terror at first, but afterward this very same belief that God is just becomes the foundation of our confidence and peace! If God is just, I, a sinner, standing alone must be punished. But Jesus takes my place and is punished for me. And now, if God is just, I, a sinner, standing in Christ, can never be punished. God would have to change His nature before one soul for whom Jesus was a substitute could possibly suffer the lash of the law. My hope lives not because I am not a sinner, but because I am a sinner for whom Christ died. My trust is not that I am holy, but that being unholy, He is my righteousness.[1079] My faith rests not upon what *I am*, but in what *Christ is*, in what He has done, and in what He is now doing for me.

The myrtle trees in a ravine (Zechariah 1:8).

The vision in this chapter describes the condition of Israel in Zechariah's day, but it equally describes Christ's Church as we find it now in the world. The Church is compared to a myrtle grove flourishing in a ravine. It's hidden, unobserved, secreted. It pursues no honor and draws no consideration from the unconcerned observer. The Church has a glory but it's concealed from carnal eyes, for the time of its breaking forth in all its splendor has not come yet. The idea of tranquil security is also suggested to us, for the myrtle grove in the ravine is still and calm while the storm sweeps over the mountain summits. The inward tranquility of God's Church is great! Even when opposed and persecuted, it has a peace that the world doesn't give,[1080] and which, therefore, it can't take away. The peace of God that transcends all understanding guards the hearts and minds of God's people.[1081] The metaphor forcibly pictures the peaceful and perpetual growth of the saints. The myrtle doesn't shed its leaves, it's always green, and the Church in its worst times still has a blessed vigorous condition of grace about it. Sometimes it exhibited the most vigorous condition when its winter was sharpest. It's prospered most when its adversities have been severest. The myrtle is also the emblem of peace, and a significant token of triumph. The brows of conquerors were bound with myrtle and with laurel, and the Church is always victorious. Every Christian is more than a conqueror through Him who loves us.[1082] Living in peace, we fall asleep in the arms of victory.

September 27

Blessed are you, O Israel! Who is like you, a people saved by the LORD? (Deuteronomy 33:29)

The person who believes that Christianity makes people miserable is a complete stranger to it. It were strange indeed if it made us wretched, since it exalts us to such a grand position. It makes us children of God.[1083] Do you suppose that God will give all the happiness to His enemies, and reserve all the mourning for His own family? Will His foes have gladness and joy, and His Spirit-born children[1084] inherit sorrow and wretchedness? No, we will rejoice in the LORD always,[1085] and glory in our inheritance, for we "did not receive a spirit that makes you a slave again to fear, but you received the Spirit of sonship. And by Him we cry, "Abba, Father."[1086] The rod of chastisement is applied to us according to what we need, but it works for us the comfortable fruits of righteousness.[1087] Therefore, by the aid of the divine Comforter, we who are the "people saved by the LORD" will joy in the God of our salvation.[1088] We are married to Christ; and our great Bridegroom won't permit His spouse to remain in constant grief. Even though we may suffer for a while as He once suffered, we are even now blessed with heavenly blessings in Him. We have the earnest of our inheritance in the comforts of the Spirit, which are neither few nor small—but are foretastes of our share. Our riches are beyond the sea. Gleams of glory from the spirit-world cheer our hearts, and urge us onward. Truly it's said of us, "Blessed are you! Who is like you, a people saved by the LORD?"

September 28

From heaven the LORD looks down and sees all mankind (Psalm 33:13).

Perhaps no figure of speech represents the LORD in a more gracious light than when He's spoken of as looking down from heaven to attend to the needs and distresses of humanity. We love Him who would not destroy the iniquity-filled cities of Sodom and Gomorrah until He had personally visited them.[1089] We can't help pouring out our heart in affection for our LORD who inclines His ear from the highest glory, and puts it to the lip of the dying sinner whose failing heart longs for reconciliation. How can we but love Him when we know that He numbers the very hairs of our heads,[1090] marks our path, and orders our ways? This great truth is especially brought near to our heart when we recollect how attentive He is, not merely to the temporal interests of His creatures, but to their spiritual concerns. Though leagues of distance lie between the finite creature and the infinite Creator, yet there are links uniting both. When a tear is wept by you, don't think God doesn't see it, "As a father has compassion on his children, so the LORD has compassion on those who fear Him."[1091] Your sigh is able to move the heart of Jehovah. Your whisper can incline His ear to you, your prayer can stay His hand, and your faith can move His arm. Don't think God sits on high and doesn't consider you. No matter how poor and needy you are, the LORD thinks about you. "For the eyes of the LORD range throughout the earth to strengthen those whose hearts are fully committed to Him."[1092]

If the disease has covered his whole body, he shall pronounce that person clean (Leviticus 13:13).

This regulation sounds strange, yet there was wisdom in it, for the throwing out of the disease proved that the constitution was sound. This morning it may be well for us to consider the typical teaching of so remarkable a rule. We, too, are lepers, and may read the law of leper as applicable to ourselves. When sinners see themselves to be altogether lost and ruined, covered all over with the defilement of sin, and plead guilty before the LORD, then they are made clean through the blood of Jesus and the grace of God. Hidden, unfelt, unconfessed sin is the true leprosy, but when sin is seen and felt it's received its death blow, and the LORD looks with eyes of mercy upon the soul afflicted with it. Nothing is more deadly than self-righteousness, or more hopeful than contrition. We must confess that we are "nothing else but sin," for no confession short of this will be the whole truth, and if the Holy Spirit is at work with us, convincing us of sin,[1093] there'll be no difficulty about making such an acknowledgment—it will spring spontaneously from our lips. Sin mourned and confessed, however black and foul, will never shut a person out from the LORD Jesus. Whoever comes to Him, He will in no way cast out.[1094] Though dishonest as the thief,[1095] though unchaste as the woman who was a sinner,[1096] though rebellious as the prodigal,[1097] the great heart of love will look upon those who feel they have no righteousness in themselves, and will pronounce them clean, when they trust in Jesus Christ crucified.[1098]

Sing the glory of His name; make His praise glorious! (Psalm 66:2)

It's not left up to us as to whether or not we'll praise God. Praise belongs to God, and as the recipient of His grace every Christian should praise God every day. It's true we have no authoritative rule for daily praise, and no commandment prescribing certain hours of song and thanksgiving, but the law written upon the heart teaches us that it is right to praise God.[1099] The unwritten mandate comes to us with as much force as if it had been recorded on the tables of stone, or handed to us from the top of thundering Sinai. Yes, it is the *duty* of Christians to praise God. It's not only a pleasurable exercise, but it's the absolute obligation of our lives. Don't think that you who are always mourning are guiltless in this respect, or imagine that you can discharge your duty to your God without songs of praise. You're bound by the bonds of His love to bless His name so long as you live. His praise should always be in your mouth,[1100] for you're blessed so that you may bless Him: "the people I formed for Myself that they may proclaim My praise."[1101] If you don't praise God, you're not bringing forth the fruit that He has a right to expect at your hands.[1102] Arise and sing His praise. With every morning's dawn, lift up your notes of thanksgiving, and let every setting sun be followed with your song. Encircle the earth with your praises, surround it with an atmosphere of melody, and God Himself will listen from heaven and accept your music.

October

≈ October 1 ≈

Every delicacy, both new and old, that I have stored up for you, my lover (Song of Songs 7:13).

The spouse desires to give Jesus all that she produces. Our heart has "every delicacy, both old and new," and they are laid up for our Beloved. At this rich autumn season of fruit, let's survey our stores. We have *new* fruits. We want to feel new life, new joy, new gratitude. We want to make new resolves and carry them out by new labors. Our heart blossoms with new prayers, and our soul is pledging itself to new efforts. But we have some *old* fruits too. There's our first love—a choice fruit that Jesus delights it! There's our first faith—that simple faith by which, having nothing, we became possessors of all things. There's our joy when we first knew the LORD—let's revive it. We have our old memories of the promises. How faithful has God been! His mercies have been more than the hairs of our head. Old sins we must regret, but then we repented and wept our way to the Cross and learned the merit of His blood. We have fruits this morning, both new and old. But here's the point—*they are all laid up for Jesus*. Let our many fruits be laid up only for our Beloved. Let us display them when He is with us, and not hold them up before the eyes of others. Jesus, we will turn the key in our garden door, and no one will enter to rob You of one good fruit from the soil that You have watered with Your bloody sweat.[1103] Our all will be Yours—Yours only, O Jesus, our Beloved!

⊲ October 2 ⊳

The hope that is stored up for you in heaven
(Colossians 1:5).

Our hope in Christ for the future is the motivating force of our joy here. It animates our hearts to think often of heaven, for all that we desire is promised there. Here we're weary and worn, but heaven is the land of *rest* where fatigue will be banished forever. To those who are weary and spent, the word *rest* is full of heaven. We're always in the field of battle—tempted internally, and so molested by foes externally that we have little peace. But in heaven we'll enjoy the victory, and we'll hear our Captain say, "Well done, good and faithful servant."[1104] We've suffered multiple bereavements, but we're going to the land of the *immortal* where graves are unknown. Here sin is a constant grief to us, but there we'll be perfectly *holy*, for nothing will enter that kingdom that can defile us. What a joy that you aren't to be in banishment forever, that you're not to dwell eternally in this wilderness, but will soon inherit Canaan! Nevertheless, let it never be said of us that we're dreaming about the *future* and forgetting the *present*—let the future sanctify the present to its highest uses. Through the Spirit of God the hope of heaven is the most potent force for holiness. Those who have this hope in them go about their work with vigor, for the joy of the LORD is their strength. They fight against temptation with enthusiasm, for the hope of the next world repels the flaming arrows of the adversary.[1105] They labor without reward, for their reward is in the world to come.

⊰ *October 3* ⊱

Are not all angels ministering spirits sent to serve those who will inherit salvation? (Hebrews 1:14)

Angels are the unseen attendants of the saints of God—they bear us up in their hands, lest we strike our foot against a stone.[1106] Loyalty to their LORD leads them to take a deep interest in the children of His love. They rejoice over the return of the prodigal to his father's house below,[1107] and they welcome the advent of the believer to the King's palace above. In ancient times the children of God were favored with their visible appearance, and in this day, although unseen by us, heaven is still opened. The angels of God ascend and descend upon the Son of man,[1108] that they may visit the heirs of salvation. Seraphim still fly with live coals from off the altar to touch the lips of those greatly beloved.[1109] If our eyes could be opened, we would see horses of fire and chariots of fire about the servants of the LORD,[1110] for we have come to an innumerable company of angels,[1111] who are all watchers and protectors of the royal seed. Imagine the dignity to which the chosen are elevated when the brilliant attendants of heaven become their willing servants! What a communion we raised into since we have communication with spotless celestials! How well we are defended since the chariots of God are armed for our deliverance! To whom do we owe all this? Let the LORD Jesus Christ be forever endeared to us, for through Him we are made to sit in heavenly places far above principalities and powers.[1112] It's His camp that is round about them that fear Him.[1113] All hail, Jesus!

October 4

When evening comes, there will be light
(Zechariah 14:7).

We often look forward with anxiety to *the time of old age.* But to many saints, old age is the choicest season in their lives. The pilgrims have reached Beulah land,[1114] that happy country whose days are as the days of heaven upon earth. Angels visit it, celestial gales blow over it, flowers of paradise grow in it, and the air is filled with seraphic music. Some dwell here for years, and others come to it but a few hours before their departure, but it's an Eden on earth. We may well long for the time when we'll recline in its shady groves and be satisfied with hope until the time of fruition comes. The setting sun seems larger than it does at midday, and a splendor of glory tinges all the clouds that surround its going down. Pain doesn't disturb the calm of the sweet twilight of age, for strength made perfect in weakness[1115] bears up with patience under it all. Ripe fruits of choice experience are gathered as the rare feast of life's evening, and the soul prepares itself for rest. The LORD's people will also enjoy light in the hour of death. Unbelief grieves, the shadows fall, night is coming, existence is ending. No, cries faith, the night is far spent,[1116] true day is at hand. Light is come—the light of immortality, the light of a Father's countenance. Gather up your feet in the bed, see the waiting bands of spirits! Angels carry you away. The pearly gates open, the golden streets shine in the jasper light.[1117] Now you have light in the evening.

∗∂ *October 5* ∗∂

He got up and ate and drank. Strengthened by that
food, he traveled forty days and forty nights
(1 Kings 19:8).

All the strength supplied to us by our gracious God is meant for service, not for immorality or boasting. When the prophet Elijah found the cake baked on the coals and the cruse of water, it wasn't so he could eat and take his rest. It was to give him strength to travel forty days and forty nights to Horeb, the mount of God. Jesus invited His disciples to "Come and eat" with Him.[1118] After the meal, He said to Peter, "Feed My sheep,"[1119] and then added, "Follow Me."[1120] So it is with us. We eat the bread of heaven.[1121] that we may use our strength in the Master's service. Many Christians are all for living *on* Christ, but aren't so anxious to live *for* Christ. Earth is a preparation for heaven, and heaven is where saints feast most and work most. They sit at the table of our LORD, and they serve Him day and night in His temple.[1122] They eat of heavenly food and render perfect service. Believer, work for Christ in the strength you daily receive from Him. Some of us have yet to learn much concerning the design of our LORD in giving us His grace. We're not to hold the precious grains of truth for ourselves, we are to sow and water them. Why does the LORD send the rain down upon the thirsty earth, and give the warm sunshine? It's to enable the fruits of the earth to yield food for humanity. Even so the LORD feeds our souls that we may afterwards use our renewed strength to promote His glory.

❧ *October 6* ☙

Whoever drinks the water I give him will never thirst (John 4:14).

Believers in Jesus find enough in the LORD to satisfy them now and keep them content forever. Believers aren't people whose days are weary for comfort, and nights are long without cheerful thought. They find in Christ such a spring of joy, such a foundation of consolation, that they're content and happy. Put them in a dungeon, and they'll find good company. Place them in a barren wilderness, and they'll eat the bread from heaven.[1123] Drive them away from friendship, and they'll meet the friend that sticks closer than a brother.[1124] Sap the foundation of their earthly hopes, and their hearts will still be fixed, trusting in the LORD. Their heart is as insatiable as a grave until Christ enters it, and then it's a cup full to overflowing. There's such a fullness in Christ that He alone is everything to the believer. True saints are so satisfied with the all-sufficiency of Christ that they thirst only for deeper drinks of the living water.[1125] Someone said, "I've been sinking my bucket down into the well often, but now my thirst for Christ has become so great that I long to put the well itself to my lips and drink forever." Is this the feeling in your heart? Do you feel that all your desires are satisfied in Christ, and that you have no need now but to know more of Him, and have closer communion with Him? Then come continually to the fountain, and take of the water of life freely.[1126] Christ will never think you take too much, but will always welcome you, saying, "Drink, drink abundantly."[1127]

"Why have you brought this trouble on your servant? (Numbers 11:11)

Our heavenly Father often sends us troubles *to test our faith*. If our faith be worth anything, it will stand the test. It's a poor faith that can only trust God when friends are true, the body healthy, and work or business prospers. True faith holds by the LORD's faithfulness when friends are gone, when the body is sick, when spirits are depressed, and the light of our Father's countenance is hidden. A faith that can say in the worst trouble, "Though He slay me, yet will I trust Him,"[1128] is heaven-born faith. The LORD is greatly glorified in the virtues of His people, which are His own handiwork. When "suffering produces perseverance; perseverance, character; and character, hope,"[1129] the LORD is honored by these growing virtues. We would never know the music of the harp if the strings were left untouched, or enjoy the juice of the grape if it wasn't trodden in the winepress, or discover the sweet perfume of cinnamon if it wasn't pressed and beaten; or feel the warmth of fire if the wood wasn't totally consumed. The wisdom and power of the great Workman are discovered by the trials through which His vessels of mercy are permitted to pass. Present afflictions *heighten future joy*. There must be night to bring out the beauty of the day. We would not be so supremely blessed in heaven if we hadn't known the curse of sin and the sorrow of earth. Peace will be sweeter after conflict, and rest more welcome after toil. The recollection of past sufferings will enhance the bliss of the glorified.

≈ *October 8* ≈

"Put out into deep water, and let down the nets for a catch" (Luke 5:4).

We learn from this narrative, *the necessity of human means*. The catch of fish was miraculous, yet neither the fisherman nor his boat nor his fishing tackle were ignored, but all were used to take the fishes. Similarly, God works by means in saving souls. While the present grace stands, God will be pleased by the foolishness of preaching to save them that believe.[1130] When God works without means, doubtless He is glorified, but He has Himself selected the plan of using means as being that by which He is most magnified in the earth. *Means by themselves are totally useless.* "Master, we've worked hard all night and haven't caught anything."[1131] What was the reason of this? They were experienced fisherman and understood the work. Had they lacked perseverance? No, they had *toiled all the night*. Was there a lack of fish in the sea? Certainly not, for as soon as the Master came, they swam to the net in large groups. What, then, is the reason? It's because there's no power in the means themselves without the presence of Christ. Without Him we can do nothing,[1132] but with Him we can do everything.[1133] *Christ's presence confers success*. Jesus sat in Peter's boat, and by His will drew the fish to the net. When Jesus is lifted up in His Church, His presence is the Church's power—"I, when I am lifted up from the earth, will draw all men to myself."[1134] If we lift up Jesus Christ in our work of soul fishing, we won't work in vain, for He will fill our nets with fishes.

October 9

Able to keep you from falling (Jude 24).

In some sense the path to heaven is very safe, but in other respects there's *no road so dangerous.* It's filled with difficulties. One false step (and how easy it is to take that if grace is absent), and down we go. What a slippery path it is that some of us have to tread! Many times we've had to exclaim with the Psalmist, "my feet had almost slipped; I had nearly lost my foothold."[1135] If we were strong, sure-footed, mountaineers, this wouldn't matter so much—but *how weak we are in ourselves!* On the best roads we soon falter, on the smoothest paths we quickly stumble. These weak knees[1136] of ours can scarcely support our tottering weight. We're mere children tremblingly taking our first steps in the walk of faith—our heavenly Father holds us by the arms or we would soon fall. Oh, if we're kept from falling, how we must bless the patient power that watches over us day by day. Think how prone we are to sin, how strong our tendency to cast ourselves down, and these thoughts will make us sing more sweetly than we've ever done, "Glory to him who is able to keep you from falling."[1137] We have many foes who try to push us down. Enemies lurk in ambush, rush out when we least expect them, and try to trip us or hurl us down the nearest cliff. Only an Almighty arm can preserve us from these unseen foes who are trying to destroy us. He is faithful who has promised,[1138] and is able to keep us from falling.[1139]

Before His glorious presence without fault (Jude 24).

Think about that wonderful phrase, *"without fault."* We're far off from it now, but since our LORD never stops short of perfection in His work of love, we'll reach it one day. The Savior who will keep His people to the end, will also present them at last to Himself, "as a radiant church, without stain or wrinkle or any other blemish, but holy and blameless." All the jewels in the Savior's crown are of the highest quality and without flaw. But how will Jesus make us without fault? He'll wash us from our sins in His own blood[111140] until we're white and fair as God's purest angel. We'll be clothed in His righteousness[1141]—righteousness that makes the saint who wear it positively without fault, perfect in the sight of God. We'll be blameless and unreproveable even in His eyes. His law will not only have no charge against us, but it'll be magnified in us. Moreover, the work of the Holy Spirit within us will be altogether complete. He'll make us so perfectly holy we'll have no lingering tendency to sin. We'll be holy even as God is holy, and we'll live in His presence forever. Saints won't be out of place in heaven, their beauty will be as great as that of the place prepared for them. Oh, the rapture of that hour when the everlasting doors will be lifted up, and we who have been made fit for the inheritance, will live with the saints in light. Sin gone, Satan shut out, temptation past forever, and we ourselves "without fault" before God—that's heaven indeed!

✂ *October 11* ✄

Let us lift up our hearts and our hands to
God in heaven (Lamentations 3:41).

Praying teaches us our unworthiness, which is a very healthy lesson for proud beings like us. If God gave us favors without compelling us to pray for them, we would never know how poor we are. True prayer is an inventory of wants, a catalogue of necessities, and a revelation of hidden poverty. While it's an application to divine wealth, it's a confession of human emptiness. The most healthy state of a Christian is to be always empty in self and constantly depending upon the LORD for supplies, always poor in self and rich in Jesus, and weak as water personally but mighty through God to do great exploits. Thus the need for prayer that lays the creature where it should be—in the dust before God. Prayer in itself is a great benefit to the Christian. As the runner gains strength for the race by daily exercise, so for the great race of life we acquire energy by prayer. Prayer plumes the wings of God's young eaglets, that they may learn to mount above the clouds.[1142] Prayer armors God's warriors with righteousness and sends them forth to combat.[1143] Prayer is the uplifted hand of Moses that routs the Amalekites more than the sword of Joshua.[1144] It's the arrow shot from the prophet chamber's foreboding defeat to the Syrians.[1145] Prayer girds human weakness with divine strength, turns human folly into heavenly wisdom, and gives to troubled mortals the peace of God. We don't know what prayer cannot do! Thank you, God, for the throne of grace where we receive mercy and help.[1146] Help us to pray this day!

☙ October 12 ❧

*I meditate on Your precepts and consider
Your ways (Psalm 119:15).*

There are times when solitude is better than society, and silence is wiser than speech. We should be better Christians if we were more alone, waiting upon God, and gathering through meditation on His Word spiritual strength for labor in His service. We should meditate upon the things of God, because that way we get the real nourishment out of them. Truth is like the cluster of the vine. If we want the juice from it, we must press and squeeze it many times. Similarly, by meditation we must press and squeeze the clusters of truth if we would get the juice of consolation from them. Our bodies aren't supported by merely taking food into the mouth. The process that really supplies our muscles, nerves, sinews, and bones is the process of digestion. It's by digestion that the outward food becomes assimilated with the inner life. Our souls aren't nourished merely by listening awhile to this and then to that and then to the other part of divine truth. Hearing, reading, marking, and learning, all require inward digesting to complete their usefulness, and the inward digesting of the truth lies for the most part in meditating upon it. Why is it that some Christians, although they hear many sermons, make such slow advances in the divine life? Because they neglect their prayer closets and don't thoughtfully meditate on God's Word. The fruit hangs upon the tree but they won't pick it, the water flows at their feet but they won't stoop to drink it. LORD, deliver us from such foolishness as we resolve to meditate upon Your Word.[1147]

October 13

Godly sorrow brings repentance (2 Corinthians 7:10).

Genuine repentance for sin is the work of the Holy Spirit.[1148] Repentance is too choice a flower to grow in nature's garden. Pearls grow naturally in oysters, but penitence never shows itself in sinners unless divine grace works it in them. If you've one particle of real hatred for sin, God must have given it to you. "Flesh gives birth to flesh."[1149] True repentance has a distinct reference to the Savior. When we repent of sin, we must have one eye upon sin and another upon the Cross. But it'll be even better if we fix both our eyes upon Christ and see our transgressions only in the light of His love. True sorrow for sin is eminently practical. None say they hate sin if they live in it. Repentance makes us see the evil of sin, not merely as a theory but experimentally—we will fear it as much as a burnt child fears fire. True mourning for sin will make us be very careful with our tongue, lest we say a wrong word,[1150] and we will be very watchful of our daily actions, lest in anything we offend. Each night we'll close the day with painful confessions of our shortcoming, and each morning awaken with anxious prayers that this day God will help us not to sin against Him. Sincere repentance is continual. Believers repent until their dying day. Every other sorrow yields to time, but sorrow for sin grows with our growth, and it's so sweet a bitterness that we thank God we're permitted to enjoy and to suffer it until we enter our eternal rest.

✍ *October 14* ✎

I consider everything a loss compared to the surpassing greatness of knowing Christ Jesus my LORD *(Philippians 3:8).*

Spiritual knowledge of Christ will be a *personal* knowledge. I cannot know Christ through another person's acquaintance with Him. No, I must know Him *myself.* It'll be an *intelligent* knowledge. I must know *Him*, not as the visionary dreams of Him, but as the Word reveals Him. I must know His natures, divine and human. I must know His offices, attributes, works, shame, and glory. I must meditate upon Him until I "have power, together with all the saints, to grasp how wide and long and high and deep is the love of Christ, and to know this love that surpasses knowledge."[1151] It'll be an *affectionate* knowledge of Him—if I know Him at all, I must love Him. An ounce of heart knowledge is worth a ton of head learning. Our knowledge of Him will be a *satisfying* knowledge. When I know my Savior, my mind will be full to the brim—I'll feel that I have what my spirit panted after.[1152] At the same time it will be an *exciting* knowledge—the more I know of my Beloved, the more I'll want to know. I'll want more as I get more. Like the miser's treasure, my gold will make me covet more. To conclude. This knowledge of Christ Jesus will be a most *happy* one. In fact, it'll be so elevating that sometimes it will completely bear me up above all trials, doubts, and sorrows, and will fling about me the immortality of the ever-living Savior, and gird me with the golden belt of His eternal joy. Sit today at Jesus' feet and learn about Him.[1153]

⊰ October 15 ⊱

But who can endure the day of his coming?
(Malachi 3:2)

His first coming was without external pomp or show of power, and yet there were few who could abide its testing might. Herod and all Jerusalem with him were stirred at the news of the wondrous birth. Those who supposed themselves to be waiting for Him, showed the fallacy of their professions by rejecting Him when He came. But what will His second advent be? What sinner can endure to think of it? "He will strike the earth with the rod of His mouth; with the breath of His lips He will slay the wicked." His death shook earth[1155] and darkened heaven.[1156] What will be the dreadful splendor of that day in which, as the living Savior and Judge, He will summon the living and the dead before Him? Oh, that the terrors of the LORD would persuade people to forsake their sins and kiss the Son, lest He be angry![1157] Though a lamb, He is still the lion of the tribe of Judah,[1158] rending the prey in pieces. Although He does not break the bruised reed, He will still break His enemies with a rod of iron, and dash them in pieces like a potter's vessel.[1159] None of His enemies will bear up before the fury of His wrath, or hide themselves from the sweeping hail of His indignation. But His beloved blood-washed people[1160] look for His appearing with love and joy,[1161] and hope to witness it without fear. Let us search ourselves this morning and make our calling and election sure,[1162] so that the coming of the LORD may cause no dark forebodings in our mind.

⊰ *October 16* ⊱

Jesus said to them, "Come and have breakfast"
(John 21:12).

In these words the believer is invited to *a holy nearness to Jesus*. "Come and have breakfast," implies the same table, the same meat. Sometimes it even means to sit side by side, and lean our head upon the Savior's chest. "Come and have breakfast," gives us a vision of *union with Jesus*, because the only food we can feast upon when we dine with Jesus is *Himself*. Oh, what union this is! It's a depth that reason cannot fathom, that we feed upon Jesus. "Whoever eats My flesh and drinks My blood remains in me, and I in him." It is also an invitation to enjoy *companionship with the saint*s. Christians may differ on a variety of points, but they have all one spiritual appetite. If we can't all *feel* alike, we can all *feed* alike on the bread of life sent down from heaven. Get nearer to Jesus, and you'll find yourself linked more and more in spirit to all who are like yourself. If we were nearer to Christ we would be nearer to each other. We also see in these words the *source of strength* for every Christian. To look at Christ is to live, but for strength to serve Him you must "come and have breakfast." We labor in unnecessary weakness because of neglecting this percept of the Master. We should fatten on the marrow and fatness of the gospel so we may accumulate strength from it. Therefore, if you want *nearness* to Jesus, *union* with Jesus, *love* to His people and *strength from Jesu*s,[1163] "come and have breakfast" with Him by faith.

*But David thought to himself, "One of these days
I will be destroyed by the hand of Saul"
(1 Samuel 27:1).*

The thought of David's heart at this time was a *false*
thought. He had no ground for thinking that God's
anointing him by Samuel was intended to be left as an
empty, meaningless, act. The LORD had never deserted
His servant. He had been placed in perilous positions very
often, but not once had divine intervention failed to deliver
him. He had been exposed to various trails, yet in every one
of them God had ordained a way of escape. He should have
realized from what God had done for him, that God would
be his defender still. But isn't this the same way that we
doubt God's help? Isn't it mistrust without a reason? Have
we ever had the slightest reason to doubt God's goodness?
Hasn't His loving-kindnesses been marvelous? Has He
once failed to justify our trust? No, our God hasn't left us
at any time. We've had dark nights, but the star of love
has shone forth amid the blackness. We've been in stern
conflicts, but over our head He's held aloft the shield of our
defense. We've gone through many trials, but never to our
harm, always to our advantage. Therefore, the conclusion
from our past experience is that He who has been with us
in six troubles won't forsake us in the seventh. What we
have known of our faithful God, proves that He will keep
us to the end. Let's not, then, reason contrary to evidence.
How can we ever be so ungenerous as to *doubt* our God?
LORD, throw down the Jezebel of our unbelief, and let the
dogs devour it.[1164]

Your [paths] overflow with abundance (Psalm 65:11).

Many of the Lord's paths "overflow with abundance, but a special one is the path of prayer. No believer who is much in the prayer closet will need to cry, "My leanness, my leanness, woe is me." Starving souls live at a distance from the throne of grace and become like the parched fields in times of drought. Prevalence with God in wrestling prayer is sure to make the believer strong. The nearest place to the gate of heaven is the throne of heavenly grace.[1165] Be often alone with Christ, and you'll have much assurance. Be seldom alone with Him, and your religion will be shallow and polluted with many doubts and fears. Since the soul-enriching path of prayer is open to the weakest saint, since no high attainments are required, see to it that you're often in private devotion. Stand often before the throne of God, like Elijah.[1166] There's another special path dropping with fatness to those who walk in it—it's the secret walk of communion. Earth has no words that tell of the holy joy of spending time with Christ. Few Christians understand it, they live in the lowlands and seldom climb to the top of Nebo.[1167] They live in the outer court, but never enter the holy place. They see the sacrifice at a distance, but they don't sit down with the priest to eat of it and enjoy the fat of the burnt offering.[1168] Oh, reader, sit under the shadow of Jesus. Let your Beloved be to you as the apple-tree among the trees of the wood, and you'll be fed beyond measure.

≤ *October 19* ≥

Mere infants in Christ (1 Corinthians 3:1).

Are you mourning, believer, because you're so weak in the divine life—because your faith is so little, and your love so feeble? Cheer up, for you have cause for gratitude. In some things you're equal to the greatest and most full-grown Christians. You're as much bought with blood as they are. You're as much an adopted child of God as any other believer. An infant is as truly a child of its parents as is the full-grown adult. You are as completely justified, for your justification is not a thing of degrees. Your little faith has made you every bit as clean. You have as much right to the precious things of the covenant as the most advanced believers, for your right to covenant mercies lies not in your growth but in the covenant itself. Your faith in Jesus is not the measure of your inheritance in Him, but the token of it. You're as rich as the richest, if not in enjoyment, yet in real possession. In the family register of glory, the small and the great are written with the same pen. You're as dear to your Father's heart as the greatest in the family. Jesus is very tender over you. You're like a bruised reed, and He will never break the bruised reed.[1169] Instead of being downcast by reason of what you are, you should triumph in Christ. In Him I'm made to sit in heavenly places.[1170] Am I poor in faith? Still in Jesus I'm heir of all things. I will rejoice in the LORD, and glory in the God of my salvation.

≈ *October 20* ≈

In all things grow up into Him (Ephesians 4:15).

Many Christians remain stunted and dwarfed in spiritual things, and so are the same year after year. No development of advanced and refined feeling is manifest in them. They exist but do not "in all things grow up into Him." But should we rest content with being in the "green blade," when we might advance to "the ear," and eventually ripen into the "full corn in the ear?"[1171] Should we be satisfied to believe in Christ, and to say, "I am safe," without wishing to know in our own experience more of the fullness that is to be found in Him. It shouldn't be so. As good traders in heaven's market, we should desire to be enriched in the knowledge of Jesus. Why should it always be wintertime in our hearts? We must have our seed time, it is true, but, Oh, for a springtime—and a summer season, that gives promise of an early harvest. If we would ripen in grace, we must live near to Jesus—in His presence—ripened by the sunshine of His smiles. We must hold sweet communion with Him. We must leave the distant view of His face and come near, as John did, and pillow our head on His breast. Then we will find ourselves advancing in holiness, love, faith, hope—in every precious gift. As the sun rises first on mountaintops and adorns them with its glorious light, so it's one of the most delightful contemplations in the world to see the glow of the Spirit's light on the face of a saint who has risen high in Jesus Christ.

For Christ's love compels us (2 Corinthians 5:14).

How much do you owe Jesus Christ? Has He ever done anything for you? Has He forgiven your sins?[1172] Has He covered you with a robe of righteousness? Has He set your feet upon a rock?[1173] Has He established your goings?[1174] Has He prepared heaven for you?[1175] Has He prepared you for heaven? Has He written your name in His book of life?[1176] Has He given you countless blessings? Has He laid up for you a store of mercies, which eye has not seen nor ear heard?[1177] Then do something for Jesus worthy of His love. Don't give just a verbal offering to a dying Redeemer. How will you feel when your Master comes, if you have to confess that you *did* nothing for Him, but kept your love shut up, like a stagnant pool, neither flowing forth to His poor or to His work. What do people think of a love that never shows itself in action? Why, they say, "Better is open rebuke than hidden love."[1178] Who will accept a love so weak that it doesn't inspire you to a single deed of self-denial, generosity, heroism, or zeal! Think how *He* has loved you, and given Himself for you! Do you know the power of that love? Then let it give wings to the feet of your service, and strength to the arms of your labor. Fixed on God with a constancy that cannot be shaken, resolute to honor Him with a determination that cannot be turned aside, and pressing on with an ardor that cannot be wearied, let us manifest the compelling love of Christ.

October 22

I will ... love them freely (Hosea 14:4).

This sentence is a body of divinity in miniature. Those who understand its meaning are theologians, and those who can dive into its fullness are true masters in Israel. It's a condensation of the glorious message of salvation that was delivered to us in Christ Jesus our Redeemer. The sense hinges upon the word "freely." This is the glorious way that love streams from heaven to earth—a spontaneous love flowing forth to those who neither deserved it nor sought after it. It's the only way that God can love creatures like us. The text is a death-blow to all sorts of spiritual fitness: "I will love them *freely.*" Now, if there were any spiritual fitness necessary in us, then He wouldn't love us freely. We complain, "Lord, my heart is so hard." "I will love you *freely.*" "But I don't feel any need of Christ." "I will not love you because you feel your need. I will love you freely." "But I don't feel that softening of spirit that I should." The softening of spirit isn't a condition, for the covenant of grace has no conditions whatever. Therefore, we may freely claim the promise of God: "Whoever believes in Him is not condemned." The grace of God is free to us at all times, without preparation, without fitness, and without price! "I will love them freely." These words *invite backsliders to return.* Indeed, the text was specially written for them. "I will heal their waywardness[1179] and love them freely." Backslider! surely the generosity of the promise will break your heart, and you'll return to your grieving Father.

≋ *October 23* ≋

"You do not want to leave too, do you?" (John 6:67)

Many have forsaken Christ, but what reason do YOU have to do the same? Hasn't Christ proved Himself all-sufficient? Haven't you found your LORD to be a compassionate and generous friend to you, and hasn't simple faith in Him given you all the peace your spirit could desire? Can you possibly dream of a better friend than He's been to you? Then don't change the old and tried for something new and false. What could compel you to leave Christ? When we're surrounded by the difficulties of this world, or with the severer trials within the Church, we find it a most blessed thing to pillow our head upon the heart of our Savior. We have the joy today of knowing that we're saved in Him—and if this joy is satisfying, why would we think of changing? We will not give up the sun until we find a brighter light, nor leave our LORD until a better lover appears. Since this can never be, we'll hold Him with a grasp immortal, and bind His name as a seal on our arm. Can you suggest anything that can arise that will make it necessary for you to desert Him? If we're poor, what comfort to have Christ who can make us rich.[1181] When we're sick, what joy to have Jesus console us. When we die, how grand that it's written, "neither death nor life, neither the present nor the future, will be able to separate us from the love of God that is in Christ Jesus our LORD!"[1182] We say with Peter, "LORD, to whom shall we go?"[1183]

*The trees of the LORD are full of sap
(Psalm 104:16, KJV).*

Without sap a tree cannot flourish or even exist. *Vitality* is essential to a Christian. There must be *life*—a vital principle infused into us by the Holy Spirit, or we cannot be trees of the LORD. The mere name of being a Christian is just a dead thing—we must be filled with the spirit of divine life. This life is *mysterious*. Regeneration[1184] is the work of the Holy Spirit entering into a person and becoming that person's life. Afterwards, this divine life in the believer feeds upon the flesh and blood of Christ and is thus sustained by divine food. But who can explain where it comes from and where it goes?[1185] What a *secret* thing the sap is! Hidden below the surface of the soil the roots search for the life force of the tree. Our root is Christ Jesus, and our life is hidden in Him.[1186] The source of the Christian life is as secret as the life itself. Sap is permanently active in the tree. In the Christian the divine life is always full of energy—not always in fruit-bearing, but in inward operations. Not all of the believer's virtues are in constant motion, but life never ceases working within. Christians aren't always working for God, but His life is always working within them.[1187] As the sap manifests itself in producing the tree's foliage and fruit, so it is with truly healthy Christians. Their virtues are externally manifested in their walk and conversation. If you talk with them, they cannot help speaking about Jesus. If you watch their actions you'll see they've been with Jesus.[1188]

Because of the truth, which lives in us and will be with us forever (2 John 2).

Once the truth of God gains entrance into the human heart and subdues the whole person to itself, no human or infernal power can dislodge it. We entertain it not as a guest but as the master of the house—this is a *Christian necessity*, no person is a Christian who doesn't believe in this way. Those who feel the vital power of the gospel, and know the might of the Holy Spirit as He opens, applies, and seals the LORD's Word, would sooner be torn to pieces than be torn away from the gospel of their salvation. A thousand mercies are wrapped up in the assurance that the truth will be with us forever—will be our living support, our dying comfort, our rising song, our eternal glory. Some truths we outgrow and leave behind, but we cannot so deal with Divine truth, for though it's sweet food for babes, it's in the highest sense solid food for adults.[1189] The truth that we are sinners is painfully with us to humble and make us watchful. The more blessed truth that whoever believes on the LORD Jesus will be saved,[1190] abides with us as our hope and joy. Experience doesn't loosen our hold on the doctrines of grace, but ties them to us more and more firmly. Our grounds and motives for believing are now stronger and more numerous than ever, and we have reason to expect that it will be so until in death we clasp the Savior in our arms. When we receive truth mingled with error, we should discard the error, but love the truth.

⤝ *October 26* ⤜

"You expected much, but see, it turned out to be little.
What you brought home, I blew away. Why?" declares
the LORD *Almighty. "Because of My house, which*
remains a ruin, while each of you is busy with his own
house" (Haggai 1:9).

Miserly souls skimp their contributions to the ministry and call such saving good economy. They little dream that by so doing they're impoverishing themselves. Their excuse is that they must care for their own families, and they forget that to neglect the house of God is the sure way to bring ruin upon their own houses. God has a method by which He can prosper our efforts beyond our expectation, or can defeat our plans to our confusion and dismay. Scripture teaches that the LORD enriches the liberal and leaves the miserly to find out that withholding inclines to poverty. In a very wide sphere of observation, I've noticed that the most generous Christians have been always the most happy, and almost invariably the most prosperous. I've seen liberal givers rise to wealth of which they never dreamed; and I've seen the miserly descend to poverty by the very thriftiness by which they thought to rise. People trust good stewards with increasing sums, and so it often is with the LORD. He gives by wagonloads to those who give by bushels.[1191] Where wealth is not bestowed, the LORD makes the little much by the contentment that the sanctified heart feels in what was received.[1192] Selfishness looks first at home, but godliness seeks first the kingdom of God and His righteousness.[1193] Ultimately, selfishness is loss and godliness is great gain. It takes faith to act toward our God with an open hand, but surely He deserves it from us.

October 27

Here is a trustworthy saying (2 Timothy 2:11).

Paul has four of these *"trustworthy sayings."*[1194] The first is in 1 Timothy 1:15, "Here is a trustworthy saying that deserves full acceptance: Christ Jesus came into the world to save sinners." The next is in 1 Timothy 4:8-9, "Godliness has value for all things, holding promise for both the present life and the life to come. This is a trustworthy saying that deserves full acceptance." The third is in 2 Timothy 2:11-12, "Here is a trustworthy saying: . . . if we endure, we will also reign with him." The fourth is in Titus 3:8, "This is a trustworthy saying. . . . that those who have trusted in God may be careful to devote themselves to doing what is good." There's a connection between these trustworthy sayings. The first one lays the foundation of our eternal salvation in the free grace of God. The second affirms the double blessedness that we obtain through this salvation—blessings of time and of eternity. The third shows one of the duties to which the chosen people are called—to endure for Christ with the promise that "if we endure, we will also reign with Him." The last sets forth the active form of Christian service, bidding us to diligently maintain good works. Treasure up these trustworthy sayings. Let them be the guides of our life, comfort, and instruction. The apostle to the Gentiles[1195] proved them to be faithful, and they are still faithful. They're worthy of full acceptation. Accept them now and prove their faithfulness. Let these four trustworthy sayings be written on the four corners of your house.

But I have chosen you out of the world
(John 15:19).

Here is distinguishing grace and discriminating regard, for some are made the special objects of divine affection. Don't be afraid to dwell upon this high doctrine of election. When your mind is heavy and depressed, you'll find it to be most comforting. Those who doubt the doctrines of grace, or who cast them into the shade, miss one of God's richest blessings. There's no balm in Gilead comparable to it.[1196] If the honey Jonathan ate enlightened his eyes,[1197] this is honey that will enlighten your heart to love and learn the mysteries of the kingdom of God. Eat, and don't fear an excess. Live upon this choice dainty, and don't fear that it will be too delicate a diet. Meat from the King's table will hurt no one. Desire to have your mind enlarged so you may increasingly understand the eternal, everlasting, discriminating love of God. When you've mounted as high as election, stay awhile on its sister mount, the covenant of grace. Covenant promises are the protections of stupendous rock that we lie securely behind. Covenant promises coupled with the guarantee, Christ Jesus,[1198] are the quiet resting places of trembling spirits. If Jesus undertook to bring me to glory, and if the Father promised He would give me to His Son to be a part of the infinite reward of the travail of His soul, then until God Himself is unfaithful, until Jesus ceases to be the truth, my soul you are safe. When David danced before the ark, he told Michal that election made him do so.[1199] My soul, dance before the God of loving grace.

◁ *October 29* ▷

"This, then, is how you should pray:
"'Our Father in heaven'" (Matthew 6:9).

This prayer begins where all true prayer must commence, with the spirit of adoption, "Our Father." There's no acceptable prayer until we can say, "I will arise and go to my Father."[1200] This child-like spirit soon perceives the grandeur of the Father "in heaven," and ascends to *devout adoration*, "Hallowed be Your name." The child lisping, "Abba, Father,"[1201] grows into the cherub crying, "Holy, holy, holy."[1202] There's but a step from rapturous worship to the *missionary spirit*, which is a sure outgrowth of filial love and reverent adoration—"Your kingdom come, Your will be done on earth as it is in heaven." Next follows the heartfelt *expression of dependence* upon God—"Give us today our daily bread." Being further illuminated by the Spirit, we discover that we're not only dependent, but sinful, hence we *entreat for mercy*, "This, then, is how you should pray: 'Our Father in heaven.'" Being pardoned, having the righteousness of Christ imputed, and knowing our acceptance with God, we humbly *supplicate for holy perseverance*, "lead us not into temptation." Those who are really forgiven are anxious not to offend again—the possession of justification leads to an anxious desire for sanctification. "Forgive us our debts," that's justification. "Lead us not into temptation, but deliver us from the evil one," that's sanctification in its negative and positive forms. As the result of all this, there follows a *triumphant ascription of praise*, "Yours is the kingdom and the power and the glory forever. Amen." From adoption to fellowship with our holy Father, this short model of prayer conducts the soul. LORD, teach us thus to pray.

I will praise You, O LORD *(Psalm 9:1).*

Praise should always follow answered prayer, as the mist of earth's gratitude rises when the sun of heaven's love warms the ground. Has the LORD been gracious to you, and inclined His ear to the voice of your supplication?[1203] Then praise Him as long as you live. Don't deny a song to Him who has answered your prayer and given you the desire of your heart. To be silent over God's mercies is to be guilty of ingratitude. It's to act as ungracious as the nine lepers, who after they had been cured of their leprosy did not return to give thanks to the LORD.[1204] To forget to praise God is to refuse to benefit ourselves, for praise is a great means of promoting the growth of the spiritual life. It helps to remove our burdens, excite our hope, and increase our faith. It's a healthful and invigorating exercise that quickens the pulse of believers and nerves them for fresh enterprises in their Master's service. To bless God for mercies received is also the way to benefit others: "let the afflicted hear and rejoice."[1205] Others who have been in like circumstances will be comforted if we can say, "Glorify the LORD with me; let us exalt his name together... This poor man called, and the LORD heard him."[1206] Weak hearts will be strengthened, and drooping saints will be revived as they listen to our "songs of deliverance." Their doubts and fears will leave them as we speak to one another in psalms and hymns and spiritual songs, making melody in our hearts to the LORD.[1207]

October 31

Renew a steadfast spirit within me (Psalm 51:10).

To renew our backsliding, the same exercise of grace is required as at our conversion. We needed repentance then, we certainly need it now. In the beginning we needed the grace of faith to come to Jesus, and only the same grace can bring us to Jesus now. We wanted a word from the Most High, a word from the lip of the loving One, to end our fears then. Under a sense of present sin, we will soon discover that we need it now. We cannot be renewed without as real and true a manifestation of the Holy Spirit's energy as we felt at first, because the work is as great, and flesh and blood are as much in the way now as ever they were. Let your personal weakness, Christian, be an argument to make you pray earnestly to your God for help. Remember, when David felt himself to be powerless, he did not fold his arms or close his lips, but he hurried to the mercy seat with "renew a steadfast spirit within me." Don't let the doctrine that unaided you can do nothing make you sleep, but let it be a goad in your side to drive you with an awful earnestness to Israel's strong Helper. Plead with God as though you were pleading for your very life: "LORD, renew a steadfast spirit within me." Be much in prayer, live much upon the Word of God. Kill the lusts that drove your LORD from you, and be careful to watch over the future uprisings of sin. "LORD, renew a steadfast spirit in me!"

November

✑ *November 1* ✑

The church that meets in your home (Philemon 2).

Is there a church in this home? Are parents, children, friends, all members of it? Or are some still unconverted? How a father's heart would leap for joy and a mother's eyes fill with holy tears if all were saved from the youngest to the oldest! Let's pray for this great mercy until the Lord grants it to us. It was probably the dearest object of Philemon's desires to have all his household saved, but it was not at first granted him in its fullness. He had a wicked servant, Onesimus, who wronged him and ran away from his service. His master's prayers followed him, and at last, as God would have it, Onesimus was led to hear Paul preach. His heart was touched and he returned to Philemon, not only to be a faithful servant but a beloved brother, adding another member to the church in Philemon's house. Is there someone away from home this morning? Make special supplication that on their return home they will gladden all hearts with good news of what grace has done! Is there someone present who is unconverted? Let that person share in the same earnest plea. If there is such a church in your house, conduct it well and let all act as in the sight of God. Further, conduct yourselves in the common affairs of life with studied holiness, diligence, kindness, and integrity. More is expected of a church than of an ordinary household. Family worship must be more devout and hearty, internal love must be more warm and unbroken, and external conduct must be more sanctified and Christlike.

"I the Lord *do not change" (Malachi 3:6).*

In the middle of all the changes in life, it's good for us that there is One whom change cannot affect, whose heart can never alter, and on whose brow mutability can make no furrows. Everything else changes. The sun grows dim with age, the world is growing old, and the heavens and earth will soon pass away and perish. But there is One who alone has immortality, of whose years there is no end, and in whose person there is no change. The delight that sailors feel when they step upon solid shore after having been tossed about for many days is like what Christians feel when, in the middle of all the changes of this troubled life, they rest their faith upon this truth: "I the Lord do not change." The stability that the anchor gives the ship when it has at last obtained a secure hold, is like that which the Christian's hope gives when it fastens itself upon this glorious truth. God "does not change like shifting shadows."[1208] Whatever His attributes were in time past, they are now. His power, wisdom, justice, and truth, are alike unchanged. He's been the refuge of His people,[1209] their stronghold in the day of trouble,[1210] and He is still their sure Helper. He is unchanged in His love. He has loved His people with "an everlasting love,"[1212] and He loves them now as much as He ever did. When all earthly things have melted in the last conflagration, His love will still wear the dew of its youth. Precious is the assurance that He does not change!

He is praying (Acts 9:11).

Prayers are instantly noticed in heaven. The moment Saul began to pray the Lord heard him. Here's comfort for the distressed but praying soul. Oftentimes a poor broken-hearted person can only kneel and groan in the language of sighs and tears, unable to speak.[1213] Yet that groan has made all the harps of heaven thrill with music, and that tear has been caught by God and treasured in golden bowls in heaven.[1214] "You ... put my tears into Your bottle,"[1215] implies that they're caught as they flow. Christians whose depths of agony prevent their words will be well understood by the Most High. They may only look up with misty eyes, but prayer is the falling of a tear. Tears are the diamonds of heaven, sighs are a part of the music of Jehovah's court. Don't think that your prayer, however weak or trembling, won't be considered. Jacob's ladder is lofty,[1216] but our prayers lean upon the Head of the covenant and so climb on starry ladders. Our God not only hears prayer but also loves to hear it. "He does not ignore the cry of the afflicted."[1217] True, He doesn't regard proud looks and lofty words. He doesn't care for the pomp and pageantry of kings. He doesn't regard the triumph and pride of humankind. But wherever there's a heart big with sorrow, or a lip quivering with agony, or a deep groan of sadness, the heart of Jehovah is open. He marks it down in the registry of His memory, and puts the prayers, like rose leaves, between the pages of His book of remembrance.

⊰ *November 4* ⊱

My power is made perfect in weakness
(2 Corinthians 12:9).

A primary qualification for serving God with any amount of success, and for doing God's work well and triumphantly, is an awareness of our own weakness. When God's warriors march forth to battle, strong in their own might, when they boast, "I know that I will conquer, my own right arm and my conquering sword will get me the victory," defeat is not far away. God will not go forth with those who march in their own strength. Those who plan on victory in that way have planned wrongly, for it is "Not by might nor by power, but by My Spirit,' says the Lord Almighty."[1218] Those who go forth to fight, boasting of their power, will return with their proud banners trailing in the dust, and their armor stained with disgrace. Those who serve God must serve Him in His own way, and in His strength, or He will never accept their service. That which we do, unaided by divine strength, God can never accept. God will empty out all the strength that you have before He will put His own strength into you. The river of God is full of water, but not one drop of it flows from earthly springs. God will have no strength used in His battles but the strength that He Himself imparts.[1219] Are you mourning over your own weakness? Take courage, for there must be a consciousness of weakness before the Lord will give you victory. Your emptiness is but the preparation for your being filled, and your casting down is but the making ready for your lifting up.[1220]

*No weapon forged against you will prevail
(Isaiah 54:17).*

This day is notable in England's history for two great deliverances brought about by God for us. On this day in 1605 the plot of the Papists to destroy our Houses of Parliament was discovered. Secondly, today is the anniversary of the landing of King William III at Torbay in 1688, by which the hope of Popish ascendancy was crushed, and religious liberty was secured. This day should be celebrated but by the songs of saints. Our Puritan forefathers most devoutly made it a special time of thanksgiving. There still exists a record of the annual sermons preached by Matthew Henry on this day. Our Protestant feeling and love of liberty should make us regard its anniversary with holy gratitude. Let our hearts and lips exclaim, "We have heard with our ears, O God; our fathers have told us what you did in their days, in days long ago."[1221] You have made this nation the home of the gospel, and when the foe has risen against her, You have shielded her. Help us to offer repeated songs for repeated deliverances. Grant us more and more a hatred of the spirit of antichrist, and hasten the day of its entire extinction. Until then and ever, we believe the promise, "No weapon forged against you will prevail." It should be laid upon the heart of every lover of the gospel of Jesus on this day to plead for the overturning of false doctrines and the extension of divine truth. It would be well to search our own hearts, and tear out any tentacles of self-righteousness that may lie concealed therein.

✑ *November 6* ✐

I will pour water on him who is thirsty
(Isaiah 44:3, NKJV).[1222]

When believers fall into a low, sad state of feeling, they often try to lift themselves out of it by chastening themselves with dark and mournful fears. That isn't the way to rise from the dust, but to continue in it. It's not the law but the gospel that saves the seeking soul at first, and it's not legal bondage but gospel liberty that can restore fainting believers afterward. Slavish fear doesn't bring backsliders back to God, but the sweet invitations of love draws them to Jesus' heart. Are you thirsting this morning for the living God, and unhappy because He isn't the delight of your heart? Have you lost the joy of Christianity, and is your prayer, "Restore to me the joy of Your salvation?"[1223] Are you conscious also that you're like the dry ground and not bringing forth the fruit God has a right to expect of you? Then here is exactly the promise you need, "I will pour water upon him who is thirsty." Water refreshes the thirsty—you will be refreshed and your desires will be gratified. Water awakes sleeping vegetable life—your life will be awakened by fresh grace. Water refreshes the tree and makes its fruits ripen—you will be made fruitful in the ways of God. Whatever good quality there is in divine grace, you will enjoy it to the full. You will receive in plenty all the riches of divine grace. As sometimes the meadows become flooded by the bursting rivers, and the fields are turned into pools, so will you be—the thirsty land will be springs of water.

*See, I have engraved you on the palms of My hands
(Isaiah 49:16).*

No doubt a part of the wonder concentrated in the word
"*See,*" is caused by the unbelieving complaint of the
preceding sentence. Zion said, ""The LORD has forsaken
me, the Lord has forgotten me."[1224] How amazed God
seems to be at this wicked unbelief! What can be more
astounding than the unfounded doubts and fears of
God's chosen people? The Lord's loving word of rebuke
should make us blush. He literally cries, "How can I have
forgotten you, when I've engraved you on the palms of
My hands?" How strange a marvel unbelief is! We don't
know which to wonder at most, the faithfulness of God
or the unbelief of His people. He keeps His promise a
thousand times, and yet the next trial makes us doubt Him.
He never fails, and yet we're as continually troubled with
anxieties, molested with suspicions, and disturbed with
fears, as if our God were a hallucination. "See," is a word
intended to excite admiration. Here we have a theme for
marveling. Heaven and earth may well be astonished that
rebels should have such a great nearness to the heart of
infinite love as to be engraved on the palms of His hands.
"I have engraved *you.*" It doesn't say, "Your name." The
name is there, but that's not all: "I have engraved *you.*"
See the fullness of this! I've engraved your person, image,
situation, circumstances, sins, temptations, weaknesses,
needs, and works. I've engraved everything about you and
all that concerns you. Will you ever say again that your
God has forsaken you when He has engraved *you* on His
own palms?

⊰ *November 8* ⊱

As you received Christ Jesus as Lord
(Colossians 2:6).

The life of faith is represented as *receiving*[1225]— *an act that implies the very opposite of anything like merit.* It's simply the acceptance of a gift. As the earth drinks in the rain, as the sea receives the streams, as night accepts light from the stars, so we give nothing and partake freely of the grace of God. The saints are not wells or streams, they're but cisterns into which the living water flows. They're empty vessels into which God pours His salvation.[1226] The idea of receiving implies *a sense of realization*, making the matter a *reality*. One cannot very well receive a shadow—we receive something substantial. In the life of faith, Christ becomes real to us. While we're without faith, Jesus is just a name to us—a person who lived long ago, so long ago that His life is only history to us now. By an act of faith, however, Jesus becomes a real person in the consciousness of our heart. Receiving also means *getting possession of.* The thing I receive becomes my own. When I receive Jesus, He becomes my Savior, so much mine that neither life nor death will take Him from me. Salvation may be described as the blind receiving sight, the deaf receiving hearing, the dead receiving life[1227]—but we haven't only received these blessings, we've received Christ Jesus Himself. All He gives us are precious things, but we've received Christ Himself. The Son of God has been poured into us,[1228] and we have received Him. How full of Christ our heart must be,[1229] for heaven itself cannot contain Him!

≈ *November 9* ≈

So walk in Him (Colossians 2:6, NKJV).

If we've received Christ Himself into our hearts, our new life will manifest its intimate acquaintance with Him by a walk of faith in Him. Walking implies *action*. Our Christianity isn't to be confined to our closet, we must display daily what we believe. If we walk in Christ, then we act as Christ would act. Christ being in us—our hope, love, joy, life—we are the reflection of the image of Jesus. So people will say of us, "They live like Jesus Christ." Walking signifies *progress*. "So walk in Him." Proceed from grace to grace and run forward until you reach the highest degree of knowledge that a Christian can attain about our Beloved. Walking implies *continuance*. There must be a continual abiding in Christ. Many Christians think that in the morning and evening they should come into the company of Jesus, but give their hearts to the world all day. This is poor living. We should always be with Him, walking in His steps and doing His will. Walking also implies *habit*. When we speak of a person's walk and conversation, we mean their habits. Now, if we sometimes enjoy Christ and then forget Him, sometimes call Him ours and soon lose our hold, that's not a habit—we don't *walk* in Him. We must keep to Him, cling to Him, and never let Him go. In the beginning of your walk, Christ Jesus was the trust of your faith, the source of your life, the principle of your action, and the joy of your spirit. Make Him the same to you until life's end.

✍ *November 10* ✍

The eternal God is your refuge
(Deuteronomy 33:27).

The word refuge may be translated "mansion," or "abode," which gives the thought that *God is our home*. There's a fullness and sweetness in the metaphor, for our *Christian* home is dear to our hearts, though it may be the poorest of rooms. Dearer by far is our blessed God, in whom we live and move and have our being. It's at home that we *feel safe*. We shut the world out and dwell in quiet security. So when we're with our God we "fear no evil."[1231] He's our shelter and retreat, our abiding refuge. At home *we rest* after the work of the day. And so our hearts find rest in God. When we're wearied with life's conflict, we turn to Him and our soul dwells at ease. At home, also, we *let our hearts loose*. We're not afraid of being misunderstood or our words being misconstrued. So when we are with God we can commune freely with Him, laying open all our hidden desires, for if "The secret of the LORD is with those who fear Him," the secrets of those who fear Him must equally be with their Lord. Home is also the place of our *truest and purest happiness*, and it's in God that our hearts find their deepest delight. *It's also for home that we work*. The thought of it gives strength to bear the daily burden, and quickens the fingers and mind to perform the task. In this sense, also, God is our home. Love for Him strengthens us to work for Him. Happy are those who have God for their refuge!

◁ *November 11* ▷

Underneath are the everlasting arms
(Deuteronomy 33:27).

God Himself is our support at all times, and especially when we're sinking into deep trouble. There are times when Christians *sink very low in humiliation.* Under a deep sense of their sinfulness, they're humbled before God until they hardly know how to pray. To themselves, they look worthless. Well, child of God, remember that when you're at your worst, underneath you are the everlasting arms. Sin may drag you low, but Christ's great atonement is still under everything. You may have descended into deep despair, but it's impossible for you to fall so low that He can't save you. Sometimes Christians sink very deep in *severe external trials.* Every earthly prop is taken away. What then? Underneath you are the everlasting arms. No matter how deep you sink, the covenant grace of an ever-faithful God still encircles you. You may sink under *fierce internal conflicts,* but even then you can't be brought so low as to be beyond the reach of the everlasting arms. While you're held by them, all Satan's efforts to harm you are useless. This assurance of support is a comfort to every Christian. It promises strength for each day, grace for each need, and power for each duty. Further, *when death comes,* the promise still holds good. When we stand in the middle of the Jordan, we'll be able to say with David, "I will fear no evil, for You are with me."[1235] We'll descend into the grave but no lower, for the eternal arms prevent our further fall. All through life and at its close, we're upheld by God's everlasting arms.

✑ November 12 ✎

The trial of your faith (1 Peter 1:7, KJV).

Untried faith may be true faith, but it's sure to be little faith, and it'll remain stunted so long as it's without trials. Faith never prospers so well as when everything is against it. Storms are its trainers, and lightnings are its illuminators. When a calm reigns on the sea, you can hoist the sails all you want, the ship won't move into its harbor. But when the winds howl and the waters rage, the ship makes headway toward its desired haven. No flowers wear a lovelier blue than those that grow at the foot of a frozen glacier, no water tastes so sweet as that which springs from desert sand, and no faith is so precious as that which lives and triumphs in adversity. Tried faith brings experience. You wouldn't have believed your own weakness if you hadn't been compelled to pass through the rivers, and you would never have known God's strength if you hadn't been supported in the middle of the floods. Faith increases in solidity, assurance, and intensity the more it's exercised with tribulation. Faith is precious, and its trial is precious, too. Don't let this, however, discourage those who are young in faith. You'll have trials enough without seeking them. Your full portion will be measured out to you in due season. Meanwhile, if you can't yet claim the result of long experience, thank God for what grace you have. Praise Him for that degree of holy confidence you've attained. Walk according to that rule, and you'll have more and more of God's blessings, until your faith will remove mountains[1236] and conquer impossibilities.[1237]

No branch can bear fruit by itself (John 15:4).

How did you begin to bear fruit? It was when you came to Jesus and cast yourselves on His great atonement, and rested on His finished righteousness. What fruit you had then! Do you remember those early days? Have you declined since then? If you have, we charge you to remember that time of love, and repent and do your first works.[1238] *Dedicate yourself to those things that you know draw you closest to Christ,* because it's from Him that all your fruits proceed. Any holy exercise that will bring you to Him will help you to bear fruit.[1239] The sun is a great worker in creating fruit in the trees of the orchard, and Jesus is still more so in the trees of His garden of grace. When have you been the most fruitless? Hasn't it been when you've lived furthest from the Lord Jesus Christ, when you've slackened in prayer, when you've departed from the simplicity of your faith, when you've said, "My mountain stands firm, I will never be moved," and when you've forgotten where your strength comes from? Hasn't it been *then* that your fruit has ceased? Some of us have been taught that we have nothing outside of Christ, by terrible humiliation of heart before the Lord. When we've seen the utter barrenness and death of all creature power, we've cried in anguish, "From Him all my fruit must be found, for no fruit can ever come from me."[1240] Past experience teaches us that the more simply we depend upon the grace of God in Christ, the more we'll bring forth fruit.

*I will cut off ... those who bow down and swear
by the* LORD *and who also swear by Molech
(Zephaniah 1:5).*

Such persons thought themselves safe because they were
with both parties. They went with the followers of Jehovah,
and bowed at the same time to Molech. But duplicity is
abominable with God, and He hates hypocrisy. Idolaters
who distinctly give themselves to their false God, have one
sin less than those who bring their sacrifice to the LORD's
altar while their heart is with the world. In the ordinary
matters of daily life, a double-minded person is despised,
but in Christianity such a person is loathsome.[1241] The
penalty pronounced in the verse before us is terrible,
but it's well deserved. For how could divine justice spare
sinners who know righteousness, approve it, profess to
follow it, and all the while love evil and give it dominion
in their hearts? My soul, search yourself this morning, and
see whether you're guilty of double-dealing. You profess
to be a follower of Jesus, but do you truly love Him? Is
your heart right with God? To have one foot on truth and
the other on falsehood will result in a terrible fall. Christ
will be all or nothing. God fills the whole universe, and
there's no room for another God. If He reigns in my heart,
there'll be no room for another reigning power. Do I rest
alone on Jesus crucified,[1242] and live alone for Him? Is it
my desire to do so? Is my heart set upon so doing? If so,
blessed be the mighty grace that has led me to salvation.
If not so, O LORD, pardon my sad offense, and unite my
heart to fear Your name.

*The LORD's portion is His people
(Deuteronomy 32:9).*

How are they His? By His own *sovereign choice*. He chose them and set His love upon them. This He did separate from any goodness in them at the time, or any goodness He foresaw in them. He had mercy on whom He would have mercy,[1243] and ordained a chosen company to eternal life. Therefore, they're His by His unconstrained election. They're also His by *purchase*. He's bought and paid for them completely, hence there can be no dispute about His title. We've been fully redeemed—not with corruptible things, as with silver and gold, but with the precious blood of the LORD Jesus Christ.[1244] See the blood mark upon all the chosen, invisible to the human eye, but known to Christ, for "The LORD knows those who are His."[1245] He forgets none whom He has redeemed from among humanity. He counts the sheep for whom He laid down His life,[1246] and remembers well the Church for which He gave Himself. They're also His by *conquest*. What a battle He had in us before we would be won! How long He laid siege to our hearts! Do we not remember that glorious hour when He carried our hearts by storm? When He placed His cross against the wall, scaled our ramparts, and raised the blood-red flag of His omnipotent mercy over our hearts? We're the conquered captives of His omnipotent love. Thus chosen, purchased, and subdued, the rights of our divine possessor are inalienable. We rejoice that we never can be our own, and we desire daily to do *His* will, and to show forth *His* glory.

I say to myself, "The Lord is my portion"
(Lamentations 3:24).

It's not "The Lord is *partly* my portion," nor "The Lord is *in* my portion." He Himself makes up the sum total of my soul's inheritance. Within the circumference of that circle lies all that we possess or desire. The Lord is my portion. Not His grace only, nor His love, nor His covenant, but Jehovah Himself. He's chosen us for His portion, and we've chosen Him for ours. It's true that the Lord must first choose our inheritance for us, or else we'll never choose it for ourselves. The Lord is our *all-sufficient* portion. God fills Himself, and if God is all-sufficient in Himself, He must be all-sufficient for us. It's not easy to satisfy our desires. When we dream that we're satisfied, we soon wake to the perception that there's still something more, and immediately the leech in our heart cries, "Give, give."[1247] But all that we can wish for is to be found in our divine portion, so that we ask, "Whom have I in heaven but You? And earth has nothing I desire besides You."[1248] Well may we delight ourselves in the Lord,[1249] who gives us drink from the river of His delights.[1250] Our faith stretches its wings and mounts like an eagle[1251] into divine love as to its proper dwelling place. "The lines have fallen to me in pleasant places; Yes, I have a good inheritance."[1252] Let's rejoice in the Lord always. Let's show to the world that we're a happy and blessed people, and so induce them to exclaim, "Let us go with you, because we have heard that God is with you."[1253]

*To Him be the glory forever! Amen
(Romans 11:36).*

"To Him be the glory forever!" This should be *the single
desire* of Christians. All other wishes must be subservient to
this one. Christians may wish for prosperity in their lives,
but only so far as it helps them to promote this: "To Him
be the glory forever!" We may desire to attain more gifts
and more graces, but it should only be that "To Him be
the glory forever!" You're not acting as you should when
you're moved by any other motive than a single eye to your
LORD's glory. Let nothing ever set your heart beating so
mightily as love for Him. Let this ambition fire your soul.
Let it be the foundation of every enterprise upon which
you enter, and your sustaining motive whenever your zeal
would grow cold. Make God your only object. Depend
upon it, where self begins sorrow begins. Let your desire
for God's glory be a growing desire. You blessed Him in the
beginning, don't be content with such praises as you gave
Him then. Has God prospered you in life? Give Him more
as He has given you more. Has God given you experience?
Praise Him by stronger faith than you exercised at first.
Does your knowledge grow? Then sing more sweetly. Do
you enjoy happier times than you once had? Have you been
restored from sickness, and has your sorrow been turned
into peace and joy? Then give Him more music, and put
more fire and sweet frankincense into the censer of your
praise. In every aspect of life, give honor to your Lord by
your service and increasing holiness.

ᘏ *November 18* ᘃ

*A spring enclosed, a sealed fountain
(Song of Songs 4:12).*

In this metaphor, which has reference to the inner life of
a believer, the idea of secrecy is quite plain. It's a spring
enclosed. In the East, an edifice was built over springs so
none could reach them except those who knew the secret
entrance. Such is the heart of a believer when it's renewed
by grace—there's a mysterious life within that no human
skill can touch. It's a secret that no other person knows,
and which even the person who is the possessor of it cannot
tell to a friend. The Scripture includes not only secrecy, but
separation. It's not a common spring from which every
passerby may drink, it's one kept and preserved from all
others. It's a fountain bearing a particular mark—a king's
royal seal, so that all can perceive that it's not a common
fountain, but a fountain owned by a proprietor, and placed
specially by itself alone. So is it with the spiritual life. The
chosen of God were separated in the day of redemption,
and they are separated by the possession of a life that others
don't have.[1254] It's impossible for them to feel at home with
the world, or to delight in its pleasures. There's also the
idea of *sacredness*. The enclosed spring is preserved for
the use of some special person, and such is the Christian's
heart. It's a spring kept for Christ. All Christians should
feel that they have God's seal on them, and should be able
to say like Paul, "let no one cause me trouble, for I bear
on my body the marks of Jesus."[1255]

❧ November 19 ❧

Avoid foolish controversies (Titus 3:9).

Our days are few, and are far better spent in doing good than in disputing over matters which are of minor importance. Our churches suffer much from petty wars over unsolvable points and unimportant questions. After everything has been said that can be said, neither party is any the wiser, and therefore the discussion no more promotes knowledge than love. Questions upon points where Scripture is silent, upon mysteries that belong to God alone, upon prophecies of doubtful interpretation, and upon methods of observing human ceremonies, are all foolish, and wise people avoid them. Our business is neither to ask nor answer foolish questions, but to avoid them altogether. If we observe the apostle's precept to be careful to devote themselves to doing good,[1256] we'll find ourselves far too occupied with profitable business to take much interest in unworthy, contentious, and needless strivings. There are, however, some questions that we must not avoid, but fairly and honestly meet, such as these: Do I believe in the Lord Jesus Christ?[1257] Am I renewed in the spirit of my mind?[1258] Am I walking not after the flesh, but after the Spirit?[1259] Am I growing in grace?[1260] Does my conversation adorn the doctrine of God my Savior? Am I looking for the coming of the LORD, and watching as a servant should do who expects his master?[1261] What more can I do for Jesus? Such questions as these urgently demand our attention. If we've been at all given to quibbling, let's stop immediately and become peace-makers, and endeavor to lead others by our precept and example to "avoid foolish controversies."

✐ *November 20* ✎

O Lord, You took up my case;
You redeemed my life (Lamentations 3:58).

Notice how *positively* the prophet speaks. He doesn't say,
"I hope, I trust, I sometimes think, that God takes up my
case." He speaks of it as a fact not to be disputed. "You
took up my case." By the aid of the gracious Comforter,
let's shake off those doubts and fears that so much mar
our peace and comfort. Notice how *gratefully* the prophet
speaks, ascribing all the glory to God alone! There's not a
word concerning himself or his own pleadings. He doesn't
ascribe his deliverance in any measure to any person,
much less to his own merit; but it's *"you"*—"O Lord,
You took up my case; you redeemed my life." Christians
should always cultivate a grateful spirit, and especially
after deliverances we should prepare a song for our God.
Earth should be a temple filled with the songs of grateful
saints, and every day should be a golden bowl smoking
with the sweet incense of thanksgiving.[1262] How *joyful*
Jeremiah seems to be while he records the Lord's mercy.
How triumphantly he lifts up the words! He's been in the
low dungeon, and is even now no other than the weeping
prophet. Yet in the book called *Lamentations,* Jeremiah's
voice speaks clear as the song of Miriam when she dashed
her fingers against the tambourine,[1263] shrill as the note of
Deborah when she met Barak with shouts of victory:[1264]
"You took up my case; you redeemed my life!" O children
of God, seek after a vital experience of the Lord's loving-
kindness, and when you have it, speak positively of it, sing
gratefully, shout triumphantly.

Do not grieve the Holy Spirit of God
(Ephesians 4:30).

All that the believer has must come from Christ, but it comes solely through the channel of the Spirit of grace.[1265] Moreover, even as all blessings flow to you through the Holy Spirit, so also no good thing can come out of you in holy thought, devout worship, or gracious act, apart from the sanctifying operation of the same Spirit. Even if the good seed is sown in you, it lies dormant except He works in you to will and to do of His good pleasure.[1266] Do you desire to speak for Jesus? You can't unless the Holy Ghost touches your tongue. Do you desire to pray? It's dull work unless the Spirit makes intercession for you.[1267] Do you desire to subdue sin? Would you be holy? Would you imitate your Master? Do you desire to rise to great heights of spirituality? Do you want to be made full of zeal and ardor for the Master's cause? You can't without the Spirit. "Apart from Me you can do nothing."[1268] Child of God, you have no life within you apart from the life that God gives you through His Spirit. So let's not grieve Him by our sins. Let's not quench Him in one of His faintest movements in our soul. Let's watch for every suggestion, and obey every prompting. The Holy Spirit is mighty, so let's attempt nothing without Him. Let's begin no project, and carry on no enterprise, and conclude no transaction, without imploring His help. Let's do Him the due homage of feeling our entire weakness apart from Him, and then depending upon Him alone.

Israel served to get a wife, and to pay for her he tended sheep (Hosea 12:12).

While reasoning with Laban, Jacob describes his own labor: "I have been with you for twenty years now. Your sheep and goats have not miscarried, nor have I eaten rams from your flocks. I did not bring you animals torn by wild beasts; I bore the loss myself. And you demanded payment from me for whatever was stolen by day or night. This was my situation: The heat consumed me in the daytime and the cold at night, and sleep fled from my eyes."[1269] Even more toilsome than this was the earthly life of our Savior. He watched over all His sheep until He gave as His last account, "Those whom You gave Me I have kept; and none of them is lost."[1270] Often He prayed all night.[1271] One night He had to pray especially for Simon.[1272] No shepherds could ever voice the kind of complaints for their hard labor that Jesus might have, if He had chosen to do so, because of the hardness of His work to obtain His spouse. It's sweet to dwell upon the spiritual parallel of Laban having required all the sheep at Jacob's hand. If they were torn by beasts, Jacob must make it good. If any of them was stolen, he must pay for them.[1273] Wasn't the labor of Jesus for His Church the labor of one who was under guarantee obligations to bring every believing one safe to the hand of Him who had committed them to His charge? Look at Jacob, and you see a representation of Him of whom we read, "He tends His flock like a shepherd."[1274]

Fellowship with Him (1 John 1:6).

When we were united by faith to Christ, we were brought into such complete companionship with Him, that we were made one with Him, and His interests and ours became mutual and identical. We have companionship with Christ in His *love.* What He loves we love. He loves the saints, so do we. He loves sinners, so do we. We have companionship with Him in His *desires.* He desires the glory of God, we labor for the same. He desires that the saints may be with Him where He is, we desire to be with Him there, too. He desires that His Father's name may be loved and adored by all His creatures, we pray daily, "Your kingdom come, Your will be done on earth as it is in heaven."[1275] We have companionship with Christ in His *sufferings.*[1276] We're not nailed to the Cross, nor do we die a cruel death, but when He's reproached, we're reproached. When the world hates Him, it hates us.[1277] The disciples aren't above their Lord.[1278] We're to minister to people by the word of truth and deeds of love. Our food, like His, is to do the will of Him who sent us and to finish His work.[1279] We have also companionship with Christ in His *joys.* We're happy in His happiness, and we rejoice in His exaltation. Have you tasted that joy, believer? There's no purer delight this side of heaven than having Christ's joy fulfilled in us, that our joy may be full.[1280] His *glory* awaits us to complete our companionship, for His Church will sit with Him on His throne.

The LORD will be our Mighty One. It will be like a place of broad rivers and streams (Isaiah 33:21).

Broad rivers and streams produce fertility and abundance in the land. Places near broad rivers are remarkable for the variety of their plants and their plentiful harvests. God is all this to His Church. Having God it has *abundance*. What can it ask for that He won't give it? What need can it mention that He won't supply? "On this mountain the LORD Almighty will prepare a feast of rich food."[1281] Want the bread of life? It drops like manna from the sky. Want refreshing streams? The rock follows you, and that Rock is Christ.[1282] If you suffer any need it's your own fault. Broad rivers and streams also point to *commerce*. Our glorious LORD is to us a place of heavenly merchandize. Through our Redeemer we have commerce with the past—the wealth of Calvary, the treasures of the covenant, the riches of the ancient days of election, the stores of eternity, all come to us down the broad stream of our gracious LORD. We have commerce, too, with the future. Ships loaded down to the water's edge come to us from the millennium! What visions we have of the days of heaven upon earth! Broad rivers and streams are specially intended to set forth the idea of *security*. In ancient times rivers were a defense. Oh, what a defense God is to His Church! The devil can't cross this broad river of God. How he wishes he could turn the current, but don't be afraid, for God is always the same. Satan may nag us, but he can't destroy us. Only gallant ships travel God's river.

To proclaim freedom for the prisoners
(Luke 4:18).[1283]

No one but Jesus can give freedom to prisoners. Real freedom comes only from Him. It's a freedom *righteously bestowed,* for the Son, who is Heir of all things, has a right to make people free. It's a freedom that's been *dearly purchased.* Christ speaks it by His power, but He bought it by His blood. You go free because He bore your burden for you. You're set free because He suffered in your place. It's a freedom *He freely gives.* Jesus asks nothing of us as a preparation for this freedom. He finds us dressed in sackcloth and clothes us with joy.[1284] He saves us just as we are, and all without our help or merit. When Jesus sets free, the freedom is *permanent*—no chains can bind again. Let the Master say to me, "Prisoner, I've delivered you," and it's done forever. Satan may scheme to enslave us, but "if God is for us, who can be against us?"[1285] The world, with its temptations, may seek to ensnare us, but mightier is He who is for us than all those who be against us.[1286] The workings of our own deceitful hearts may harass and annoy us, but He who has begun the good work in us will carry it on and perfect it to the end.[1287] If we're no more under the law, but free from its curse,[1288] let our freedom be *practically exhibited* by our serving God with gratitude and delight. "I am your servant, the son of your maidservant; you have freed me from my chains."[1289] "LORD, what do You want me to do?"[1290]

≫ November 26 ≪

Whatever your hand finds to do, do it with all your might (Ecclesiastes 9:10).

"Whatever your hand finds to do" refers to works that are *possible*. There are many things that our heart finds to do that we will never do. We must not be content, however, with just forming schemes in our heart and talking of them. We must practically carry out "whatever our hand finds to do." One good deed is worth more than a thousand brilliant theories. Let's not wait for large opportunities or a different kind of work. Let's do just the things we find to do each day. We've no other time in which to live. The past is gone, the future hasn't arrived. We'll never have any time but the present. So don't wait until your experience has ripened into maturity before you attempt to serve God. Endeavor now to bring forth fruit.[1291] Serve God now, but be careful as to the way in which you perform what you find to do: *"do it with all your might."* Do it *promptly*. Don't throw away your life in thinking of what you intend to do tomorrow, as if that could make up for your idleness of today. No one ever served God by doing things tomorrow. If we honor Christ and are blessed, it's by the things we do *today*. Whatever you do for Christ throw your whole soul into it. Don't give Christ a little token labor, done as a matter of course now and then. Serve Him with heart, soul, and strength—getting your strength form Him.[1292] Then when we've done "whatever our hand finds to do," let's wait upon the Lord for His blessing.

Joshua the high priest standing before the Angel of the LORD (Zechariah 3:1).

In Joshua *the high priest* we see a picture of every child of God who has been brought near by the blood of Christ and has been taught to minister in holy things. Jesus has made us priests and kings unto God,[1293] and even here upon earth we exercise the priesthood of consecrated living and hallowed service. But this high priest is said to be "*standing* before the Angel of the LORD," that is, standing to minister.[1294] This should be the perpetual position of every true believer. Every place is now God's temple, and His people can as truly serve Him in their daily work as in His house. They're to be always ministering, offering the spiritual sacrifice of prayer and praise,[1295] and presenting themselves a "living sacrifice."[1296] But notice where it is that Joshua stands to minister, it is *before the angel* of Jehovah. It's only through a mediator that we poor defiled ones can ever become priests to God.[1297] I present what I have before the messenger, the angel of the covenant, the LORD Jesus. Through Him my prayers find acceptance wrapped up in His prayers.[1298] If I can bring Him nothing but my tears, He will put them with His own tears, for He once wept.[1299] If I can bring Him nothing but my groans and sighs,[1300] He will accept these as an acceptable sacrifice, for He once was broken in heart. I myself, standing in Him, am accepted in the Beloved.[1301] God is content and I am blessed. See, then, the position of the Christian: "a priest—standing—before the angel of the LORD."

It gave me great joy to have some brothers come and tell about your faithfulness to the truth and how you continue to walk in the truth (3 John 3).

The truth was in Gaius, and Gaius walked in a the truth. If the first had not been the case, the second could never have occurred. If the second could not be said of him, the first would have been just a pretence. Truth must enter into the soul, penetrate and saturate it, or else it's of no value. Doctrines held as a matter of creed are like bread in the hand, which gives no nourishment to the body. But doctrines accepted by the heart are like food digested, which sustains and builds up the body. In us truth must be a living force, an active energy, an indwelling reality, a part of the foundation of our being. If it's in us, we cannot part with it. A person may lose clothing or limbs, but inward parts cannot be torn away without absolute loss of life. Christians can die but they can't deny the truth. Now it's a rule of nature that the inward affects the outward, as light shines from the center of the lantern through the glass. Therefore, when the truth is lit within, its brightness soon beams forth in the outward life and conversation. The spiritual life upon which our inward nature feeds gives color to every word and deed proceeding from us. To walk in the truth brings a life of integrity, holiness, faithfulness, and simplicity—the natural product of those principles of truth that the gospel teaches, and which the Holy Spirit enables us to receive. We may judge of the secrets of a soul by their manifestation in a person's conversation.

✧ *November 29* ✧

*Do not go about spreading slander among your people
... Rebuke your neighbor frankly so you will not share
in his guilt (Leviticus 19:16-17).*

Spreading slander emits a threefold poison—it injures the teller, the hearer, and the person about whom the story is told. Whether the report is true or false, God's Word forbids us to spread it. The reputations of the Lord's people should be very precious in our sight,[1302] and we should be ashamed to help the devil dishonor the Church and the Lord's name. Many glory in tearing down their brothers and sisters, as if by so doing they elevate themselves. There may be a day in which we ourselves will need tolerance and silence from others. Let's give it cheerfully to those who require it now. Make this our Christian rule—speak no evil of any person! The Holy Spirit does, however, permit us to censure sin, and prescribes the way in which we're to do it. It must be done by rebuking the person directly, not by talking behind their back. This course is godly, loving, Christlike, and under God's blessing, which will make it effective. Does the flesh shrink from it? Then we must put greater pressure upon our conscience and keep ourselves to the work, lest by allowing sin in our friend we ourselves become partakers of it. Hundreds have been saved from gross sins by the timely, wise, affectionate warnings of faithful ministers and brothers and sisters.[1303] Our Lord Jesus set us a gracious example of how to deal with erring friends in His warning given to Peter, the prayer with which He preceded it, and the gentle way in which He endured Peter's boastful denial that he needed such a warning.[1304]

Amaziah asked the man of God, "But what about the hundred talents I paid for these Israelite troops?" The man of God replied, "The LORD can give you much more than that" (2 Chronicles 25:9).

This seemed to be a very important question to the king of Judah, and possibly it's of even more importance to the tried and tempted Christian. To lose money is never pleasant, and when principle is involved, the flesh isn't always ready to make the sacrifice. "Why lose what may be useful to us? What will we do without it? Remember our small income!" All these things and a thousand more tempt Christians to engage in unrighteous gain, or keep themselves from carrying out the convictions of their conscience when serious loss is involved. Not everyone can view these matters in the light of faith, and even with the followers of Jesus, the doctrine of "we must live" bears a lot of weight. The only satisfactory answer to such anxious questions is, *the LORD can give you much more than that.* Our Father holds the purse strings, and what we lose for His sake He can repay a thousandfold. It's our duty to obey His will, and we may rest assured that He'll provide for us. Saints know that a grain of heart's ease is of more value than a ton of gold. Those who wrap a threadbare coat about a good conscience have gained a spiritual wealth far more desirable than any they've lost. God's smile and a dungeon are enough for a true heart.[1305] His frown and a palace would be hell to a gracious spirit. Let worst come to worst, let all the talents go, we haven't lost our treasure, for that's above where Christ sits at the right hand of God. Obey and trust.

December

You made both summer and winter (Psalm 74:17).

My soul begin this wintry month with your God. The cold snows and the piercing winds remind you that He keeps His covenant with day and night,[1306] and assure you that He will also keep that glorious covenant that He made with you in Christ Jesus.[1307] He who is true to His Word in the revolutions of the seasons of this poor sin-polluted world, will not prove unfaithful in His dealings with His own well-beloved Son. Winter in the soul is by no means a comfortable season, and if it's upon you just now it will be very painful to you. But there's this comfort, namely, that *the* LORD makes it. He does it all, He's the great Winter King, and rules in the realms of frost, and therefore you can't murmur. Many negative and burdensome situations are of the LORD's sending, and come to us with wise design. Frosts kill noxious insects, and put a stop to raging diseases—they break up the clods, and sweeten the soul. O that such good results would always follow our winters of affliction! How we prize the fire just now! How pleasant its cheerful glow is! Let's in the same manner prize our LORD, who's the constant source of warmth and comfort in every time of trouble. Let's draw near to Him, and in Him find joy and peace in believing. Let's wrap ourselves in the warm garments of His promises, and go forth and perform works that befit the season. Don't be like the sluggard who won't plow because it's cold. That one will beg in summer and have nothing.

All beautiful you are, my darling (Song of Songs 4:7).

The Lord's admiration of His Church is wonderful, and His description of her beauty is glowing. She's not merely *beautiful*, but *"all beautiful."* He views her in Himself, washed in His blood and clothed in His righteousness, and He sees her full of comeliness and beauty. No wonder that is so, since it's but His own perfect excellency that He admires. The holiness, glory, and perfection of His Church are His own glorious garments on the back of His well-beloved spouse. She's not simply pure, she's positively lovely and fair! Her deformities of sin are removed. Further, through her Lord she has obtained a meritorious righteousness by which an actual beauty is conferred upon her. Believers have a positive righteousness given to them when they become "accepted in the beloved."[1308] And the Church isn't barely beautiful, she's *superlatively* so. Her Lord calls her "most beautiful of women."[1309] She has a real worth and excellence that cannot be equaled by all the royalty of the world. If Christ could exchange His elect bride for all the queens and empresses of earth, or even for the angels in heaven, He would not, for He puts her first and foremost—"most beautiful of women." Like the moon, she far outshines the stars, and Christ invites everyone to hear His opinion of her. He sets an "oh" before a special exclamation, inviting and calling attention. *"How beautiful you are, my darling! Oh, how beautiful!"*[1310] Soon He'll avow this truth before the assembled universe. "Come, you who are blessed by my Father" will be His solemn affirmation of the loveliness of His elect.

↭ *December 3* ↩

There is no flaw in you (Song of Songs 4:7).

Having pronounced His Church beautiful, our Lord confirms His praise by a precious negative, "There is no flaw in you." It's as if the thought occurred to the Bridegroom that the fault-finding world would insinuate that He had only mentioned her comely parts, and had purposely omitted those features that were deformed or defiled, He sums all up by declaring her universally and entirely fair and utterly devoid of flaws. A flaw may soon be removed, and is the very least thing that can disfigure beauty, but even from this little blemish the believer is delivered in the LORD's sight. If He had said there's no hideous scar, no horrible deformity, or no deadly ulcer, we might even then have marveled. But when He testifies that she's free from the slightest flaw, all these other forms of defilement are included, and the depth of wonder is increased. If He had only promised to remove all spots eventually, we would have eternal reason for joy. But when He speaks of it as already done, who can restrain the most intense emotions of satisfaction and delight. Christ Jesus has no quarrel with His spouse. She often wanders from Him, and grieves His Holy Spirit,[1311] but He does not allow her faults to affect His love. He sometimes chides, but it's always in the tenderest manner, and with the kindest intentions. He doesn't cherish ill thoughts of us, but He pardons and loves as well after the offense as before it. Our precious Husband knows our silly hearts too well to take any offense at our ill manners.

ᴀ *December 4* ᴃ

"I have many people in this city" (Acts 18:10).

This should be a great encouragement to try to do good, since God has among the vilest of the vile an elect people who *must* be saved.[1312] When you take the Word to them, you do so because God has ordained you to be the messenger of life to their souls, and they *must* receive it, for so the decree of predestination runs.[1313] They're as much redeemed by blood as the saints before the eternal throne. They're Christ's property, and yet perhaps they're lovers of bars and haters of holiness—but if Jesus Christ purchased them[1314] He will have them. God isn't unfaithful to forget the price that His Son has paid. He will not suffer His substitution to be an ineffectual dead thing in any way. Tens of thousands of redeemed ones are not regenerated yet, but regenerated they must be, and this is our comfort when we go forth to them with the life-giving Word of God. Further, these ungodly ones are prayed for by Christ before the throne. ""My prayer is not for them alone," says the great Intercessor. "I pray also for *those who will believe in me* through their message."[1315] They know nothing about prayer for themselves, but Jesus prays for them. Their predestinated moment has not come. But when it comes *they will obey*, for God will have His own. *They must*, for the Spirit cannot be resisted when He comes forth with power. "My people will be willing in the day of my power."[1316] "My righteous servant will justify many."[1317] "He shall see the labor of His soul, and be satisfied."[1318]

⊰ *December 5* ⊱

"Ask and it will be given to you" (Matthew 7:7).

We know of a place in England that still exists today, where a ration of bread is served to every passerby who chooses to ask for it. Whoever the traveler may be, they have but to knock at the door of St. Cross Hospital, and they will receive their ration of bread. Jesus Christ so loves sinners that He's built a St. Cross Hospital, so that whenever sinners are hungry, they have but to knock and have their needs supplied. He's done better. He's attached a bath to this Hospital of the Cross, and whenever a soul is filthy, it has but to go there and be washed. The fountain is always full, always effective. No sinners ever went into it and found that it couldn't wash away their stains. Sins that were scarlet and crimson have all disappeared, and the sinners have been whiter than snow.[1319] As if this weren't enough, there's a wardrobe attached to this Hospital of the Cross, and sinners making application simply as a sinners, may be clothed from head to foot.[1320] They'll be denied nothing that is good for them. They'll have spending money as long as they live, and they'll have an eternal heritage of glorious treasure when they enter into the joy of their Lord. If all these things are to be had by merely knocking at mercy's door, knock hard this morning and ask large things of your generous LORD. Don't be held back by bashfulness when Jesus invites, or hindered by unbelief when Jesus promises. And don't let cold-heartedness restrain you when such blessings are to be obtained.

December 6

As is the man from heaven, so also are those who
are of heaven (1 Corinthians 15:48).

The head and members are of one nature, and not like
that monstrous image Nebuchadnezzar saw in his dream.
The head was of fine gold, but the belly and thighs were of
brass, the legs of iron, and the feet, part of iron and part of
clay.[1321] Christ's mystical body is no absurd combination
of opposites; the members were mortal, and therefore
Jesus died. The glorified head is immortal, and therefore
the body is immortal too. Therefore Jesus said, "Because I
live, you also will live."[1322] As is our loving Head, so is the
body, and every member in particular. A chosen Head and
chosen members, an accepted Head and accepted members,
a living Head and living members. If the head is pure gold,
all the parts of the body are of pure gold, also. Pause
here, Christian, and see if you can without amazement
contemplate the infinite condescension of the Son of God
in exalting your wretchedness into blessed union with His
glory. In knowledge of your mortality, you can "say to
corruption, 'You are my father,' And to the worm, 'You
are my mother and my sister,'"[1323] Yet, in Christ you are
so honored that you can say to the Almighty, "Abba,
Father,"[1324] and to the Incarnate God, Jesus Christ, "You
are my brother and my husband."[1325] Surely if relationships
to ancient and noble families make people think highly of
themselves, we have more to glory about then them all.
Let the poorest and most despised believer lay hold upon
this privilege—the wonder of the exclusion of this glorious,
heavenly, honor of union with Christ.

*He chose the lowly things of this world
(1 Corinthians 1:28).*

Walk the streets by moonlight, if you dare, and you will see sinners then. Go to the jail and walk through the cell blocks and you will see sinners there whom you would not like to meet alone at night. Go to the most sophisticated and wealthy city in the world and you see sinners there. Go to the most remote places on the earth where survival is barely possible and you will see sinners there. Go where you will, you needn't ransack earth to find sinners, for they're common enough. They're in every lane and street of every city, town, village, and hamlet. It's for such that Jesus died. If you find the grossest specimen of humanity, I will have hope of that person yet, because Jesus Christ came to seek and to save *sinners*.[1326] Electing love has selected some of the worst to be made the best. Grace turns rocks in the brook into jewels for the royal crown. He transforms worthless dross into pure gold. Redeeming love has set apart many of the worst of humankind to be the reward of the Savior's passion. Effectual grace calls forth many of the vilest of the vile to sit at the table of mercy. Therefore, let none despair. Reader, by that love looking out of Jesus' tearful eyes, by that love streaming from those bleeding wounds, by that faithful love, that strong love, that pure, disinterested, and abiding love, by the Lord's compassion, we urge you not to turn away as though it were nothing to you. Believe in Him and you will be saved.[1327]

≼ *December 8* ≽

Yet you have a few people in Sardis who have not soiled their clothes. They will walk with me, dressed in white, for they are worthy (Revelation 3:4).

This refers to *justification*. "They will walk with me, dressed in white." That is, they'll enjoy a constant sense of their own justification by faith, and will understand that the righteousness of Christ is imputed to them and they've been made whiter than the newly-fallen snow. It refers also to *joy and gladness*, for white robes were holiday clothes at that time. These people will understand what Solomon meant when he said "Go, eat your food with gladness, and drink your wine with a joyful heart, for it is now that God favors what you do."[1328] Those accepted by God will wear white garments of joy, while they walk in sweet communion with the LORD Jesus. Why are there so many doubts, so much misery and mourning? It's because so many believers defile their garments with sin, and so they lose the joy of their salvation and the intimate companionship of the LORD Jesus. The promise also refers to *walking in white before the throne of God*. Those who haven't defiled their garments here will most certainly walk in white up there, where the white-robed hosts sing perpetually to the Most High.[1329] They'll possess inconceivable joys, happiness beyond a dream, bliss that imagination doesn't know, blessedness that even the stretch of desire hasn't reached. The "undefiled in the way"[1330] will have all this. Not by merit, nor by works, but by grace. They'll walk with Christ in white, for He's made them "worthy." In His glorious company they'll drink of the living fountains of waters.[1331]

⚜ *December 9* ⚜

Yet the LORD *longs to be gracious to you*
(Isaiah 30:18).

God often delays in answering prayer. We've several instances of this in Scripture. Jacob didn't get the blessing from the angel until near the dawn of day—he had to wrestle all night for it.[1332] The poor Canaanite woman wasn't answered for a long while.[1333] Paul asked the Lord *three times* that "the thorn in the flesh" be taken from him, and he received no assurance that it should be taken away. Instead, he was promised that God's grace would be sufficient for him.[1334] If you've been knocking at the gate of mercy and haven't received an answer, shall I tell you why God hasn't opened the door and let you in? Our Father has reasons peculiar to Himself for keeping us waiting. Sometimes it's to show His power and His sovereignty, that people may know that Jehovah has a right to give or to withhold. More frequently the delay is for our profit. You are perhaps kept waiting so your desires will be more fervent. God knows that delay will quicken and increase desire, and that if He keeps you waiting you'll see your necessity more clearly, will seek more earnestly; and will prize the mercy all the more for its long delay. There may also be something wrong in you that needs to be removed. Perhaps you're putting some little reliance on yourself, instead of trusting simply and entirely to the Lord Jesus. Don't give up,[1335] your prayers are all filed in heaven. In a little while they'll be fulfilled to your delight and satisfaction. Don't let despair make you silent. Continue your earnest supplication.

ᴈ᷉ *December 10* ᵎ᷉

So we will be with the LORD *forever*
(1 Thessalonians 4:17).

Even the sweetest visits from Christ are short and temporary! One moment our eyes see Him, and we "are filled with an inexpressible and glorious joy."[1336] Then in a little while we don't see Him, for our beloved withdraws Himself from us. like a roe or a young hart He leaps over the rugged mountains.[1337] He is gone to the land of spices, and feeds no more among the lilies.[1338] Oh, how sweet the prospect of the time when we won't see Him at a distance, but will see Him face to face.[1339] Then He will not be as a wayfaring man tarrying for only a night, but will eternally enfold us in the arms of His glory. In heaven there will be no interruptions from care or sin—no weeping will dim our eyes. No earthly business will distract our happy thoughts. We will have nothing to hinder us from looking forever with unwearied eyes on the Sun of Righteousness. Oh, if it is so sweet to see Him now and then, how sweet to look on that blessed face for eternity, and never have a cloud rolling between, and never have to turn our eyes away to look on a world of weariness and woe! Blessed day, when will you dawn? Rise, O unsetting sun! The joys of sense may leave us as soon as they will, for this will make glorious amends. If to die is but to enter into uninterrupted communion with Christ, then death is indeed gain,[1340] and the black drop into physical death is swallowed up in a spiritual sea of victory.

The one who calls you is faithful and He will do it
(1 Thessalonians 5:24).

Heaven is a place where we'll never sin, and where we'll cease our constant watch against an untiring enemy, because there'll be no tempter to ensnare our feet. There the weary saints are at rest. Heaven is the "undefiled inheritance."[1341] It's the land of perfect holiness, and therefore of complete security. But don't even the saints on earth sometimes taste the joys of blissful security? The doctrine of God's Word is that all who are in union with the Lamb are safe, and that those who have committed their souls to the keeping of Christ will find Him a faithful and immutable preserver. Sustained by such a doctrine we can enjoy security even on earth. Not that high and glorious security that renders us free from every slip, however, but that holy security that comes from the sure promise of Jesus that none who believe in Him will ever perish,[1342] but will be with Him where He is. Believer, let's often reflect with joy on the doctrine of the perseverance of the saints, and honor the faithfulness of our God by a holy confidence in Him. May our God bring home to you a sense of your safety in Christ Jesus! May He assure you that your name is engraved on His hand[1343] and whisper in your ear the promise, "Fear not, I am with you to the end."[1344] Look upon Him, the great Guarantee of the covenant, as faithful and true, and, therefore, bound to present you with all the chosen before the throne of God.[1345] "The one who calls you is faithful and He will do it."[1346]

✠ December 12 ✠

His ways are eternal (Habakkuk 3:6).

What God has done at one time, He will do yet again. Our ways are variable, but God's ways are eternal. There are many reasons for this comforting truth, among them the following. The LORD's ways are *the result of wise deliberation*; He works everything according to the counsel of His will.[1347] Human action is frequently the hasty result of passion or fear, and is followed by regret and alteration. But nothing takes the Almighty by surprise, or happens other than He has foreseen. His ways are *the outgrowth of an immutable character*. Unless the Eternal One Himself can undergo change, His ways, which are Himself in action, must remain forever the same. He is eternally just, gracious, faithful, wise, and tender, and so His ways are always distinguished by the same excellences. Human beings act according to their nature. When those natures change, their conduct varies also. But with God there is "no variation or shadow of turning."[1348] His ways will always be the same. Moreover, there's nothing outside Him that could reverse His ways, since they're the *embodiment of irresistible might*. When Jehovah marches forth for the salvation of His people, who can restrain His hand?[1349] But it's not might alone that gives stability. God's ways are *the manifestation of the eternal principles of right*, and therefore can never pass away. Wrong breeds decay and ruin, but the true and the good have a vitality that time cannot diminish. This morning let's go to the throne of our heavenly Father with confidence, remembering that "Jesus Christ is the same yesterday, today and forever."[1350]

≈⊲ *December 13* ⊳≈

Salt without limit (Ezra 7:22).

Salt was used in every offering made by fire to the Lord, and from its preserving and purifying properties it was the grateful emblem of divine grace in the soul. When Artaxerxes gave salt to Ezra the priest, he set no limit to the quantity, and we may be certain that when the King of kings distributes grace among His royal priesthood, the supply isn't cut short by *Him*. We're often limited in ourselves, but never in the LORD. Those who choose to gather much manna will find that they may have as much as they desires. Some things in the economy of grace are measured. For instance, God never lets us to "be tempted beyond what [we] can bear."[1351] But as for the salt of grace there's no limit: "Ask and it will be given to you."[1352] Parents sometimes need to lock up the candy, but there's no need to keep the salt under lock and key, for few children will eat too much of that. People may have too much money, or too much honor, but they can't have too much grace. When Jeshurun grew fat he kicked against God,[1353] but there's no fear of a person becoming too full of grace. More wealth brings more care, but more grace brings more joy. Believer, go to the throne for a large supply of heavenly salt. It will season your afflictions, which are unsavory without salt. It will preserve your heart, which corrupts if salt is absent. And it will kill your sins, even as salt kills snakes. You need much, so seek much, and have much.

≤⃗ *December 14* ⃗≥

They go from strength to strength (Psalm 84:7).

They go from *strength to strength*. There are various renderings of these words, but all of them contain the idea of progress—to grow stronger and stronger. Usually, if we're walking, we go from strength to weakness. We start fresh, but after awhile the road is rough and the sun is hot. So we sit down by the roadside to rest, and then again painfully pursue our weary way. But Christian pilgrims who obtain fresh supplies of grace are as vigorous after years of toilsome travel and struggle as when they first started. They may not be quite as elated and buoyant, nor quite as zealous as they once were, but they're much stronger in all that constitutes real power. Now they travel more surely, even if more slowly. Some gray-haired veterans have remained as firm in their grasp of truth, and as zealous in spreading it, as they were in their younger days. It must be confessed, however, it's often otherwise, for the love of many waxes cold and iniquity abounds.[1354] But this is their own sin and not the fault of the promise: "Even youths grow tired and weary, and young men stumble and fall; but those who hope in the LORD will renew their strength. They will soar on wings like eagles; they will run and not grow weary, they will walk and not be faint."[1355] Fretful spirits sit down and whine about the future. "Alas!" say they, "we go from affliction to affliction." True, but you'll never find a bundle of affliction that doesn't have sufficient grace bound up in the middle of it.

≥ *December 15* ≥

Orpah kissed her mother-in-law good-by,
but Ruth clung to her (Ruth 1:14).

Both women had an affection for Naomi, and so set out
with her upon her return to the land of Judah. But the
hour of testing came. Naomi most unselfishly set before
each of them the trials that awaited them, and urged them
to return to their Moabitish friends if they cared for ease
and comfort. At first both of them declared they would
cast in their lot with the LORD's people, but on still further
consideration Orpah, with much grief and a respectful
kiss, left Naomi and went back to her idolatrous friends.
Ruth, however, gave herself up to Naomi's God with
all her heart. It's one thing to love the ways of the Lord
when all is well, and quite another to cling to them under
all discouragements and difficulties. The kiss of outward
profession is cheap and easy, but the practical clinging
to the Lord, which must show itself in godly decision for
truth and holiness, isn't so small a matter. Where do we
stand? Is our heart fixed upon Jesus, is the sacrifice bound
with cords to the horns of the altar?[1356] Have we counted
the cost?[1357] Are we ready to suffer all worldly loss for
the Master's sake?[1358] The reward is greater than the cost.
Nothing more is heard of Orpah, but Ruth lives in history
and in heaven, for grace placed her in the noble line from
which came the King of kings.[1359] Blessed among women
will be those who for Christ's sake renounce all. Believer,
never be content with the form of devotion that may be
no better than Orpah's kiss.

≈ *December 16* ≈

"Come to Me" (Matthew 11:28).

The cry of Christianity is the gentle word, "Come." The Jewish law harshly said, "Go, take heed to your steps as to the path in which you walk. Break the commandments, and you'll perish. Keep them, and you'll live." The law was a dispensation of terror, that drove people before it as with a scourge. The gospel draws with bands of love. Jesus is the good Shepherd going before His sheep, bidding them follow Him, and always leading them onward with the sweet word, "Come." The law repels, the gospel attracts. The law shows the distance that there is between God and man. The gospel bridges that awful chasm, and brings the sinner across it. From the first moment of your spiritual life until you're ushered into glory, the language of Christ to you will be, *"Come, come to me."* He will always be ahead of you, bidding you follow Him. He'll always go before you to pave your way and clear your path. You'll hear His animating voice calling you after Him all through life. When you're in the solemn hour of death, the sweet words with which He'll usher you into the heavenly world will be, "Come, you who are blessed by My Father."[1360] Further, this isn't only Christ's cry to you, but, if you're a believer, this is your cry to Christ: "Come! come!" You'll be longing for His second advent. You'll be saying, "Come quickly, LORD Jesus."[1361] As His voice to you is "Come," your response to Him will be, "Come, LORD, and occupy the throne of my heart and make me wholly Yours."

≼ *December 17* ≽

"I remember you" (Jeremiah 2:2, NKJV).

Christ delights to think upon His Church and look upon her beauty. As the bird returns often to its nest, and as the traveler hastens home, so the mind continually pursues the object of its choice. We can't look too often at the one we love—our LORD Jesus. From all eternity He has been "rejoicing in His whole world and delighting in mankind."[1362] His thoughts looked forward to the time when His elect would be born into the world; He viewed them in the mirror of His foreknowledge. "All the days ordained for me were written in your book before one of them came to be."[1363] When the world was created, He was there.[1364] Many times before His incarnation, He descended to this earth in the appearance of a man. On the plains of Mamre.[1365] By the brook of Jabbok.[1366] Beneath the walls of Jericho.[1367] In the fiery furnace of Babylon.[1368] Often the Son of Man visited His people. Because His soul delighted in them, He couldn't stay away from them, for His heart longed after them. They were never absent from His heart, for He had written their names upon His hands.[1369] As the breastplate containing the names of the tribes of Israel was the most brilliant ornament worn by the high priest,[1370] so the names of Christ's elect were His most precious jewels, and glittered on His heart. We may often forget to meditate upon the perfections of our LORD, but He never ceases to remember us. Let's admonish ourselves for past forgetfulness, and pray for grace to always keep Him in our fondest memories.

❧ *December 18* ❧

Rend your heart and not your garments (Joel 2:13).

Outward signs of religious emotion are easily manifested and are *frequently hypocritical*. To feel true repentance is far more difficult and, consequently, far less common. People will attend to the most multiplied and minute ceremonial regulations, for such things are *pleasing to the flesh*. But true religion is too humbling, too heart-searching, too thorough for the tastes of carnal people. They prefer something more ostentatious and worldly. Outward observances are *temporarily comfortable*—eye and ear are pleased, self-conceit is fed, and self-righteousness is puffed up. However, they are *ultimately deceptive*, for at the day of judgment the soul needs something more substantial than ceremonies and rituals to lean upon. Apart from vital godliness all religion is utterly vain. When offered without a sincere heart, every form of worship is a mockery of the majesty of God. Heart-rending is *divinely wrought and solemnly felt*. It's a secret grief that is *personally experience*d as a deep, heart-felt work of the Holy Spirit. It's not a matter to be just talked about and believed in, but keenly and sensitively felt in every living child of the living God. It's *powerfully humiliating*, and completely sin-purging. But it's also *sweet preparation* for those gracious consolations that the proud are unable to receive. Further, it's *distinctly discriminating*, for it belongs to the elect of God, and to them alone. The text commands us to rend our hearts, but how can we do this? We must take them to the Cross on Calvary. A dying Savior's voice rent the rocks once, and it's as powerful now.[1371]

The lot is cast into the lap, but its every decision is from the LORD (Proverbs 16:33).

If the disposal of the lot is the Lord's, whose is the arrangement of our whole life? If the simple casting of a lot[1372] is guided by Him, how much more the events of our entire life—especially when we're told by our blessed Savior that not a sparrow falls to the ground apart from the will of our Father, "and even the very hairs of your head are all numbered."[1373] It would bring a holy calm to your mind if you always remembered this. It would so relieve your mind from anxiety that you would be better able to walk in patience, quietness, and cheerfulness as a Christian should. When we're anxious we can't pray with faith, when we're troubled about the world we can't serve our Master—our thoughts are serving ourselves. "Seek first the kingdom of God and His righteousness, and all these things shall be added to you."[1374] You're meddling with Christ's business and neglecting your own when you fret about your situations and circumstances. You've been trying work that provides and forgetting that it's yours to obey. Be wise and attend to the obeying, and let Christ manage the providing. Come and survey your Father's storehouse, and ask whether He'll let you starve while He has laid up such a great abundance in Christ?[1375] Look at His heart of mercy and see if that can ever prove unkind! Look at His inscrutable wisdom and see if that will ever be at fault. Above all, look to Jesus Christ your Intercessor,[1376] and ask yourself, while He pleads, can your Father deal ungraciously with you?

December 20

"I have loved you with an everlasting love"
(Jeremiah 31:3).

Sometimes the LORD Jesus tells His Church His love thoughts. The Holy Spirit often witness to our spirits of the love of Christ. He takes of the things of Christ and reveals them to us. No voice is heard from the clouds, and no vision is seen in the night, but we have a testimony more sure than either of these. If an angel flew from heaven and informed the saints personally of the Savior's love to them, the evidence would not be one bit more satisfactory than that which is borne in the heart by the Holy Ghost. Ask those of the LORD's people who have lived the nearest to the gates of heaven, and they will tell you that they have had seasons when the love of Christ toward them has been a fact so clear and sure, that they could no more doubt it than they could question their own existence. Yes, beloved believer, you and I have had times of refreshing from the presence of the LORD,[1377] and then our faith has mounted to the topmost heights of assurance. We've had confidence to lean our heads upon the bosom of our LORD, and we have no more questioned our Master's affection to us than John did when in that blessed posture.[1378] Not even that much, for the dark question, "LORD, is it I that will betray you?"[1379] has been put far from us. He has kissed us with the kisses of His mouth, and killed our doubts by the closeness of His embrace. His love has been sweeter than honey[1380] to our souls.

December 21

*Has He not made with me an everlasting covenant
(2 Samuel 23:5).*

This covenant is *divine in its origin.* Oh that great word
HE! God, the everlasting Father, has made a covenant with
you. Yes, that God who spoke the world into existence
by a word. He, stooping from His majesty, takes hold
of your hand and makes a covenant with you. It's a
deed that might enrapture our hearts forever if we could
really understand it. "HE ... made with me an everlasting
covenant." A king has not made a covenant with me. The
Prince of the kings of the earth, Shaddai, the Lord All-
sufficient, the Jehovah of ages, the everlasting Elohim, "HE
... made with me an everlasting covenant." But notice,
it's *particular in its application.* "HE ... made with ME an
everlasting covenant." Here lies the sweetness of it to each
believer. It's not enough for me that He made peace for the
world, I want to know whether He made peace for *me!*
Neither is it enough that He's made a covenant, I want to
know whether He's made a covenant *with me.* Blessed is
the assurance that He's made a covenant with me! If the
Holy Ghost gives me assurance of this, then His salvation
is mine, His heart is mine, He Himself is mine—*He's my
God.* This covenant is *everlasting.* An everlasting covenant
means a covenant that has no beginning and no ending.
How marvelous amid all the uncertainties of life to know
that "God's solid foundation stands firm,"[1381] and to have
God's own promise, "I will not violate My covenant or
alter what My lips have uttered."[1382]

⊰ *December 22* ⊱

I will strengthen you (Isaiah 41:10).

God is able to do all things! Believer, until you can drain dry the ocean of omnipotence, until you can break into pieces the towering mountains of almighty strength, you never need to fear. Don't think that human strength will ever be able to overcome the power of God. While the earth's huge pillars stand,[1383] you have enough reason to hold firm in your faith. The same God who directs the earth in its orbit, who feeds the burning furnace of the sun, and trims the lamps of heaven, has promised to supply you with daily strength. While He's able to uphold the universe,[1384] don't dream that He'll prove unable to fulfill His own promises. Remember what He did in past ages and generations. Remember how He spoke and it was done[1385]—how He commanded and it stood fast.[1386] Will He that created the world grow weary?[1387] He hangs the earth on nothing.[1388] Will He who does this be unable to support His children? Will the Almighty be unfaithful to His word for lack of power? Who restrains the tempest?[1389] Doesn't He ride upon the wings of the wind,[1390] make the clouds His chariots,[1391] and measure the waters in the hollow of His hand?[1392] How can He fail you? When He's put such a faithful promise as this on record, will you for a moment indulge the thought that He has out-promised Himself, and gone beyond His power to fulfill? Surely you can no longer doubt. O my God and my strength, Your promise will be fulfilled, for the boundless reservoir of Your grace can never be exhausted.

December 23

"Friend, move up to a better place" (Luke 14:10).

When the life of grace first begins in the soul, we do draw near to God, but it's with great fear and trembling. The soul, conscious of guilt and humbled by it, is overawed with the solemnity of its position. It's cast to the earth by a sense of the grandeur of Jehovah, in whose presence it stands. But as Christians grow in grace—although they'll never forget the solemnity of their position or lose that holy awe of realizing they're in the presence of the God who can create or can destroy—their fear has all its terror taken out of it. It becomes a holy reverence, and no longer an overshadowing dread. They're called up higher to greater access to God in Christ Jesus. Then the children of God, walking amid the splendors of Deity, and veiling their face like the glorious cherubim,[1393] with those twin wings that are the blood and righteousness of Jesus Christ, will reverently approach the throne. There they will see a God of love, goodness, and mercy, and will realize the covenant character of God rather than His absolute Deity. They will see in God His goodness rather than His greatness, and more of His love than of His majesty. Then will the soul enjoy a more sacred liberty of intercession, for while prostrate before the glory of the Infinite God, it will be sustained by the refreshing consciousness of being in the presence of boundless mercy and infinite love, and by the realization of acceptance "in the Beloved."[1394] Thus the believer draws near in holy confidence, crying, "Abba, Father."[1395]

◁ *December 24* ▷

For your sakes He became poor (2 Corinthians 8:9).

The LORD Jesus Christ was eternally *rich*, glorious, and exalted, but "though he was rich, yet for your sakes he became poor." Rich saints cannot be true in their relations with poor brothers and sisters unless they share their substance with them. Similarly, it's impossible that our LORD could have communion with us unless He imparted to us of His own wealth and became poor to make us rich. Had He remained upon His throne of glory, and had we continued in the ruins of The Fall without receiving His salvation, communion would have been impossible on both sides. The Fall made it as impossible for humankind to communicate with God as it is for Christ to be in harmony with Belial.[1396] To achieve communion, it was necessary that the righteous Savior give to sinners His own perfection, and that we sinners receive of His fullness grace for grace.[1397] Thus in giving and receiving, the One descends from the heights and the others ascend from the depths, and so can embrace each other in true companionship. Poverty must be enriched by Him in whom are infinite treasures before it can commune, and guilt must lose itself in imputed and imparted righteousness[1398] before the soul can walk in companionship with purity. Christ must clothe His people in His own garments[1399] or He cannot admit them into His palace of glory, and He must wash them in His own blood[1400] or they will be too defiled for the embrace of His companionship. For *your sake* the Lord Jesus "became poor" so He might lift you up into communion with Himself.

"The virgin will be with child and will give birth to a Son, and will call Him Immanuel" (Isaiah 7:14).

Let's go today to Bethlehem, and in company with wondering shepherds and adoring Magi see Him who was born King of the Jews, for we by faith can claim an interest in Him and can sing, *"To us* a Child is born, *to us* a Son is given."[1401] Jesus is Jehovah incarnate,[1402] our LORD and our God,[1403] and yet our brother and friend. Let us adore Him. Let's look first at *His miraculous conception.* It was a thing unheard of before, and unparalleled since, that a virgin should conceive and bear a Son. The first promise was like this, *"The seed of the woman,"*[1404] not the offspring of the man. Since the woman led the way in the sin that lost the Garden, she alone ushers in the Restorer. Our Savior, although truly man, was as to His human nature the Holy One of God. Let's reverently bow before the holy Child whose innocence restores to humanity its ancient glory. And let's pray that He will truly be formed in us, the hope of glory.[1405] Don't fail to note *His humble parentage.* His mother has been described simply as "a virgin," not a princess, or prophetess, or matron of a large estate. How humble her position, how poor the man to whom she was betrothed, and how miserable the accommodation provided for the new-born King. *Immanuel,* God with us[1406] in our nature, in our sorrow, in our lifework, in our punishment, in our grave, and now with us, or rather we with Him, in resurrection, ascension, triumph, and Second Advent splendor. All blessings to Him on this day!

The last Adam (1 Corinthians 15:45).

Jesus is the head of His elect. Under the law of grace every redeemed soul is one with the LORD from heaven, since He is the sponsor and substitute of the elect in the new covenant of love. The apostle Paul declares that Levi was in the body of Abraham when Melchizedek met him.[1407] It's also true that the believer was in the body of Jesus Christ, the Mediator, when in eternity the covenant settlements of grace were decreed, ratified, and made sure forever. Thus, whatever Christ has done, He has done for the whole body of His Church. We were crucified in Him and buried with Him,[1408] and to make it still more wonderful, we're risen with Him and even ascended with Him to the seats on high.[1409] It's in that way the Church has fulfilled the law, and is "accepted *in the Beloved*."[1410] It's in that way it's regarded with complacency by the just Jehovah, for He views it in Christ, and doesn't look upon it as separate from its covenant head. As the Anointed Redeemer of Israel, Christ Jesus has nothing separate from His Church, but all that He has He holds for it. All that the last Adam is or does, is ours as well as His, seeing that He is our representative. Here is the foundation of the covenant of grace. This gracious system of representation and substitution moved Justin Martyr[1411] to cry out, "O blessed change, O sweet permutation!"[1412] This is the very foundation of the gospel of our salvation, and is to be received with strong faith and rapturous joy.

Can papyrus grow tall where there is no marsh?
(Job 8:11)

Papyrus is spongy and hollow, and so are hypocrites—there's no substance or stability in them. It's shaken to and fro in every wind just as formalists yield to every influence. For this reason the papyrus isn't broken by the storm, and neither are hypocrites troubled with persecution. The papyrus by nature lives in water, and owes its very existence to the marsh and moisture in which it has taken root. Let the marsh become dry, and the papyrus withers quickly. Its greenness is absolutely dependent upon circumstances, a present abundance of water makes it flourish, and a drought destroys it at once. Is this our case? Do we only serve God when we're in good company, or when Christianity is profitable and respectable? Do we love the LORD only when temporal comforts are received from His hands? If so we're base hypocrites, and like the withering papyrus, we'll perish when death deprives us of outward joys. But can we honestly assert that when bodily comforts have been few, and our surroundings have been harmful to grace rather than helpful to it, we've still held fast our integrity? If so, then we've hope that there's genuine vital godliness in us. The papyrus can't grow without wet soil, but those planted by the LORD can and do flourish even in years of drought. Godly people often grow best when their worldly circumstances decay. Those who follow Christ for their prosperity are Judases. Those who follow for loaves and fishes are children of the devil. But those who follow Him out of love for Him are His own beloved ones.

⇜ *December 28* ⇝

The life I live in the body, I live by faith in the Son of God (Galatians 2:20).

When the LORD in mercy passed by and saw us in our blood, He first of all said, "Live."[1413] This He did *first*, because life is one of the essential things in spiritual matters, and until it is bestowed we're incapable of partaking in the things of the kingdom. Now the life that grace confers upon the saints at the moment of their life-giving is none other than the life of Christ. This life runs into us, like the sap from the vine into the branches,[1414] and establishes a living connection between our souls and Christ. Faith is the grace that perceives this union, having proceeded from it as its firstfruits. It's the neck that joins the body of the Church to its all-glorious Head. Faith lays hold upon the LORD Jesus with a firm and determined grasp. It knows His excellence and worth, and no temptation can induce it to place its trust elsewhere. Christ Jesus is so delighted with this heavenly grace, that He never ceases to strengthen it by the loving embrace and all-sufficient support of His eternal arms. Here is established a living, sensible, and delightful union that brings forth love, confidence, sympathy, complacency, and joy, of which both the bride and bridegroom love to drink. When the soul clearly perceives this oneness between itself and Christ, the pulse is sensed as beating for both, and the one blood as flowing through the veins of each. Then the heart is as near heaven as it can be on earth, and is prepared for the enjoyment of the most sublime and spiritual kind of companionship.

December 29

"Thus far has the Lord *helped us"*
(1 Samuel 7:12).

The words "thus far" seem like a hand pointing toward the past. Twenty years or seventy, and yet, "thus far the Lord has helped!" Through poverty, wealth, sickness, health; at home, abroad, on the land or on sea; in honor, dishonor, perplexity, joy, trial, triumph, prayer, and temptation, "thus far has the Lord helped us!" We delight to look down a long avenue of trees. It's delightful to gaze from end to end of the long vista, a sort of vegetation temple, with its branching pillars and its arches of leaves. In the same way, look down the long aisles of your years, at the green boughs of mercy overhead, and the strong pillars of loving kindness and faithfulness that bear up your joys. Are there no birds in yonder branches singing? Surely there must be many, and they all sing of mercy received "thus far." But the words also point *forward.* For when a person gets up to a certain mark and writes "thus far," they're not yet at the end, there's still a distance to be traveled. More trials, joys, temptations, triumphs, prayers and answers, toils, strength; battles, and victories. Then come old age, affliction, death. Is it over now? No! There is more yet—awakening in Jesus' likeness, thrones, harps, songs, psalms, white raiment, the face of Jesus, the society of saints, the glory of God, the fullness of eternity, the infinity of bliss. O be of good courage, believer, and with grateful confidence raise your "Ebenezer."[1415] When read in heaven's light, how glorious a prospect your "thus far" will unfold to your grateful eye!

The end of a matter is better than its beginning
(Ecclesiastes 7:8).

Look at our LORD and Master and see His beginning. He was despised and rejected by people, a man of sorrows and acquainted with grief.[1416] Would you see the end? He sits at His Father's right hand, waiting until His enemies are made his footstool.[1417] "In this world we are like Him."[1418] You must bear the cross,[1419] or you'll never wear the crown.[1420] You must wade through the mire, or you'll never walk the golden street.[1421] Cheer up, "the end of a matter is better than its beginning." See that creeping worm, how contemptible its appearance. It's the beginning of a thing. Mark that insect with gorgeous wings, playing in the sunbeams, sipping at the flower bells, full of happiness and life. It's the end of the thing. That caterpillar is you, until you're wrapped up in the chrysalis of death. But when Christ appears you'll be like Him, for you'll see Him as He is.[1422] Be content to be like Him, a worm and not a person,[1423] so you'll be satisfied when you wake up in His likeness. That rough-looking diamond is put upon the cutting wheel. He cuts it on all sides. It loses much—much that seemed costly to itself. The king is crowned, the diadem is put upon His head with trumpet's joyful sound. A glittering ray flashes from that crown, and it beams from the very diamond that was so sorely troubled by the cutting wheel. Let faith and perseverance have their perfect work,[1424] for in the day when the crown is set upon the King's head,[1425] one ray of glory will stream from you.

ᚫ *December 31* ᚫ

*On the last and greatest day of the Feast, Jesus
stood and said in a loud voice, "If anyone is thirsty,
let him come to Me and drink" (John 7:37).*

Patience had her perfect work in the Lord Jesus, and
until the last day of the feast He pleaded with the Jews.
On this last day of the year He pleads with us, and waits ⋅
to be gracious to us. The longsuffering of the Savior
in bearing with some of us year after year is admirable
indeed, considering our provocations, rebellions, and
resistance to His Holy Spirit. It's a wonder we're still in
the land of mercy. Christ pleads with us to be reconciled.
"We *implore* you," says the Apostle, "as though God were
pleading through us." [1426] How deep must be the love that
makes the Lord weep over sinners. [1427] Surely at the call
of such a cry our willing hearts will come. Everything
is provided that anyone can need to quench their soul's
thirst. To the conscience the atonement brings peace, to
the understanding the gospel brings the richest instruction,
to the heart Christ is the noblest object of affection, to
the whole person the truth that is in Jesus [1428] supplies the
purest nourishment. Thirst is terrible, but Jesus can remove
it. [1429] Though the soul were utterly famished, Jesus could
restore it. Every one who is thirsty is welcome. No other
distinction is made but that of thirst. Whatever is causing
the thirst, sin, sorrow, or sickness, come and drink freely.
The sinner must come to Jesus, not to works, ordinances,
or doctrines, but to a personal Redeemer—Jesus Christ.
Dear reader, hear the dear Redeemer's loving voice as He
cries to each of us, "If anyone is thirsty, let him come to
me and drink."

ENDNOTES

1. Deuteronomy 26:9
2. Joshua 5:12
3. Philippians 1:23
4. Hebrews 4:9
5. Some consider the Jordan River to be symbolic of death, which we must cross to reach our promised land of heaven.
6. 1 Thessalonians 4:17
7. Hebrews 4:3
8. 2 Corinthians 5:5
9. Zephaniah 3:17
10. Isaiah 26:3
11. Revelation 5:8-13
12. Psalm 78:25
13. The land of Canaan, the Promised Land, is considered by some to be symbolic of heaven.
14. Genesis 4:26
15. Revelation 22:20
16. 1 Corinthians 15:18
17. Colossians 2:9
18. 2 Corinthians 5:21
19. John 17:3
20. Genesis 1:3
21. Ecclesiastes 11:7
22. 1 King 17:16
23. Exodus 39:30, KJV
24. Deuteronomy 32:49
25. John 17:9, 24
26. Revelation 5:9
27. Romans 8:17
28. Ephesians 6:13, KJV
29. Isaiah 9:6
30. Philippians 1:6
31. Romans 8:3, Hebrews 10:12
32. Matthew 28:18, KJV
33. Isaiah 1:18
34. Matthew 15:28
35. Hebrews 4:16
36. *Granary*: A building for storing threshed grain.
37. John 1:29
38. Revelation 21:4
39. *The Pilgrim's Progress* by John Bunyan, updated by L. E. Hazelbaker, published by Bridge-Logos
40. Genesis 4:4
41. Hebrews 12:24
42. Hebrews 9:24-25, 13:11-12
43. Romans 5:1
44. Exodus 15:13
45. Revelation 15:3
46. John 18:9
47. Romans 8:33, Ephesians 1:11, Colossians 3:12, James 2:5, 1 Peter 2:9
48. Romans 1:6, 8:28-30
49. Ephesians 2:5, 8
50. Hebrews 4:15
51. Psalm 23:4
52. Jeremiah 3:22
53. Matthew 11:28
54. Galatians 4:3, 9, 5:1, Hebrews 2:15
55. Exodus 2:3
56. Psalm 25:6
57. Matthew 6:9
58. Malachi 1:6
59. Romans 6:13
60. Romans 8:15, Galatians 6:6
61. 1 John 1:7
62. Romans 8:1
63. Hebrews 7:25
64. Hebrews 2:14
65. 1 Peter 1:3
66. Colossians 1:28
67. Colossians 2:10, KJV
68. Ephesians 1:6, KJV
69. Ephesians 5:27, KJV

70. Believed by some to be symbolized by the Jordan River, which the Israelites had to cross to enter the Promised Land.
71. Romans 8:37
72. Revelation 3:21
73. Numbers 13:24
74. 2 Samuel 23:15
75. Matthew 6:10
76. Psalm 102:13
77. Romans 8:26-27
78. Colossians 1:28
79. 1 Corinthians 1:30
80. John 19:30
81. Philippians 3:9
82. *The Pilgrim's Progress* by John Bunyan, updated by L. E. Hazelbaker, published by Bridge-Logos
83. Isaiah 44:22
84. Psalm 34:1
85. Romans 3:3, Hebrews 2:17, 1 John 2:2
86. John 19:30
87. 1 Corinthians 6:11, Revelation 1:5, 7:14
88. Colossians 2:14
89. Ephesians 2:1, 5, Colossians 2:13
90. Exodus 16:3
91. Deuteronomy 8:15-16
92. 2 Corinthians 12:9
93. Revelation 1:5, KJV
94. Psalm 23:4
95. Revelation 1:8, 17
96. Joshua 1:9, Matthew 28:20
97. Some believe that the Jordan River symbolizes death, which must be crossed to get into the Promised Land, which symbolizes heaven.
98. Romans 8:38-39
99. John 6:57
100. 1 Timothy 2:5
101. Daniel 7:9, 13, 22
102. Exodus 3:14
103. Isaiah 44:22
104. 1 Corinthians 12:9, Ephesians 2:8
105. Philippians 4:19
106. Numbers 7:89, Hebrews 4:16
107. Psalm 103:2
108. Psalm 23:4
109. Hebrews 11:10
110. Psalm 45:8
111. Psalm 32:8
112. Deuteronomy 8:10-11
113. Matthew 26:41
114. Mark 8:38
115. Luke 23:34
116. Luke 6:27, 35, Romans 12:21
117. Psalm 130:1
118. 2 Corinthians 1:3-5
119. 1 John 3:1
120. Matthew 6:34
121. Philippians 4:19
122. Matthew 6:11
123. Genesis 16:13-14
124. Genesis 21:19
125. See the Pure Gold Classics version of *The Practice of the Presence Of God* by Brother Lawrence, published by Bridge-Logos Publishers.
126. John 4:13-14
127. Acts 27:28
128. Psalm 34:4
129. 2 Corinthians 1:3
130. Jeremiah 8:22
131. Exodus 15:26
132. John 16:24
133. Psalm 94:19
134. John 4:14
135. John 15:5
136. Genesis 28:12-13
137. Romans 4:13, 16, NKJV
138. Genesis 13:14-15
139. Ephesians 2:8-9

140. Malachi 3:10
141. Ephesians 2:1
142. Revelation 1:8, 11 KJV
143. 1 Corinthians 4:7
144. Galatians 2:20
145. Romans 15:16, 1 Corinthians 6:11, Hebrews 10:10, 14
146. 2 Corinthians 6:17
147. Romans 8:28, Hebrews 12:10
148. Psalm 121:2
149. John 15:5
150. Exodus 13:21-22, Numbers 14:14
151. Psalm 90:1
152. Hebrews 13:8, James 1:17
153. Hebrews 11:13, 1 Peter 2:11, KJV
154. Philippians 4:19
155. A famous German family of bankers who established banks throughout Europe.
156. Hebrews 4:16
157. Hebrews 6:19
158. Hebrews 1:14
159. Galatians 3:13, 1 Peter 1:18, Revelation 5:9, KJV
160. Matthew 25:34
161. 1 John 3:2
162. Romans 5:1-2, Colossians 1:27
163. Galatians 3:24
164. Romans 2:4, Titus 1:3-7
165. Luke 15:11-24
166. John 1:12
167. Acts 2:39, 1 Corinthians 1:23-24
168. Romans 8:28
169. Luke 10:2
170. Ephesians 6:12-18
171. 2 Corinthians 11:3, 1 Peter 5:8
172. Acts 1:14, 2:1, 46, 4:24
173. Revelation 3:18

174. Isaiah 41:10
175. 2 Corinthians 20:17
176. Romans 8:28
177. Luke 6:48-49
178. 2 Corinthians 12:9
179. The Pilgrim's Progress by John Bunyan, updated by L. E. Hazelbaker, published by Bridge-Logos
180. Hebrews 10:25
181. 1 Peter 5:8
182. Numbers 35:6-12
183. 2 Timothy 4:8
184. Luke 22:46
185. Philippians 1:6, 2:13
186. 2 Corinthians 5:17
187. Romans 8:15-16, Galatians 4:6
188. John 1:12, Romans 5:1-2
189. Romans 8:16
190. Ephesians 2:12
191. Mark 9:23
192. Acts 6:5-8
193. Matthew 8:26, 14:31
194. Matthew 15:28
195. Hebrews 11:6
196. 2 Timothy 3:12
197. Romans 4:16, Galatians 3, Hebrews 11:8-10, 17
198. Acts 5:40-41
199. Hebrews 4:15, 13:5-6
200. 2 Corinthians 12:9-10
201. Romans 8:18
202. Luke 24:32
203. Song of Songs 5:15
204. Song of Songs 1:3
205. Jeremiah 48:11
206. Romans 5:8, 1 Thessalonians 5:9-10
207. 2 Corinthians 5:21
208. Deuteronomy 5:21, Romans 13:9
209. Philippians 4:11, 1 Timothy 6:6-8, Hebrews 13:5
210. Acts 17:26
211. 1 Corinthians 13:3
212. Galatians 6:2

213. 2 Kings 7:1-11
214. Mark 10:29, John 3:15, 5:39, 10:28, 17:2; Acts 13:48, Romans 5:21, 6:23; 1 John 5:11-13
215. Jonah 3:9
216. Jeremiah 29:13
217. John 6:37
218. Matthew 18:14, Luke 21:18, John 3:15-16, 10:28
219. 2 Kings 7:8
220. *Grace*: Divine love and protection bestowed freely on people. The state of being protected or sanctified by the favor of God. An excellence or a power granted by God.
221. Acts 4:13
222. Psalm 119:116
223. Hebrews 4:16
224. 2 Corinthians 12:9
225. Exodus 29:1, Leviticus 8:30
226. John 1:10
227. Luke 2:48, John 7:5
228. *Tartar*: A member of any of the Turkic and Mongolian peoples of central Asia who invaded western Asia and eastern Europe in the Middle Ages.
229. *Cheapside*: A street and district in medival London, England. It was the market center and the site of the Mermaid Tavern, a gathering place for Elizabethan poets and playwrights.
230. Psalm 39:12, Hebrews 11:9, KJV
231. Psalm 50:10
232. Mark 10:21, Galatians 6:2
233. Matthew 25:40-45
234. Matthew 6:30, 8:26, 14:31, 16:18
235. Characters in *The Pilgrim's Progress* by John Bunyan, updated by L. E. Hazelbaker, published by Bridge-Logos
236. John 1:12, 1 John 3:1-2, 10
237. Matthew 6:9, Galatians 4:6
238. Luke 17:5
239. Romans 8:15-16
240. 1 John 4:18
241. Isaiah 65:24
242. Hebrews 10:36
243. Hebrews 4:16
244. Psalm 62:7-8, 91:2, 94:22
245. Psalm 57:2, 91:1, Daniel 7:18
246. 2 Samuel 22:41, Psalm 18:40
247. James 1:6-8
248. Mark 9:23, KJV (Compare with Matthew 19:26)
249. Isaiah 61:1; Luke 4:18
250. Song of Songs 2:16, KJV
251. Isaiah 5:1, KJV
252. Song of Songs 5:10, 16, KJV
253. Romans 8:35, 37, KJV
254. Luke 22:44, KJV
255. 1 Corinthians 3:1
256. Exodus 3:3
257. Matthew 26:37
258. Philippians 3:10
259. Isaiah 49:21
260. 2 Corinthians 9:15
261. Revelation 8:3-4
262. Luke 22:41
263. Genesis 32:28
264. Matthew 23:12, 1 Peter 5:6
265. Mark 14:36, Galatians 4:6
266. Romans 8:15

267. Psalm 61:1
268. Luke 11:5-10
269. Luke 18:1-8
270. Philippians 4:6, Colossians 4:2
271. Matthew 26:39
272. Numbers 21:17
273. Hebrews 3:1, KJV
274. He was heard because of His reverent submission. (NIV)
275. Matthew 26:40
276. Ephesians 6:16
277. Luke 22:53, John 14:30
278. Luke 22:43
279. Matthew 26:41
280. Mark 13:22
281. Matthew 10:16
282. Proverbs 7:5-23
283. Proverbs 7:21
284. Mark 14:21
285. Isaiah 53:7
286. John 10:11
287. John 18:12
288. 2 Corinthians 5:21, 1 John 4:10
289. Despair, Much-afraid, and Despondency are characters in *Pilgrim's Progress*.
290. John 5:28-29, 1 Thessalonians 4:16
291. Hebrews 11:13, 12:22-24
292. Matthew 26:35, John 11:16
293. Matthew 26:53
294. Hebrews 6:6
295. John 17:5
296. John 1:3, 10
297. Isaiah 53:3
298. Luke 1:35, John 1:34, 3:18
299. Matthew 27:46
300. 1 John 4:19
301. Hebrews 5:9
302. Hebrews 4:15
303. Acts 5:40-41
304. 2 Timothy 4:8
305. 2 Timothy 2:12, KJV
306. *Ransom*. A redemption from sin and its consequences.
307. 2 Corinthians 5:21
308. Matthew 27:26, Mark 15:15, John 19:1-3
309. 2 Corinthians 11:24
310. Isaiah 50:6, Matthew 26:67, Mark 14:65, Luke 22:64
311. Mark 14:3
312. Luke 10:39
313. Esther 4:10-11
314. 1 John 4:18
315. 2 Corinthians 5:7
316. John 4:10
317. John 7:46
318. *Apologist*: A person who argues in defense or justification of Something, such as a doctrine a policy, or an institution.
319. Isaiah 53:7
320. John 1:29, 36, Revelation 13:8
321. Leviticus 16:8-10, 20-22
322. Isaiah 53:6
323. 2 Corinthians 5:21
324. Acts 2:36-38, 3:19, 17:30
325. Colossians 2:10
326. Hebrews 10:14
327. Jeremiah 23:6
328. Ephesians 1:6
329. Revelation 3:12, 21:2
330. Revelation 3:21
331. Luke 9:23
332. 2 Corinthians 4:17
333. John 17:14, 16
334. Matthew 7:14
335. 2 Timothy 4:8
336. Mark 15:23
337. John 19:28
338. Psalm 69:21, Matthew 27:34, John 19:29

339. John 1:10
340. Matthew 2:2, Matthew 27:37
341. Matthew 27:16-22
342. Mark 15:27
343. John 17:5
344. Revelation 20:15
345. Psalm 22:1, Mark 15:34
346. Proverbs 1:25-26
347. Romans 5:8, 1 Thessalonians 5:10
348. John 3:15-16
349. John 19:2
350. Luke 23:21
351. Luke 7:11-15
352. Mark 1:30-31
353. Mark 16:9
354. Luke 10:38-39
355. Hebrews 13:5
356. John 19:34
357. 2 Samuel 15:30
358. Exodus 19:20, Judges 4:14
359. John 19:13
360. Daniel 10:8
361. Isaiah 53:5
362. Job 19:29
363. Luke 22:42
364. Hebrews 4:16
365. Mark 10:38-39
366. Romans 8:16
367. 1 Corinthians 3:13-15
368. Proverbs 18:14
369. Psalm 24:7-10
370. Hebrews 4:15
371. Psalm 51:11
372. Psalm 42:1-2
373. Psalm 43:5
374. Colossians 2:9
375. John 14:15, 15:10
376. Mark 4:15
377. Hebrews 9:26, 1 Peter 1:19-20, Revelation 13:8
378. Luke 8:53
379. Luke 23:11
380. Mark 15:17-19
381. Matthew 27:39-43
382. Isaiah 53:3
383. Romans 5:8
384. Romans 5:11, KJV
385. Galatians 3:13
386. Romans 5:10, 2 Corinthians 5:19
387. 1 Corinthians 8:6, Galatians 3:28, Ephesians 1:10
388. 1 John 1:7
389. Isaiah 1:18
390. Revelation 1:5, KJV
391. Ephesians 5:27
392. Exodus 12:21-23
393. Hebrews 13:12
394. Revelation 12:11
395. John 6:44
396. Ephesians 2:12-13
397. Luke 13:3, Acts 2:38
398. John 19:30
399. Hebrews 12:2, KJV
400. Exodus 12:7-8, 22-23
401. According to legend, Alexander the Great was shown a curious knot at Gordium in Asia Minor. An oracle had said that the man who untied it would rule Asia. Alexander dramatically cut the Gordian knot with his sword.
402. Mark 8:38
403. Exodus 12:23, 27
404. In the tabernacle in the wilderness, the curtain separated the Holy Place from the Most Holy Place. The ark of the Testimony, with the broken tablets inside, was placed behind the curtain, in the Most Holy Place. (Exodus 26:33) In Solomon's Temple in Jerusalem, the curtain still separated the Holy Place from the Most Holy Place, but the

ark of the Testimony was
not behind the curtain.
It had been lost centuries
before—no one knows
when or how.
405. Exodus 25:17-22, 30:6
406. Exodus 25:22
407. Romans 16:25-26
408. Hebrews 9:7, 12
409. Romans 5:1-2, Ephesians
2:18
410. Hebrews 4:16, KJV
411. John 14:6
412. 1 Corinthians 15:55
413. John 14:2-3
414. 2 Corinthians 5:8, KJV
(away from the body ...
at home with the Lord,
NIV)
415. John 6:20-21
416. Matthew 17:20
417. Psalm 139:11-12, 1 Thessalonians 5:5
418. Romans 12:5, 1 Corinthians 12:12, Ephesians 1:10
419. Revelation 4:21; Hebrews
1:3, 10:12
420. 2 Timothy 4:8
421. Revelation 19:12
422. 1 John 3:2
423. John 14:3
424. Romans 6:6, Galatians
2:20
425. Matthew 1:21
426. John 15:5
427. Romans 8:37
428. "In view of all this, we
are making a binding
agreement" (NIV).
429. Psalm 118:27, KJV
430. Psalm 50:14, 61:8,
116:18
431. "Arise, my darling, my
beautiful one, and come
with Me" (NIV).
432. 2 Corinthians 6:17, 1
John 2:15

433. Psalm 40:2
434. Revelation 5:9, IJV
435. 1 Peter 5:7
436. Philippians 4:19
437. Genesis 15:1
438. Psalm 84:11
439. Isaiah 40:29
440. Matthew 5:6
441. 2 Samuel 7:25, 1 Chronicles 17:23
442. Isaiah 43:25
443. Isaiah 55:11
444. Isaiah 54:10
445. Proverbs 4:18
446. Psalm 23:2
447. Exodus 15:23
448. Ephesians 6:13
449. Hebrews 12:6-11
450. Lamentations 3:33
451. Hebrews 12:10
452. Hebrews 12:6-7
453. Matthew 26:67, Mark
14:65
454. Luke 19:41, John 11:35
455. Matthew 27:30, Mark
15:19
456. Matthew 27:29, Mark
15:17, John 19:2
457. 1 Timothy 6:12
458. Matthew 25:21, 23, KJV
459. John 17:24
460. Psalm 55:6
461. 1 Thessalonians 4:17
462. John 19:30
463. Revelation 3:18
464. Matthew 5:48
465. John 12:31, 14:30, 16:11,
Ephesians 2:2
466. 1 Peter 5:8
467. Genesis 23:4
468. James 4:4
469. Jeremiah 17:9
470. Psalm 91:15
471. Revelation 5:9
472. John 20:28
473. Psalm 71:3
474. Luke 4:38-39

475. Mark 9:20
476. Luke 8:27
477. Luke 17:12
478. Mark 10:46
479. Luke 7:22
480. Exodus 15:26, Luke 4:18
481. Luke 7:21
482. Matthew 8:16-17
483. Isaiah 53:4-5
484. Matthew 12:15, KJV
485. Romans 8:16
486. Ephesians 3:11, 1 John 3:8
487. *Penitent*: Feeling or expressing remorse for one's misdeeds or sins.
488. John 5:14-15
489. John 17:24, Ephesians 1:4
490. Ephesians 1:5
491. Romans 8:14-16
492. John 1:12
493. Hebrews 13:20
494. Hebrews 7:22 (surety, KJV; guarantee, NIV)
495. Hebrews 13:20
496. 2 Corinthians 1:3-4
497. Ephesians 1:5, 8
498. John 17:2, 6, Ephesians 1:4
499. Galatians 3:13, 1 Peter 1:18, Revelation 5:9
500. Romans 8:34, Hebrews 7:25
501. Colossians 2:15
502. 1 Corinthians 15:14, 17
503. Romans 1:4
504. Romans 14:9
505. Romans 4:25, 5:1
506. 1 Peter 1:3
507. Romans 8:11
508. 1 Corinthians 15:18
509. Mark 6:50
510. Matthew 7:24-25
511. Hebrews 13:8
512. Psalm 138:6
513. Psalm 116:11
514. Galatians 6:7

515. Revelation 19:11-14
516. James 5:7
517. Revelation 22:12
518. Hebrews 1:2
519. Revelation 21:21
520. Revelation 22:1-2
521. 1 Peter 2:9
522. Revelation 1:6, 5:10
523. Revelation 3:21
524. John 17:22
525. John 15:11
526. Romans 5:1
527. Revelation 7:9
528. Revelation 5:8, 14:2
529. Luke 23:42-43
530. Ephesians 1:6
531. Romans 8:1
532. Revelation 20:12
533. Romans 8:33
534. Ephesians 5:27, Hebrews 9:14
535. Romans 4:25, 5:16-18
536. 2 Kings 4:1-6
537. Psalm 103:2
538. Psalm 68:19, KJV
539. Psalm 103:4, KJV
540. Psalm 57:8
541. 2 Corinthians 11:1, NKJV
542. 1 Corinthians 3:2-3
543. Deuteronomy 33:23
544. John 13:16, 15:20
545. Matthew 19:30, Mark 10:31
546. Esther 3:1, 2:19
547. 1 Chronicles 12:8
548. 1 Kings 19:2-3, 9-10
549. James 1:5
550. 2 Timothy 1:12
551. Romans 8:16
552. Isaiah 55:3, Acts 13:34
553. Hebrews 6:19
554. Psalm 30:6-7
555. Revelation 20:15
556. Deuteronomy 34:1
557. Psalm 107:30
558. Acts 14:22

559. James 1:2
560. Philippians 1:6
561. Isaiah 61:10
562. Philippians 3:9
563. Psalm 107:30
564. Genesis 32:24
565. Genesis 32:26
566. Exodus 25:17, Hebrews 4:16
567. *Shekinah*: A visible manifestation of the divine Presence as described in Jewish theology.
568. Exodus 25:20
569. Ephesians 6:18
570. Psalm 119:117
571. John 15:5
572. Hebrews 13:20
573. John 15:1
574. 2 Corinthians 12:10
575. Matthew 23:37
576. Psalm 22:11
577. Psalm 27:9
578. *Care*: Worry, anxiety
579. Matthew 6:34
580. Philippians 4:6
581. Matthew 11:28
582. Psalm 1:1-2, 33:11, 106:13, Proverbs 3:5-7
583. Jeremiah 2:13
584. Jeremiah 9:24
585. Philippians 4:6, NKJV
586. Isaiah 26:3
587. 2 Samuel 9:6-7
588. 2 Samuel 9:8
589. Romans 8:15
590. 2 Samuel 2:18
591. 2 Corinthians 12:9
592. 2 Samuel 4:4
593. Isaiah 35:6
594. Revelation 21:4
595. 2 Kings 2:11
596. Romans 8:35-39
597. Ephesians 4:26
598. Matthew 23:14, NKJV (verse not contained in NIV)

599. 1 John 3:8
600. 1 Corinthians 15:25
601. 2 Corinthians 6:15
602. Matthew 25:41
603. Psalm 45:7, Hebrew 1:9
604. John 15:10
605. Song of Songs 2:15
606. Judges 15:4
607. 2 Samuel 13:19, Esther 4:1, Daniel 9:3
608. Revelation 17:14
609. Hebrews 4:15
610. Isaiah 63:9
611. Isaiah 12:3
612. John 18:1
613. Genesis 8:22
614. Revelation 22:5
615. Job 2:10
616. Ephesians 6:11-13
617. *The Pilgrim's Progress* by John Bunyan, updated by L. E. Hazelbaker, published by Bridge-Logos
618. Hebrews 2:10
619. Romans 8:37
620. Hebrews 12:2, KJV
621. KJV: dwelt among plants and hedges
622. 1 Corinthians 7:20-24
623. 1 Corinthians 2:9
624. Genesis 41:49
625. Ephesians 3:20, Philippians 4:19
626. 1 Corinthians 13:12
627. 1 John 5:19
628. John 17:14, 16
629. Genesis 7:1, NKJV
630. John 14:23, Acts 17:28
631. Luke 13:25, NKJV
632. Matthew 25:1-12
633. 1 Corinthians 15:9
634. 1 John 4:19
635. Matthew 9:13
636. Romans 5:8
637. Hebrews 10:22
638. 1 John 1:9
639. John 16:8

640.	Ephesians 1:6, KJV	680.	Matthew 7:11, Romans 8:32
641.	Isaiah 61:10, Revelation 7:9-10	681.	Isaiah 41:13
642.	2 Corinthians 6:2, KJV	682.	Psalm 23:4
643.	Romans 4:5	683.	Joshua 5:13-15
644.	1 Corinthians 2:4	684.	2 Kings 2:13-14
645.	Jeremiah 17:9, KJV (beyond cure, NIV)	685.	Hebrews 2:11
646.	Exodus 23:2	686.	Romans 15:13
647.	1 Corinthians 6:11	687.	1 John 2:20
648.	1 Chronicles 5:18	688.	1 Peter 2:5, 9
649.	1 Chronicles 5:20	689.	Hebrews 10:22
650.	Deuteronomy 23:9	690.	1 Thessalonians 5:23
651.	Ephesians 6:12	691.	Philippians 2:13
652.	1 Samuel 17:47	692.	Colossians 1:27
653.	Psalm 40:2-3	693.	Ephesians 5:8
654.	Psalm 126:3	694.	Matthew 3:11, Acts 2:3, Hebrews 1:7
655.	Colossians 1:12, KJV (saints in the kingdom of light, NIV)	695.	Leviticus 23:37, Romans 12:1
656.	Mark 4:14	696.	John 14:16 (Helper, NKJV; Counselor, NIV)
657.	Jeremiah 4:3	697.	Acts 2:2
658.	Mark 16:15	698.	John 3:8
659.	2 Corinthians 6:1, KJV	699.	Job 1:12, 2:6
660.	Ephesians 1:6	700.	Luke 3:17
661.	Romans 5:5 (shed abroad, KJV)	701.	Psalm 45:8
662.	Psalm 51	702.	Song of Songs 1:3, John 12:3
663.	Psalm 13:5	703.	1 Kings 5:6
664.	Psalm 116:13	704.	1 Kings 5:17
665.	Romans 8:29	705.	Ephesians 3:17
666.	Romans 7:24	706.	1 Kings 6:7
667.	1 Timothy 1:15	707.	Hebrews 20
668.	Ephesians 3:8	708.	1 Thessalonians 5:23
669.	Philippians 1:21	709.	James 4:8
670.	Matthew 16:18 (hell, KJV)	710.	Psalm 25:14
671.	Romans 8:9	711.	John 15:15
672.	Hebrews 11:11	712.	John 14:2
673.	1 Samuel 2:1	713.	Ephesians 3:19
674.	Isaiah 49:15	714.	1 Timothy 1:12
675.	Isaiah 54:10	715.	1 Chronicles 5:25, Mark 7:6
676.	John 10:28-29	716.	Proverbs 14:32
677.	Hebrews 4:16	717.	Isaiah 27:11
678.	Psalm 54:4, 124:8	718.	Revelation 20:12
679.	John 16:23, Ephesians 2:18	719.	Revelation 20:15
		720.	2 Corinthians 13:5

721. Matthew 7:26-27
722. 2 Corinthians 6:17
723. Colossians 3:11
724. Hebrews 12:2
725. Matthew 11:28-30
726. Luke 23:43
727. Revelation 7:14
728. Revelation 14:13
729. Romans 8:17
730. Hebrews 13:8
731. Job 6:15, KJV
732. Psalm 23:2
733. Jeremiah 2:18
734. Daniel 3:25
735. Revelation 22:1
736. Joshua 1:9
737. Isaiah 41:10
738. Luke 12:32
739. Hosea 11:7, KJV
740. Philippians 3:14, KJV
741. 2 Corinthians 5:17, Galatians 6:15
742. *Vivification:*The act of giving or bringing life
743. John 4:14
744. Psalm 119:105
745. Hebrews 12:2, KJV
746. 1 Kings 17:1
747. 1 Kings 17:3-4
748. 1 Kings 17:9
749. Romans 11:5
750. 1 Kings 18:3-4
751. Matthew 24:6, Mark 13:7
752. Ezekiel 33:6, Acts 18:6
753. Romans 4:20-21
754. Romans 8:32
755. Psalm 23:6
756. Psalm 23:2
757. Psalm 106:1, NKJV
758. Matthew 6:10
759. Hebrews 1:14
760. Hebrews 12:23, KJV
761. 1 Corinthians 3:22, NKJV
762. Revelation 4:10
763. John 14:23, Colossians 3:4, Hebrews 9:28
764. 1 Corinthians 3:12-15
765. Ephesians 3:17
766. Acts 16:5, KJV
767. Ephesians 5:27
768. 1 Kings 18:36-38
769. Psalm 97:10
770. 2 Timothy 4:8; Revelation 2:12, 3:11
771. 2 Corinthians 10:1
772. John 19:30
773. Leviticus 3:9
774. James 5:16
775. Revelation 3:15-16
776. Zechariah 12:10
777. Numbers 4:11, Revelation 8:3
778. 1 Kings 1:39
779. Matthew 6:11
780. Deuteronomy 33:25
781. John 15:5
782. Hebrews 12:2, KJV
783. John 6:37
784. 1 Timothy 1:15
785. Matthew 20:22, Mark 10:38
786. Romans 8:16, 1 Thessalonians 1:5
787. 2 Timothy 1:12
788. Jeremiah 31:3
789. Exodus 13:21-22
790. Exodus 16:35
791. 1 Corinthians 10:4
792. Isaiah 40:30-31, Matthew 15:32
793. Deuteronomy 25:17-18
794. Exodus 33:22
795. 1 Peter 2:3
796. Romans 8:23
797. Romans 8:23
798. Numbers 13:23
799. Matthew 16:18 (gates of hell shall not prevail, KJV)
800. Acts 9:5
801. Isaiah 41:14
802. Psalm 9:19, 17:13

803. Psalm 2:9
804. Exodus 17:14, Deuteronomy 32:26
805. Luke 14:35 (dunghill,
KJV)
806. Genesis 29:18
807. Revelation 19:9
808. Psalm 120:5
809. Malachi 2:16
810. Mark 12:5
811. "Et tu, Brute?" Caesar
was assassinated by
Roman senators and
his friend Brutus in the
Roman Senate House
on March 15, 44 BC,
the Ides of March in the
ancient Roman calendar.
812. 2 Corinthians 5:17
813. KJV: stand still
814. Job 2:9
815. Psalm 84:7
816. Exodus 14:15
817. Matthew 5:28, 26:41
818. James 1:5
819. James 4:7
820. Genesis 39:7
821. James 3:5-6
822. Job 23:10
823. John 13:34
824. Mark 12:31
825. Romans 4:20, KJV (wa-
ver, NIV)
826. Romans 4:21
827. Malachi 3:6
828. Psalm 39:34
829. NIV: I was senseless and
ignorant; I was a brute
beast before you.
830. 1 Samuel 13:14
831. Psalm 73:3, KJV
832. Philippians 3:12
833. Hebrews 12:10
834. Romans 8:28
835. Hebrews 12:15
836. Psalm 73:24
837. Psalm 33:18

838. Exodus 28:21
839. Song of Songs 8:7
840. Matthew 26:33
841. Luke 22:34
842. Luke 22:61
843. Revelation 21:21
844. Matthew 12:20
845. John 20:22
846. Matthew 11:28
847. Isaiah 41:14
848. Isaiah 44:22
849. Isaiah 1:18
850. Matthew 10:29
851. Matthew 29:30
852. Isaiah 40:12
853. Isaiah 46:10
854. Acts 4:28
855. John 12:28
856. John 15:16
857. 1 John 4:19
858. 1 Corinthians 6:20, 7:23,
1 Peter 1:18-19
859. 2 Peter 1:9, Revelation
1:5
860. Revelation 7:9
861. 1 Peter 1:5
862. Romans 8:30
863. 1 John 3:2
864. 1 Timothy 6:15, Revelation 19:16
865. Isaiah 5:13
866. Isaiah 54:13, Ephesians
1:17-18
867. 1 John 2:20 (unction,
KJV)
868. John 16:13
869. Hebrews 12:10
870. Ephesians 4:13; 2 Peter
1:8, 3:8
871. KJV: We know that all
things work together for
good to them that love
God.
872. Matthew 14:27
873. Isaiah 21:8
874. Luke 22:32
875. Matthew 16:3

876. *Polestar*: A guiding principle
877. Hebrews: 10:37
878. Malachi 4:2
879. Revelation 2:16
880. Song of Songs 2:17, 4:6
881. Revelation 4:8
882. Isaiah 54:13
883. John 6:27
884. Daniel 9:21, Luke 1:19
885. 1 Corinthians 13:12
886. Ephesians 2:1
887. John 11:43
888. Galatians 2:20
889. Colossians 1:27
890. John 6:50, NKJV
891. Psalm 63:3, KJV
892. Philippians 1:21
893. Luke 12:34
894. 1 Peter 5:5
895. James 4:10
896. Matthew 8:29
897. Job 40:15
898. Job 41:1-2
899. Mark 1:23-24
900. Revelation 4:10
901. Psalm 148:7, 9
902. Romans 12:1
903. 2 Samuel 9:3, 6-7
904. Galatians 6:2
905. Psalm 1:1-3
906. Acts 10:14
907. John 3:27
908. Micah 6:8
909. Psalm 96: 7-8
910. Psalm 115:1
911. Philippians 4:13, NKJV
912. 1 Corinthians 15:10
913. KJV: The mercy of God.
914. Isaiah 6:1, Luke 4:18
915. *The Pilgrim's Progress* by John Bunyan, updated by L. E. Hazelbaker, published by Bridge-Logos
916. Hebrews 13:5
917. Matthew 22:11-13
918. Matthew 11:14
919. Matthew 7:13 (KJV: strait is the gate, and narrow is the way—NKJV: narrow is the gate and difficult is the way)
920. 2 Samuel 6:6-7
921. 1 Corinthians 11:23-31
922. Psalm 139:23
923. 1 Peter 5:4
924. John 10:4
925. Matthew 28:8
926. Romans 14:11
927. 1 Samuel 23:29, 24:3 (Engedi, KNV)
928. 2 Samuel 15:31
929. Psalm 41:9
930. Matthew 10:36
931. Acts 18:26 (perfectly, KJV)
932. 1 Kings 17:10-16
933. Luke 6:38
934. Matthew 5:6
935. 1 Thessalonians 5:23
936. Hebrews 3:12
937. Philippians 2:15, Revelation 14:5 (NKJV, KJV)
938. Romans 8:29
939. 1 Thessalonians 4:17
940. 1 Corinthians 2:9
941. 1 Thessalonians 4:18
942. Isaiah 43:3
943. Isaiah 45:22, NKJV
944. Isaiah 55:3, KJV
945. Luke 8:43-48
946. 1 John 1:1
947. Song of Songs 2:3, KJV
948. Ephesians 1:4
949. Isaiah 55:3, Acts 13:34, KJV
950. Amos 2:13, NKJV
951. Psalm 50:10
952. Leviticus 8:10
953. William Carey (1761-1834), pioneer of the modern missionary movement and a distinguished scholar

of Indian languages. Born on Aug. 17, 1761, in Northamptonshire, Carey joined the Baptist church in 1783 and served as pastor at Moulton and Leicester. He helped found the Baptist Missionary Society and went to India as a missionary in 1793. There he translated the Bible into several Indian languages and translated the Hindu epic poem 'Ramayana' into English. Carey died in Serampore, India, on June 9, 1834.

954. Acts 10:2
955. Exodus 12:7
956. Hebrews 9:21
957. Leviticus 16:15
958. Exodus 24:6
959. Habakkuk 2:3
960. Exodus 15:24, 17:3, Numbers 14:2
961. Exodus 16:2-3
962. Luke 22:42
963. Psalm 21:1
964. Psalm 91:2
965. Psalm 61:3
966. Romans 4:20
967. Hebrews 13:6
968. Deuteronomy 33:27
969. Joshua 1:7, 23:6
970. Acts 11:12, KJV
971. Romans 8:14
972. 1 Corinthians 2:8
973. Exodus 15:26
974. James 5:14-15
975. Psalm 103:2-4
976. 2 Timothy 1:12
977. Job 19:25
978. Romans 8:16
979. 1 John 14:19
980. Galatians 1:4, 2:20, Titus 2:14

981. Romans 5:21
982. Colossians 1:20
983. 2 Corinthians 8:9
984. Song of Songs 5:16
985. Literal translation of Genesis 1:3—"Let there be light" is the translation in most Bible versions.
986. Mark 1:40, NKJV
987. John 6:37
988. Leviticus 13:45-47
989. Matthew 8:1-3
990. Leviticus 15:7
991. 2 Corinthians 5:21
992. 1 Peter 5:8
993. Daniel 6:5
994. 1 Corinthians 16:13
995. Acts 8:26-39
996. Acts 18:6
997. 2 Corinthians 1:3-4
998. Mark 2:3
999. John 15:5
1000. John 15:4
1001. John 15:1-2
1002. John 13:23
1003. 2 Corinthians 12:2
1004. 1 Kings 18:42-45
1005. Deuteronomy 34:1
1006. Matthew 17:1-2
1007. Psalm 61:2
1008. Luke 11:5-8, 18:1-8
1009. Exodus 19:20
1010. Mark 16:17, John 14:12
1011. John 12:21
1012. Hebrews 4:16
1013. Isaiah 27:13
1014. John 15:19, 17:14, 16
1015. Philippians 1:21
1016. 1 Corinthians 10:31
1017. Matthew 6:19-20
1018. James 2:5
1019. Matthew 5:16
1020. Ephesians 5:19
1021. Micah 6:8
1022. For more on the subject of the presence of God, see *The Practice of the*

Presence of God by Brother Lawrence, published by Bridge-Logos Publishers.

1023. Ephesians 5:11
1024. Ephesians 4:1
1025. Revelation 17:14
1026. Galatians 2:20
1027. 2 Chronicles 32:7, Proverbs 3:5
1028. Proverbs 3:5
1029. 2 Corinthians 1:4
1030. 1 Samuel 14:27
1031. Psalm 42:5
1032. Proverbs 21:31
1033. Malachi 3:10
1034. Mark 4:39
1035. Psalm 107:30
1036. 1 Peter 1:3
1037. Numbers 14:27, 1 Corinthians 10:10
1038. 2 Kings 17:11
1039. Psalm 37:7
1040. Exodus 14:13, KJV
1041. John 14:27
1042. Genesis 1:26
1043. 1 John 3:2
1044. 1 John 4:16
1045. 1 John 6:7
1046. Luke 18:19
1047. Matthew 5:8
1048. Colossians 3:3
1049. 2 Peter 1:4
1050. Luke 1:37, Matthew 28:18
1051. Romans 1:18, NKJV (hold, KJV)
1052. Matthew 23:27
1053. Luke 6:48-49
1054. Isaiah 43:2
1055. Isaiah 54:10
1056. Hebrews 4:16, 10:19-22
1057. Philippians 4:19
1058. *Earthen pitcher*: empty jar
1059. Matthew 5:15
1060. Matthew 5:16
1061. Acts 4:13
1062. Isaiah 62:5
1063. Proverbs 8:31
1064. Zephaniah 3:17
1065. Genesis 1:31
1066. Acts 20:28
1067. 1 Peter 2:4, 9
1068. Habakkuk 3:18
1069. Psalm 43:4
1070. Isaiah 40:7
1071. Exodus 15:1, NKJV
1072. Hebrews 13:8
1073. Ephesians 5:27
1074. Isaiah 38:17
1075. 2 Chronicles 32:8
1076. Deuteronomy 33:29
1077. Romans 5:1
1078. Hebrews 10:22
1079. 1 Corinthians 1:20, 2 Corinthians 5:21
1080. John 14:27
1081. Philippians 4:7
1082. Romans 8:37
1083. 1 John 3:1
1084. John 3:3-8
1085. Philippians 4:4
1086. Romans 8:15
1087. Philippians 1:11
1088. Psalm 68:19, KJV
1089. Genesis 18:20-21
1090. Luke 12:7
1091. Psalm 103:13
1092. 2 Chronicles 16:9
1093. John 16:8
1094. John 6:37
1095. John 10:10
1096. Luke 7:37-50
1097. Luke 15:11-24
1098. 1 Corinthians 1:23
1099. Jeremiah 31:33
1100. Psalm 34:1
1101. Isaiah 43:21
1102. John 15:8
1103. Luke 22:44
1104. Matthew 25:21
1105. Ephesians 6:16
1106. Psalm 91:12

1107. Luke 15:10
1108. John 1:51
1109. Isaiah 6:6
1110. 2 Kings 6:17
1111. Hebrews 12:22
1112. Ephesians 2:6
1113. Isaiah 29:3
1114. *Beulah Land*: The land of Israel in the Old Testament (Isaiah 62:4). The land of peace described in John Bunyan's *Pilgrim's Progress*.
1115. 2 Corinthians 12:9
1116. Romans 13:12
1117. Revelation 21:21
1118. John 21:12
1119. John 21:16-17
1120. John 21:19
1121. John 6:33, 41, 50-51
1122. Revelation 7:15
1123. John 6:32-33
1124. Proverbs 18:24
1125. John 4:10
1126. Revelation 21:6, 22:1, 17
1127. Psalm 36:8
1128. Job 13:15, NKJV
1129. Romans 5:3-4
1130. 1 Corinthians 1:21
1131. Luke 5:5
1132. John 15:5
1133. Philippians 4:13
1134. John 12:32
1135. Psalm 73:2
1136. Hebrews 12:12 (feeble, KJV)
1137. Jude 24-25
1138. Hebrews 10:23, 11:11
1139. Psalm 116:8
1140. Revelation 1:5, KJV
1141. Isaiah 61:10
1142. Isaiah 40:31
1143. Ephesians 6:12-18
1144. Exodus 17:10-12
1145. 2 Kings 13:17, KJV
1146. Hebrews 4:16
1147. Psalm 1:1-3
1148. John 16:7-8
1149. John 3:6
1150. James 3:6
1151. Ephesians 3:18-19
1152. Psalm 42:1
1153. Luke 10:39
1154. Isaiah 11:4
1155. Matthew 27:50-54
1156. Luke 23:44-45
1157. Psalm 2:12
1158. Revelation 5:5
1159. Psalm 2:9, Revelation 19:15
1160. Revelation 1:5, NKJV, 7:14
1161. 2 Timothy 4:8
1162. 2 Peter 1:10
1163. Philippians 4:13
1164. 2 Kings 9:30-36
1165. Hebrews 4:16
1166. 1 Kings 17:1
1167. Deuteronomy 34:1
1168. Leviticus 6:12, 16
1169. Matthew 12:20
1170. Ephesians 2:6
1171. Mark 4:28, KJV
1172. 1 John 2:12
1173. Psalm 40:2
1174. Psalm 40:2, KJV
1175. John 14:2-3
1176. Revelation 21:27
1177. 1 Corinthians 2:9
1178. Proverbs 27:5
1179. KJV: backsliding
1180. Luke 15:17-19
1181. 2 Corinthians 8:9
1182. Romans 8:38-39
1183. John 6:68
1184. Spiritual rebirth—John 3:3
1185. John 3:8
1186. Colossians 3:3
1187. Philippians 2:13
1188. Acts 4:13
1189. Hebrews 5:12-14
1190. Mark 16:16, Acts 16:31,

Romans 10:9
1191. Malachi 3:10
1192. Philippians 4:11-12
1193. Matthew 6:33
1194. KJV: faithful sayings
1195. Romans 11:13
1196. Jeremiah 8:22
1197. 1 Samuel 14:27
1198. Hebrews 7:22 (surety, KJV)
1199. 2 Samuel 6:20-21
1200. Luke 15:18, KJV
1201. Romans 8:15, Galatians 4:6
1202. Isaiah 6:4, Revelation 4:8
1203. Psalm 88:2, NKJV
1204. Luke 17:12-19
1205. Psalm 34:2
1206. Psalm 34:3, 6
1207. Ephesians 5:19
1208. James 1:17
1209. Psalm 62:8
1210. Nahum 1:7, KJV
1211. Psalm 54:4
1212. Jeremiah 31:3
1213. Romans 8:26
1214. Revelations 5:8
1215. Psalm 56:8, NKJV
1216. Genesis 28:12
1217. Psalm 9:12
1218. Zechariah 4:6
1219. Philippians 4:13
1220. 2 Corinthians 12:10
1221. Psalm 44:1
1222. NIV: I will pour water on the thirsty land.
1223. Psalm 51:12
1224. Isaiah 49:14
1225. John 1:12
1226. 2 Kings 4:3
1227. Matthew 11:5, Luke 7:22
1228. Colossians 1:27
1229. Ephesians 3:17
1230. Acts 17:28
1231. Psalm 23:4

1232. Psalm 46:1
1233. Psalm 25:14
1234. Some doctrines see the Jordan River as symbolizing death, which we much cross to enter the promised land of eternal life.
1235. Psalm 23:4
1236. Matthew 21:21
1237. Matthew 17:20
1238. Revelation 2:5
1239. For a study on holy exercises, see *The Practice of the Presence of God*, by Brother Lawrence, published by Bridge-Logos Publishers.
1240. John 15:5
1241. James 4:8
1242. 1 Corinthians 2:2
1243. Exodus 33:19, Romans 9:15
1244. 1 Peter 1:18-19
1245. 2 Timothy 2:19
1246. John 10:11, 15
1247. Proverbs 30:15 (horseleech, KJV)
1248. Psalm 73:25
1249. Psalm 37:4
1250. Psalm 36:8 (pleasures, KJV)
1251. Isaiah 40:31
1252. Psalm 16:6
1253. Zechariah 8:23
1254. 2 Corinthians 6:17
1255. Galatians 6:17
1256. Titus 3:8
1257. John 20:31, Acts 16:31
1258. Ephesians 4:23, KJV
1259. Romans 8:1, 4
1260. 2 Peter 3:18
1261. Matthew 24:42, 25:13
1262. Revelation 5:8
1263. Exodus 15:20 (timbrel, KJV)
1264. Judges 4:14, 5:1

1265. Zechariah 12:10, Hebrews 10:29
1266. Philippians 2:13
1267. Romans 8:26-27
1268. John 15:5
1269. Genesis 31:38-40
1270. John 17:12, NKJV
1271. Luke 6:12
1272. Luke 22:32
1273. Genesis 31:39
1274. Isaiah 40:11
1275. Matthew 6:10
1276. Romans 8:17, Philippians 3:10
1277. Luke 6:22
1278. Matthew 10:24, Luke 6:40
1279. John 4:34
1280. John 15:11
1281. Isaiah 25:6
1282. 1 Corinthians 10:4
1283. KJV: To preach deliverance to the captives.
1284. Psalm 30:11
1285. Romans 8:31
1286. 1 John 4:4
1287. Philippians 1:6
1288. Galatians 3:13
1289. Psalm 116:16
1290. Acts 9:6
1291. John 15:8
1292. Philippians 4:13
1293. Revelation 1:6
1294. Acts 7:53-55
1295. Hebrews 13:15
1296. Romans 12:1
1297. 1 Timothy 2:5
1298. Ephesians 2:18
1299. John 11:35
1300. Romans 8:26
1301. Ephesians 1:6
1302. 1 Peter 3:4
1303. 1 John 5:16
1304. Matthew 26:33-35, Luke 22:31-34
1305. Acts 16:25
1306. Genesis 8:22

1307. Hebrews 9:15
1308. Ephesians 1:6, KJV
1309. Song of Songs 1:8
1310. Song of Songs 4:1
1311. Ephesians 4:30
1312. 2 Timothy 5:21
1313. Romans 8:30, Ephesians 1:5, 11
1314. Acts 20:28
1315. John 17:20
1316. Psalm 110:3, KJV (paraphrase)
1317. Isaiah 53:11
1318. Isaiah 53:11, NKJV
1319. Isaiah 1:18
1320. Isaiah 61:10
1321. Daniel 2:31-33
1322. John 14:19
1323. Job 17:14, NKJV
1324. Galatians 4:6
1325. 2 Corinthians 11:2
1326. Luke 19:10
1327. Acts 16:31, Romans 10:9
1328. Ecclesiastes 9:7
1329. Revelation 7:9-10
1330. Psalm 119:1
1331. Revelation 7:17
1332. Genesis 32:24
1333. Matthew 15:22-23
1334. 2 Corinthians 12:7-9
1335. Luke 18:1
1336. 1 Peter 1:8
1337. Song of Songs 2:17
1338. Song of Songs 2:16 KJV
1339. 1 Corinthians 13:12
1340. Philippians 1:21
1341. 1 Peter 1:4, KJV
1342. Luke 21:18; John 3:15-16, 10:28
1343. Isaiah 49:16
1344. Matthew 28:20
1345. Revelation 17:14
1346. 1 Thessalonians 5:24
1347. Ephesians 1:11
1348. James 1:17, NKJV
1349. Daniel 4:35

1350. Hebrews 13:8
1351. 1 Corinthians 10:13
1352. Luke 11:9-10
1353. Deuteronomy 32:15
1354. Matthew 24:12
1355. Isaiah 40:30-31
1356. Psalm 118:27, NKJV
1357. Luke 14:28
1358. Matthew 19:27
1359. Matthew 1:5
1360. Matthew 25:34
1361. Revelation 22:20
1362. Proverbs 8:31
1363. Psalm 139:16
1364. Colossians 1:16
1365. Genesis 18:1
1366. Genesis 32:22-24
1367. Joshua 5:13-15
1368. Daniel 3:19-25
1369. Isaiah 49:16
1370. Exodus 28:15-21
1371. Matthew 27:50-51
1372. Lots were cast, similar to casting dice, to decide what to do, or what the Lord's will was in the matter. See Acts 1:15-26.
1373. Matthew 10:29-30
1374. Matthew 6:33
1375. Philippians 4:19
1376. Hebrews 7:25
1377. Acts 3:19
1378. John 13:23, KJV
1379. Matthew 26:25
1380. Revelation 10:10
1381. 2 Timothy 2:19
1382. Psalm 89:34
1383. 1 Samuel 2:8, Job 9:6, Psalm 75:3
1384. Hebrews 1:3
1385. Genesis 1:3
1386. Psalm 33:9
1387. Isaiah 40:28
1388. Job 26:7
1389. Matthew 8:24-26
1390. 2 Samuel 22:11
1391. Psalm 104:3

1392. Isaiah 40:12
1393. Isaiah 6:2
1394. Ephesians 1:6, NKJV
1395. Romans 8:15
1396. 2 Corinthians 6:15
1397. John 1:16
1398. Romans 4:11, KJV
1399. Isaiah 61:10
1400. Revelation 1:5
1401. Isaiah 9:6
1402. 2 Corinthians 5:19, KJV
1403. John 20:28
1404. Genesis 3:15
1405. Colossians 1:27
1406. Matthew 1:23
1407. Hebrews 7:9-10
1408. Colossians 2:10-13
1409. Ephesians 2:6
1410. Ephesians 1:6, NKJV
1411. Justin Martyr (100-165AD), Church Father; adherent of Platonic system; one of foremost Christian apologists; born in Palestine of non-Christian parents; said to have been scourged and beheaded at Rome.
1412. *Permutation*: A complete change, a transformation.
1413. Ezekiel 16:6
1414. John 15:5
1415. 1 Samuel 7:12
1416. Isaiah 53:3
1417. Psalm 110:1
1418. 1 John 4:17
1419. Luke 9:23
1420. 2 Timothy 4:8
1421. Revelation 21:21
1422. 1 John 3:2
1423. Psalm 22:6
1424. James 1:4
1425. Revelation 14:14
1426. 2 Corinthians 5:20
1427. Luke 13:24
1428. Ephesians 4:21
1429. John 4:14

TOPICAL INDEX

April 29
May 3
May 31

Trust
May 11
August 31
September 15
November 7
November 30

Truth
July 4
October 25
October 27
November 28

Unbelief
August 27
October 17

Unchangeable, God is
December 12

Vain labor
July 14

Victory
August 24
November 5

Warfare, weapons of
March 2

Wickedness
May 29

Work
February 15
June 3
July 18
September 20
October 5
November 26

SCRIPTURE INDEX

Joshua			**Nehemiah**	
2:21	April 18		9:38	April 24
5:12	January 1			
			Esther	
Judges			No entry.	
7:20	September 20			
16:6	July 8		**Job**	
			8:11	December 27
Ruth			10:2	February 18
1:14	December 15		19:25	April 21
2:2	August 1		29:2	August 11
			40:4	June 06
1 Samuel				
7:12	December 29		**Psalms**	
13:20	March 2		4:2	Apri 7
27:1	October 17		9:1	October 30
			12:01	June 17
2 Samuel			17:7	May 20
5:23	February 9		22:7	Apri 14
5:24	January 30		22:14	April 11
7:25	January 15		22:14	April 12
9:13	May 27		22:21	April 15
15:23	May 31		27:14	August 30
23:1	August 20		29:2	August 16
23:5	December 21		30:5	May 13
			30:6	March 10
1 Kings			33:13	September 28
19:8	October 5		33:21	July 2
			37:4	June 14
22:48	January 13		38:21	May 25
			39:12	March 16
2 Kings			45:2	June 21
7:3	March 13			
25:30	February 14		45:7	May 29
			51:1	Augus 29
1 Chronicles			51:10	October 31
4:23	June 3		52:8	August 17
5:22	June 8		55:22	May 26
			62:5	February 28
2 Chronicles			65:11	October 18
25:9	November 30		66:2	September 30
			66:20	May 24
Ezra			67:6	April 27
7:22	December 13		73:22	July 28
8:22	September 24		73:23	July 29
			73:24	September 1

74:17	December 1		4:16	March 1
84:6	September 13		5:8	August 22
84:7	December 14		5:13	May 1
89:19	January 23		5:16	March 9
91:3	January 24		7:13	October 1
91:9	February 27			
92:4	August 14		**Isaiah**	
97:10	June 7		7:14	December 25
97:1	August 12		14:10	June 26
103:2	July 9		21:11	August 6
104:16	August 13		30:18	December 9
104:16	October 24		33:21	November 24
107:7	May 22		37:22	July 21
119:9	August 26		40:9	June 25
112:7	September 15		41:10	December 22
119:15	October 12		41:14	January 16
119:49	April 28		44:3	November 6
120:5	September 5		48:10	March 3
126:3	June 9		49:8	January 3
138:5	February 1		49:16	November 7
138:8	May 23		51:5	August 31
149:2	September 22		53:5	March 31
			53:12	March 30
Proverbs			54:5	June 18
1:33	July 6		54:17	November 5
11:25	August 21		59:5	August 8
16:33	December 19		63:1	January 14
			63:7	January 25
Ecclesiastes			65:19	August 23
7:8	December 30			
9:10	November 26		**Jeremiah**	
10:7	May 19		2:2	December 17
			16:20	May 4
Song of Songs			17:7	April 29
1:2	April 1		23:6	January 31
1:4	August 7		31:3	February 29
1:7	September 3		31:3	December 20
1:13	April 13		31:33	January 9
2:3	August 25		32:41	September 21
2:8	March 20		33:3	September 9
2:10	April 25		51:51	August 18
2:15	May 30			
3:1	January 19		**Lamentations**	
4:7	December 2		3:41	October 11
4:7	December 3		3:24	November 16
4:12	November 18		3:58	November 20

Ezekiel		Zechariah	
15:2	January 22	1:8	September 26
34:26	February 24	3:1	November 27
36:37	February 19	6:13	June 22
		14:7	October 4
Daniel		14:8	July 1
5:27	June 12		
11:32	August 4	**Malachi**	
		3:2	October 15
Hosea		3:6	November 2
3:1	February 4		
7:8	June 23	**Matthew**	
12:12	November 22	1:21	February 8
14:4	October 22	3:7	February 25
14:8	September 8	5:43	March 12
		6:9	October 29
Joel		6:26	January 26
2:13	December 18	7:7	December 5
		11:28	December 16
Amos		12:15	May 7
9:9	June 20	26:39	March 22
		26:56	March 27
Obadiah		27:14	April 2
1:11	July 23	27:51	April 19
		28:20	May 11
Jonah			
2:9	February 26	**Mark**	
4:9	July 13	1:30	September 2
		1:41	September 4
Micah		2:4	September 7
2:10	February 7	3:13	September 10
2:13	August 24	4:36	September 14
5:4	August 19	9:19	September 17
		11:22	March 7
Nahum			
1:2	September 12	**Luke**	
		4:18	November 25
Habakkuk		5:4	October 8
3:6	December 12	8:13	January 11
		11:27	June 24
Zephaniah		14:10	December 23
1:5	November 14	22:44	March 23
		22:48	March 25
Haggai		23:26	April 5
1:9	October 26	23:27	April 9
		23:31	April 8
		23:33	April 10

John

1:16	January 27
3:7	March 6
4:14	October 6
5:13	May 8
6:67	October 23
7:37	December 31
10:28	June 16
14:21	May 12
15:4	November 13
15:19	October 28
16:32	March 21
16:33	May 3
17:15	May 2
17:17	July 4
17:22	June 30
17:23	July 31
18:8	March 26
19:16	April 3
21:12	October 16

Acts

2:4	June 19
4:13	February 11
5:31	April 22
9:11	November 3
13:39	May 15
14:22	March 8
18:10	December 4

Romans

1:7	July 5
3:26	September 25
4:20	March 19
7:13	March 11
8:12	February 3
8:17	May 14
8:28	August 5
8:30	May 28
8:37	April 23
11:26	January 21
11:36	November 17
14:8	June 10

1 Corinthians

1:28	December 7
3:1	October 19

3:23	January 12
10:12	March 14
11:24	April 26
15:20	May 10
15:45	December 26
15:48	December 6

2 Corinthians

1:5	February 12
4:18	January 29
5:14	October 21
5:21	April 4
6:16	May 5
6:17	September 11
7:10	October 13
8:9	December 24
12:9	March 4
12:9	November 4

Galatians

2:10	March 17
2:20	December 28
3:26	March 18
5:1	September 19
5:17	June 2
5:25	September 18

Ephesians

1:3	May 9
1:4-6	September 23
1:11	August 2
1:14	July 20
2:19	July 10
3:19	March 28
4:15	October 20
4:30	November 21
6:18	February 6

Philippians

1:21	January 7
2:15	September 6
3:8	October 14
4:11	February 16
4:12	February 10

Colossians

1:5	October 2

1:28	January 28	**James**	
2:6	November 8	No entry.	
2:6	November 9		
2:9-10	May 18	**1 Peter**	
3:4	August 10	1:2	July 12
4:2	January 2	1:7	November 12
		1:19	April 16
1 Thessalonians		2:3	May 21
1:4	July 17	5:7	January 6
4:14	June 29	5:10	July 11
4:17	December 10		
5:6	March 5	**2 Peter**	
5:24	December 11	1:4	July 27
5:25	July 07	1:4	September 16
		1:5-7	July 26
2 Thessalonians		3:18	January 4
No entry.		3:18	February 15
1 Timothy		**1 John**	
6:17	May 16	1:6	November 23
		2:6	May 17
2 Timothy		3:1-2a	February 13
2:1	March 15	4:13	May 6
2:11	October 27	4:14	February 5
4:8	January 10	4:19	June 11
		5:3	May 8
Titus			
3:4	June 4	**2 John**	
3:9	November 19	1:2	October 25
Philemon		**3 John**	
1:2	November 1	1:3	November 28
Hebrews		**Jude**	
1:14	October 3	24	October 9
2:14	April 20	24	October 10
4:9	January 18		
5:7	March 24	**Revelation**	
5:8	March 29	3:4	December 8
9:22	February 2	14:1	January 17
12:2	June 28	21:23	August 3
12:24	April 17	21:23	Augus 9
13:5	February 21	22:17	June 13
13:5	February 23		
13:13	April 6		

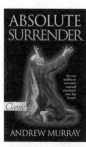
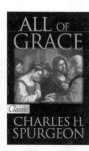

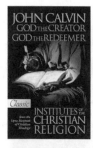
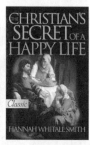

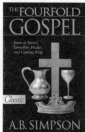

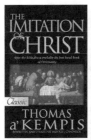

THE
IMITATION
of
CHRIST

After the Bible, this is probably the best loved book of Christianity

Classic

THOMAS
a' KEMPIS

REWRITTEN AND UPDATED BY HAROLD J CHADWICK

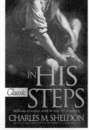

In
HIS
STEPS

Classic

Millions of copies sold, to over 45 countries

CHARLES M. SHELDON

REVISED AND UPDATED BY HAROLD J CHADWICK

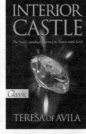

INTERIOR
CASTLE

The Soul's Spiritual Journey to Union with God

Classic

TERESA OF AVILA

THE
KNEELING
CHRISTIAN

Includes
The Life of Prayer
by A. B. Simpson
and
The True Vine:
31 Meditations
by Andrew Murray

Classic

AN
UNKNOWN CHRISTIAN

MADAME
JEANNE
GUYON

Classic

EXPERIENCING UNION WITH GOD
THROUGH INNER PRAYER
& THE WAY AND RESULTS OF
UNION WITH GOD

REVISED & MODERN ENGLISH BY HAROLD J CHADWICK

MORNING
by
MORNING

His daily devotionals moved into clear, modern English

Classic

CHARLES H.
SPURGEON

EDITED BY HAROLD J CHADWICK

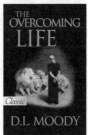

THE
OVERCOMING
LIFE

Classic

D.L. MOODY

THE PILGRIM'S
PROGRESS
IN
MODERN
ENGLISH

John Bunyan's powerful classic distinctively revised for the 21st century reader

Classic

JOHN BUNYAN

REVISED AND UPDATED BY L. EDWARD HAZELBAKER

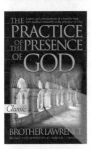

THE
PRACTICE
OF
THE PRESENCE
OF
GOD

Letters and conversations of a humble man who walked constantly in the presence of God

Classic

BROTHER LAWRENCE

REVISED AND REWRITTEN BY HAROLD J CHADWICK

POWER, PASSION
& PRAYER

Finney's Greatest Sermons on Revival through Prayer

Classic

CHARLES G. FINNEY

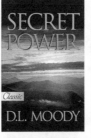

SECRET
POWER

Classic

D.L. MOODY

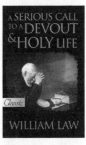

A SERIOUS CALL
TO A DEVOUT
& HOLY LIFE

Classic

WILLIAM LAW

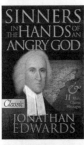

SINNERS
IN
THE HANDS OF
AN
ANGRY GOD

&
11 Short
Classic
Messages

Classic

JONATHAN
EDWARDS

THE
SOVEREIGNTY
OF
GOD

Classic

A.W. PINK

TABLE
TALK

MARTIN
LUTHER

Classic

The culmination of all that is Martin Luther revealed in conversations with his colleagues and students

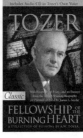

Includes Audio CD in Tozer's Own Voice

TOZER

Classic

With Prayers, a Study, and an Excerpt from the World's Winning Biography for Personal Use by James L. Snyder

FELLOWSHIP OF THE
BURNING HEART

A COLLECTION OF SERMONS BY A.W. TOZER

TOZER ON THE
HOLY SPIRIT

Classic

A.W. TOZER

WITH
CHRIST IN THE
SCHOOL OF
PRAYER

Andrew Murray begins at the simplest elementary level and takes us step by step to the highest reaches of prayer.

Classic

ANDREW MURRAY

REWRITTEN AND UPDATED BY HAROLD J CHADWICK

WILLIAM
WILBERFORCE

Classic

GREATEST WORKS

INCLUDES A KEY WORK FOR EVERY MAJOR PERIOD OF HIS LIFE

Pure Gold Classics

CHRISTIAN CLASSICS

A classic is a work of enduring excellence; a Christian classic is a work of enduring excellence that is filled with divine wisdom, biblical revelation, and insights that are relevant to living a godly life. Such works are both spiritual and practical. Our Pure Gold Classics contain some of the finest examples of Christian writing that have ever been published, including the works of John Foxe, Charles Spurgeon, D.L. Moody, Martin Luther, John Calvin, Saint John of the Cross, E.M. Bounds, John Wesley, Andrew Murray, Hannah Whitall Smith, and many others.

The timeline on the following pages will help you to understand the context of the times in which these extraordinary books were written and the historical events that must have served to influence these great writers to create works that will always stand the test of time. Inspired by God, many of these authors did their work in difficult times and during periods of history that were not sympathetic to their message. Some even had to endure great persecution, misunderstanding, imprisonment, and martyrdom as a direct result of their writing.

The entries that are printed in green type will give you a good overview of Christian history from the birth of Jesus to modern times.

The entries in red pertain to writers of Christian classics from Saint Augustine, who wrote his *Confessions* and *City of God*, to Charles Sheldon, twentieth-century author of *In His Steps*.

Entries in black provide a clear perspective on the development of secular history from the early days of Buddhism (first century) through the Civil Rights Movement.

Finally, the blue entries highlight secular writers and artists, including Chaucer, Michelangelo, and others.

Our color timeline will provide you with a fresh perspective of history, both secular and Christian, and the classics, both secular and Christian. This perspective will help you to understand each author better and to see the world through his or her eyes.

714-1770 George Whitefield, alvinist evangelist known r powerful preaching nd revivals in England nd America. Friend of John esley.

720-1760 "The Great wakening" in America. umerous revivals result widespread Church owth.

741 Handel's *Messiah* omposed.

756-1763 Seven Years ar in Europe, Britain efeats France.

759-1833 William ilberforce, British olitionist and author of *Practical View of hristianity.*

775-1783 American evolutionary War.

779 Olney Hymns ublished, John Newton's *mazing Grace.*

789 French Revolution egins.

792-1875 Charles nney, American angelist. Leads Second reat Awakening in 1824.

305-1898 George ueller, English evangelist founder of orphanages; uthor, *Answers to Prayer.*

313-1855 Soren erkegaard, Danish ilosopher & theologian; uthor, *Fear and embling.*

316-1900 J.C. Ryle, uthor of *Practical Religion* d *Holiness.*

1820-1915 "Fanny" Crosby, though blind, pens over 8,000 hymns.

1828-1917 Andrew Murray, author of *Humility, Abide in Christ, With Christ in the School of Prayer,* and *Absolute Surrender.*

1828 Noah Webster publishes a dictionary of the English Language.

1829 Salvation Army founded by William and Catherine Booth.

1832-1911 Hannah Whitall Smith, author of *The Christian's Secret to a Happy Life* and *God of All Comfort.*

1834-1892 Charles H. Spurgeon, author of *Morning by Morning* and *The Treasury of David.*

1835-1913 E.M. Bounds, author of *The Classic Collection on Prayer.*

1836-1895 A.J. Gordon, New England Spirit-filled pastor; author, *The Ministry of the Spirit.*

1837-1899 Dwight L. Moody, evangelist and founder of Moody Bible Institute in Chicago. Author of *Secret Power* and *The Way to God.*

1843-1919 A.B. Simpson, founder of Christian and Missionary Alliance, author of *The Fourfold Gospel.*

1844 Samuel Frank Morse invents the telegraph.

1847-1929 F.B. Meyer, English Baptist pastor & evangelist; author, *Secret of Guidance.*

1857-1858 Third Great Awakening in America; Prayer Meeting Revival.

1851-1897 Henry Drummond, author of *The Greatest Thing in the World … Love.*

1856-1928 R.A. Torrey, American evangelist, pastor and author.

1857-1946 Charles Sheldon, author of *In His Steps.*

1859 Theory of evolution; Charles Darwin's *Origin of Species.*

1861-1865 American Civil War.

1862-1935 Billy Sunday, American baseball player who became one of the most influential evangelists in the 20th century. *Collected Sermons.*

1867 Alexander Graham Bell invents the telephone.

1869-1948 Mahatma Gandhi makes his life's work India's peaceful independence from Britain.

1881-1936 J. Gresham Machen, "Old School" Presbyterian leader, writes *Christianity and Liberalism*; forms the new Orthodox Presbyterian Church in 1936.

1886-1952 A. W. Pink, evangelist & biblical scholar; author, *The Sovereignty of God.*

1897-1963 A.W. Tozer, author of *Fellowship of the Burning Heart.*

1898-1900 Boxer Rebellion in China deposes western influence, particularly Christian missionaries.

c. 1900-1930 *The Kneeling Christian* (Written by The Unknown Christian.)

1901 American Standard Version of Bible published.

1906 Azusa Street Revival, Los Angeles, instrumental in rise of modern Pentecostal Movement.

1906-1945 Dietrich Bonhoeffer spreads Christian faith to Germans in opposition to WWII Nazism.

1914-1918 World War I.

1917 Bolshevik Revolution in Russia.

1925 Scopes Monkey Trial pits Bible against theory of evolution.

1929 US Stock Market crashes, 12 years of Great Depression.

1939-1945 World War II. Holocaust in eastern Europe under Hitler.

1947 Dead Sea Scrolls found in caves in Judean desert.

1948 State of Israel reestablished.

1949 Communist revolution in China; religion suppressed.

1952 RSV Bible first published.

1960s Civil Rights movement in the United States.